▶ What the Reviewers Are Saying About *Building Professional Services*

HARRIS KERN'S ENTERPRISE COMPUTING INSTITUTE

- ▶ IT Architecture Toolkit
  Jane A. Carbone

- ▶ Software Development: Building Reliable Systems
  Marc Hamilton

- ▶ High Availability: Design, Techniques, and Processes
  Michael Hawkins, Floyd Piedad

- ▶ Data Warehousing: Architecture and Implementation
  Mark Humphries, Michael W. Hawkins, Michelle C. Dy

- ▶ IT Organization: Building a Worldclass Infrastructure
  Harris Kern, Stuart D. Galup, Guy Nemiro

- ▶ IT Production Services
  Harris Kern, Rich Schiesser, Mayra Muniz

- ▶ Building Professional Services: The Sirens' Song
  Thomas E. Lah, Steve O'Connor, Mitchel Peterson

- ▶ CIO Wisdom: Best Practices from Silicon Valley
  *Dean Lane, Change Technology Solutions, Inc.,
  and Members of the Silicon Valley Community of Practice*

- ▶ CIO Wisdom II
  Phillip Laplante, Thomas Costello

- ▶ IT Automation: The Quest for Lights Out
  Howie Lyke with Debra Cottone

- ▶ Managing IT as an Investment: Partnering for Success
  Ken Moskowitz, Harris Kern

- ▶ IT Systems Management
  Rich Schiesser

- ▶ IT Services: Costs, Metrics, Benchmarking, and Marketing
  Anthony F. Tardugno, Thomas R. DiPasquale, Robert E. Matthews

- ▶ IT Problem Management
  Gary Walker

ENTERPRISE COMPUTING SERIES

Building Professional Services

The Sirens' Song

Thomas E. Lah, Steve O'Connor, Mitchel Peterson

Harris Kern's Enterprise Computing Institute

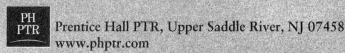

Prentice Hall PTR, Upper Saddle River, NJ 07458
www.phptr.com

A CIP catalog record for this book can be obtained from the Library of Congress.

Editorial/production supervision: *BooksCraft, Inc., Indianapolis, IN*
Executive editor: *Greg Doench*
Editorial assistant: *Brandt Kenna*
Marketing manager: *Debby vanDijk*
Manufacturing manager: *Alexis Heydt-Long*
Cover design director: *Jerry Votta*
Cover designer: *Nina Scuderi*
Project coordinator: *Anne Garcia*

© 2002 by Prentice Hall PTR
A Division of Pearson Education, Inc.
Upper Saddle River, New Jersey 07458

Prentice Hall books are widely used by corporations and government agencies for training, marketing, and resale.

For information regarding corporate and government bulk discounts please contact:

Corporate and Government Sales (800) 382-3419 or corpsales@pearsontechgroup.com

Other company and product names mentioned herein are the trademarks or registered trademarks of their respective owners.

Pearson Education LTD.
Pearson Education Australia PTY, Limited
Pearson Education Singapore, Pte. Ltd.
Pearson Education North Asia Ltd.
Pearson Education Canada, Ltd.
Pearson Educación de Mexico, S.A. de C.V.
Pearson Education—Japan
Pearson Education Malaysia, Pte. Ltd.

ISBN 0-13-035389-2

Text printed in the United States at Hamilton in Castleton, New York.

9th   Printing   March 2008

Dedications

"Come this way. Stay your ship, and listen to our voice! No man ever yet sailed past this place, without first listening to the voice which sounds from our lips sweet as honey."

The Sirens of *The Odyssey*

Thomas E. Lah's dedication:

To Ken Coleman, who provided the opportunity.
To my wife, who gave me the courage.
To my parents, who taught me how.

Steve O'Connor's dedication:

To Ken Coleman for believing in me AND providing the opportunity,
To Mike Graves for teaching me about Leadership and Excellence.
To my Parents for instilling rich values, and
To my wife and children for bringing me great joy in my life.

Mitchel Peterson's dedication:

To Patty for providing me the opportunity,
To Steve for teaching me how to think differently,
To Thomas for his enthusiasm and drive,
To my parents for their belief in me, and
To my friends for their ongoing support and friendship.

Contents

Chapter 4

Organizational Overview 51

Chapter 5

Selling 61

Chapter 6

Delivering   89

Chapter 7

Productizing   113

Chapter 8

Promoting   **145**

Chapter 9

Operational Infrastructure   167

Four Phases of Building PS   231

Chapter 13

Unique Issues   267

Chapter 14

Summary of Key Concepts   287

Appendix A

Evaluating Your Service Vendors   301

Appendix F

Customer Request and Qualification Form   **339**

Glossary

Glossary of Terms   **343**

Selected Bibliography   **350**

Index   **351**

Why Product Companies Jump In

Professional services at a product company

▶ The Sirens' Song of Services

May 31st, 2001. Bill Gates grants a live interview. He appears on CNBC's "Squawk Box" to promote Microsoft's latest software release. Two minutes into the interview, host Mark Haines wants to know about Microsoft's service strategy: Isn't Mr. Gates concerned that Microsoft doesn't enjoy the same level of service revenues that Oracle and IBM do? Mr. Gates responds that Microsoft is now offering new consulting services. A visit to the Microsoft Web page confirms the new direction (see Figure 0-1).

A quick search on *www.google.com* using the key words "Professional Services" and "Product" yields hundreds of Web sites for technology product companies also offering professional services. Besides Oracle and IBM, the who's who list includes hardware manufacturers Alcatel, Aspect, Compaq, EMC, HP, Lucent, Nortel, and Sun; software makers PeopleSoft, Sybase, WebCT, Pumatech, and Red Hat. All of these technology companies have heard it. They can't ignore it. The Sirens' song of services.

1

Microsoft Consulting Services Portfolio of Services

Microsoft® Consulting Services (MCS) provide help directly from Microsoft through every stage of the technology planning, deployment, and support process. MCS is staffed with Microsoft experts who can help you make the most of your IT investment. Specializing in real-life IT solutions, MCS offers a full range of programs for advanced technology requirements: e-commerce, enterprise application planning, distributed network architecture computing, and more. Customers around the world have used MCS to improve productivity and establish a competitive advantage. With more than 100 offices and just under 4,000 consultants worldwide, Microsoft has the experience and expertise to align your IT vision and business goals. The following are some of the services we offer.

Figure 0–1   Microsoft's new direction. © 2002 Microsoft Corporation. Reprinted with permission from Microsoft Corporation. (*www.microsoft.com/indonesia/business/services/mcs.asp*)

▶ The Product-Services Wheel

The Gartner Group has documented an identity crisis that both product and service companies constantly go through:[1] Product companies want to become service companies and service companies want to become product companies. This Product-Services wheel is shown in Figure 0-2. For product companies offering technology, the turning point begins with product services, or services offered to support the core products of the company. These are commonly known as support services. But soon, the product company may be tempted to move in a different direction. In particular, the Sirens' call of potentially high-growth and high-margin consulting services for a product company is almost too tempting to resist, especially if the product company is experiencing erosion in product margins.[2] If you visit the Web sites of product companies such as IBM, HP, Compaq, EMC, and Silicon Graphics, you see very consistent positioning of their newly developed

---

1. "There Is a Tide in the Affairs of Vendors: Product or Service Business?" Gartner Group, May 2000.

2. In Chapter 12, we review the service strategies of HP, Compaq, Sun, and EMC. From this review, it should become clear why companies like Compaq are motivated to move to offer consulting services.

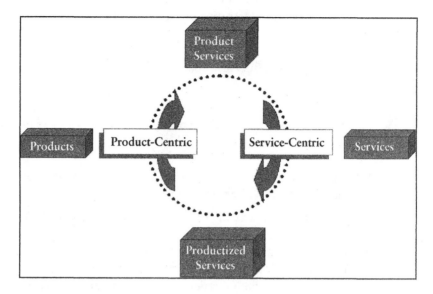

Figure 0–2   Product-Services wheel.

services. All of these product companies now offer at least four distinct flavors of services:[3]

Support Services: These are basic break-fix support services that product companies have always offered.

Education Services: These are traditional product-training services offered by product companies.

Managed Services: These are services focused on successfully implementing the core products of the company. Typically, these services are tightly scoped and very similar from customer to customer. They are usually offered at a fixed price.

Consulting (or Professional) Services: These are services that move beyond implementation and into integrating the products of the company into the customer's business. These services may involve developing custom code to integrate the product into

3. In fact, the definition of professional services is very nebulous in the industry. Figure 0-2 provides a helpful and simple way to visualize and classify the various types of service offerings in which product companies invest.

existing infrastructure. These services may also involve consulting with the customer on actual workflow and business processes.

For the larger product companies like IBM and HP, a fifth service is offered:

Outsourcing: These are services where the product company literally takes over the day-to-day operations of the customer's technical environment.

Table 0-1 provides a summary of the five types of services that product companies are now likely to offer.

And there is good reason for product companies to develop and offer all these new services: *over half of all InformationTechnology (IT) spending is on services!*[4] Key customers often turn to their preferred and trusted product vendors to provide more and more of these services. According to the Gartner Group, this behavior is being driven by three key factors: the continuing shortage of qualified technical talent, the trend of companies to refocus on their core competencies, and the ever-increasing complexity of new technology requiring specialized expertise for successful implementation.[5]

Table 0–1   Types of Services.

Service Name	Description	Tag Lines	Pricing Attributes	Length Attributes	Proposed Benefits
Support Services	Basic break-fix service for products of the company	24/7, Remote administration, Help desk	Fixed percent of product costs. Price also driven by response time you are willing to pay for.	Annual contracts, during the life of product	Insurance policy for the customer

4. "IT Service Spending in the Crosswinds," p. 4, The Gartner Group, September 25, 2000.
5. Ibid.

Table 0–1   Types of Services. (cont.'d)

Service Name	Description	Tag Lines	Pricing Attributes	Length Attributes	Proposed Benefits
Education Services	Product training	E-Learning, Web-Learning	Fixed percent of product costs OR per class. Also, as part of the sale, "training units" are available that can be applied to training.	Service measured in days of training	Increased employee productivity and employee certification
Implementation Services	Standard services designed to help customer implement the product faster or make the product efficient	Quick start, System tuning, Performance analysis	Fixed price per service requested	1 day – 4 weeks	Decreased time to implement new product and improve effectiveness of products already implemented
Consulting or Professional Services	Custom services designed to truly integrate the product into the customer's business	Business solutions, Best practices, Turnkey integration	Variable price. Driven by complexity of deliverables.	2 weeks – 6 months	ROI, reduced risk, and reduced time to implement business solution
Outsourcing Services	Staff provided by product company to actually administer the product for the customer on an ongoing basis	Staff augmentation	Fixed rate per head	Months – Years	Reduced costs and increased customer focus on core competencies

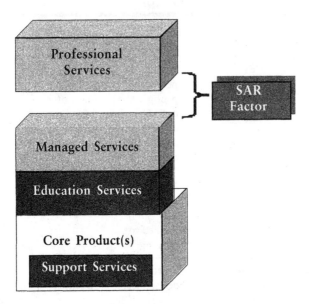

Figure 0–3 Product services.

These product companies see this opportunity for new service revenues. Figure 0-3 illustrates the traditional service opportunities on which a product company would focus: *support services and education services*—both are closely related to the core product of the company. But now, product companies are exploring new service opportunities that seem very attractive (light gray). There are *managed services,* which are more complex than standard support services but are still closely related to the products of the company. And, they are typically being delivered by support-service personnel who have downtime between support calls. This means managed services don't represent an investment in incremental staff to deliver the services. Finally, there are *professional services,* which may or may not be directly related to the product, but they do represent an incremental investment in new skill types.

The nice thing about professional-services revenues is that they don't seem to have all the messy strings attached to them that product revenues do: no product qualification process, no backwards-compatibility discussions, no never-ending support worries. With these high-level consulting services, it appears the product-service company can be "in and out." They collect their money and move on. Or do they? No, not

Introduction I Why Product Companies Jump In

really. In fact, consulting services are just as complex and risky to deliver as any new product. Every service-centric company can validate this fact. Unfortunately, no product-centric company believes it can be true. And, here begins the rub! Not only are professional services complex to deliver, there are business risks to providing professional services that many product companies do not understand at first. If the new professional services offered by the product company are not aligned and somehow anchored to their product, there is the risk that the services will be both unprofitable and counterproductive to the objectives of the product company. We refer to this risk as the services alignment risk (SAR) factor. In Chapter 2, we discuss this risk factor in more detail.

One of the oldest stories known to Western civilization is the *Odyssey* composed by the Greek poet Homer. In the story of the *Odyssey*, there is a conflict between a man named Odysseus and the Greek god Poseidon. Poseidon does not want Odysseus to return home to Ithaca, so the god hurls one challenge after another toward the tormented man. But this is not the true conflict. The defining conflict Odysseus faces is between his intelligence and his arrogance. On one hand, he is a very smart man. His wits brought about the fall of Troy (it was his idea to build the Trojan horse), and his wits allow him to survive each challenge the gods present. But his intelligence and success make him arrogant—arrogant enough to believe he needs no assistance from any man or any god. This arrogance fuels the wrath of Poseidon. Not until Odysseus acknowledges his limitations is he permitted to return home.

Product companies face the identical challenge that Odysseus faced. They are skilled and successful at bringing products to market. They have money from lucrative product margins to invest in new endeavors. They are confident in their business savvy. But this confidence becomes a harmful blinder as they enter the world of providing services. When service profits are thin or customer engagements go awry, the product company has difficulty acknowledging it has entered a new realm—a realm where the natural laws are different, requiring new frameworks to succeed. This reality leads us to our first "Sirens' Song." Throughout this book, we will be highlighting false perceptions held by many product companies regarding professional services. Because these perceptions can prove deadly, we have named them Sirens' Songs after the beautiful yet deadly monsters from the *Odyssey*. These Sirens were creatures that sang enchantingly to passing sailors, only to lead the sailors to crash into unseen boulders. The misperceptions we will be highlighting have the same effect: If they are not recognized, they can lead a product company to crash its service business.

Now, for our first Sirens' Song of Services:

> **SIRENS' SONG:** Professional services are not dramatically different from support services or education services.
> **BOULDER AHEAD:** The truth is professional services are dramatically different from other services typically offered by product companies. They are different in size, scope, and risk. They operate under a different financial model. Finally, they are the first service a product company offers that does not have to be directly linked to the product portfolio of the company.

Have we scared you? Good. But don't get too scared. Despite the potential hazards, there are many compelling reasons for a product-centric company to move forward from basic support services.

▶ Good Reasons to Offer New Services

Beyond pursuing additional revenue opportunities, there are many sound business reasons product companies offer more than just product-support services. The Services Marketing Advisors Association provides this standard list of reasons:[6]

- Client interest in business solutions as opposed to point products
- Deeper client relationships and improved account control
  - Increased revenue per customer: 50 to 100 percent higher revenues from both products and services[7]
  - Product pull-through[8]
- Increased margins
- Greater implementation control
- Improved customer satisfaction

6. "Training Fish to Fly? Seven Tips to Convert a Product Sales Force to Solutions Selling," June 2001, *www.itsma.com/education/prof_dev/pd_052901.html*.

7. "Should Professional Services Be in Your Company's Services Portfolio?" Shera Mikelson, Hahn Consulting.

8. Product pull-through is the act of leading with service sales and then pulling product sales in.

In *Living on the Fault Line*, Geoffrey Moore provides an updated list of why technology companies specifically need an internal professional-services organization:

- To help implement projects that advance the company's state of the art, featuring products that are fresh from R&D.
- To do the gritty, unglamorous work behind the scenes that has to be done to make the system work right. This is the very work that independent consulting firms want no part of.
- To develop domain expertise in one or more vertical markets to help differentiate the company's existing products.

Moore states that by providing professional services, a product company can take on problems for long-established customers that no one else will tackle. "Not only does this help secure long-term loyalty and commitment, but it can also lead to the discovery of new market opportunities."[9]

And in reality, there are benefits to the end customer. By providing consulting services directly, the product-centric company can succeed in the following ways:

- Provide one-stop shopping for implementation
- Provide hard-to-find product expertise and technical skills
- Decrease time to complete the customer solution
- Allow customers to focus on their core competencies
- Provide a single point of contact
- Provide a single point of liability

These last two points are especially attractive to understaffed, overworked IT managers who have enough vendor relationships to juggle as it is. When coauthor Steve O'Connor was CIO at Silicon Graphics, he drove his IT organization to work with a short list of seven strategic vendors. "I didn't feel my management (team) and I could build effective relationships with more than seven vendors." The practice reclaims cycles for the IT management team and creates deeper, more productive relationships with vendors.

So, with a win-win situation in mind, the product company cranks the product-service wheel and begins offering new services to the customer.

9. Geoffrey Moore, *Living on the Fault Line*, New York: HarperCollins, 2000. © 2000 by Geoffrey A. Moore. Reprinted by permission of HarperCollins Publishers Inc.

The customer buys them. And then, the real fun begins: the fun of actually delivering these services in a consistent and profitable manner. For most product companies, this is when the journey begins to get rough. Engineering and implementing products profitably is one set of skills, doing the same for services is quite another. The principles are often the same, but their application is very different. If services are not managed properly, the product company may soon find its hard-won product margins being used to subsidize unprofitable service engagements.

SIRENS' SONG: Professional services should be a high-margin component of a product company's portfolio.
BOULDER AHEAD: The truth is many product companies are experiencing lower than expected margins from their professional-services business. Gross margins for professional-services business units have been running at 15 percent to 20 percent with net operating profits of zero.

In reality, some of the best and brightest product companies have struggled to maintain a profit in the journey of building a services organization.[10] IBM is used constantly as the poster child for success—a model for how a product company can transition itself into a true service and solution provider. But how many companies have the deep pockets of IBM? How many companies have a locked-in legacy install base that can carry them through the painful and unprofitable transition IBM went through? Not many. And, how many other examples of success have you read about? How long is the list of product companies that have actually developed a successful and profitable service organization that offers more than basic support services? The number of articles describing product companies that want to offer more complex services is endless. The number of articles documenting favorable results is almost nonexistent.

We know the service waters look inviting. We know you want to set sail. But are you prepared to navigate these waters? Have you built the right ship? Do you have the right maps? If the answer is *no*, not even Poseidon himself will be able to save you from the shipwreck ahead.

10. "Should Professional Services Be in Your Company's Services Portfolio?" Shera Mikelson, Hahn Consulting.

This book is designed to help the product company listen to the Sirens' Song of services without sailing into the rocks, to help the product company succeed as it turns the product-service wheel without succumbing to blind arrogance.

1

Mapping the Voyage

Surviving the sirens' song

▶ Parameters for Success

In the ever-expanding world of business how-to books, there are two opposing camps of business philosophy. In one camp, you have the recipe philosophers. These are business gurus who believe step-by-step instructions are ideal. Step one, create business model. Step two, analyze business processes. Add a pinch of this, a dash of that, and voilà: the perfect business. Michael Hammer, coauthor of *Reengineering the Corporation* and leader of the reengineering revolution, is a solid example of a recipe philosopher. In the other camp sit the ingredient philosophers. Their goal is not to provide a detailed recipe, but to explain the current ingredients at hand. Their insight includes defining the attributes of each ingredient. The businessperson then decides how best to combine the raw ingredients to bake success. These ingredient philosophers strongly believe every company must find its own unique recipe for success. A book such as *Intellectual Capital,* by Thomas Stewart, is a fine example of ingredient philosophy.

The Sirens' Song may have the appearance of recipe philosophy but is actually based on ingredient philosophy. Yes, we will provide a step-by-step example of building a professional-services organization at a product company. But, this is only an example. The true insight comes from the frameworks offered to understand a service business that's attached to a product company. Our belief is that to successfully manage any business unit, you must clearly understand the following ten parameters (or ingredients) of your business:

1. The **mission** of your business unit
2. The **strategic objectives** (i.e., long-term objectives) for your business
3. The **guiding principles** (or policies) that apply to your business
4. The overall financial **business model** of your business
5. The key **levers** you can use to drive profitability in your business
6. The **organizational structure** (including roles and responsibilities) of your staff
7. The **metrics** you will use to manage the health of your business
8. The **compensation strategy** (i.e., how you will incite and encourage the right behaviors) for your staff
9. The **current key objectives** (i.e., short-term objectives) of your business
10. Any **unique issues** you face in running this particular business

These key parameters are different for a professional-services organization that is attached to a product company than they would be for a stand-alone professional-services firm. We cannot stress this enough. Building a service organization within a product company is different than building an independent consulting firm.

SIRENS' SONG: Services are services are services. Managing professional services within a product company is not very different than managing professional services outside a product company.

BOULDER AHEAD: The truth is there are fundamental differences in managing a professional-services organization within a product company. If those differences are not understood, it will be very difficult for the product company to build, manage, and sustain a profitable service organization.

Independent consulting organizations have dramatically different business models, alternate organizational structures, and different metrics than product-centric service firms have. Table 1-1 shows just how some of the parameters can be different.

Table 1-1 Product-Company Professional Services versus Independent Professional Services.

Parameter	Stand-Alone Professional-Services Firm	Professional Services within a Product Company
Mission	Deliver outstanding customer service, hire and retain the best talent, achieve financial success (profitability)	Customer satisfaction and product pull-through
Strategic Objectives	Grow install base Improve/maintain billable utilization rates	Educate sales force on selling and positioning services Develop software and tools to complete product offerings
Business Model	40%–50% gross margins 10%–16% operating profit	20%–30% gross margins 0–10% operating profit

We believe the business community has paid very little attention to these differences and the unique challenges a product company faces as it plunges into the consulting waters. This book has been written to provide the key frameworks a product company needs to successfully build a profitable professional-services organization.

▶ Primary Audience

This book is targeted primarily at the management team with the responsibility for establishing the new professional-services business. The text will address this audience directly. This newly formed management team will face three daunting issues:

1. On a strategic level, how does the team successfully establish the mission, objectives, guiding principles, and target business model for this new business unit?

2. On a tactical level, what levers does the team use to optimize profitability? How does it organize, evaluate, and compensate its employees?

3. On an operational level, how must the team actually deliver new services successfully and profitably?

This book will address all three issues. It will assist the team in understanding its new environment and help it focus on the right issues at the right time during the evolution of the new business. To achieve this objective, this book will run through the creation of a new consulting-services organization targeted to reach $100 million in revenue.

▶ Chapter Structure

Information on how to create a professional services business will be presented on three levels. As shown in Figure 1-1, these are the strategic level, the tactical level, and the operational level.

Figure 1–1   Levels of business planning.

In Chapter 2: Setting the Parameters, we begin with the overarching strategy required for success, including a discussion on establishing a core mission and strategic objectives. Also, there will be a review of the guiding principles that should be applied to the newly formed professional-services (PS) organization. These principles will greatly impact the financial business model the organization can execute.

Next, we present a set of tactics that can be used to establish the services unit of the business. In Chapter 3: Levers for Profitability, we will present a high-level overview of the PS organization. Then in Chapters 4 through 7, we review the following details for each separate function:

- **Charter:** What is the directive and purpose of this function?

- **Activities and Processes:** What activities must this function perform? What key processes must it implement?

- **Roles and Responsibilities:** What are the typical staffing needs, or staff roles, required to deliver this capability? What are the key responsibilities of each role?

- **Key Interfaces:** There are four key functions in a PS organization: sales, delivery, marketing, and engineering (i.e., solution development). Each of these functions has specific internal interfaces that are critical. Any PS organization must also interface with several other companies and organizations. As each PS function is overviewed, these internal and external key interfaces will be reviewed.

- **Key Metrics:** How can this function be measured? What are the key measures? How are they calculated and who is responsible for them?

- **Key Tools:** What infrastructure does this function require?

- **Compensation Strategies:** How can employees of each function be motivated to exhibit the right behaviors?

- **Organizational Structure and Sizing:** How is this function typically organized? What are some other options? When new, how should the function be sized?

- **Sample Budget:** What would the budget for this function look like?

After reviewing each function individually, we will take a look at the system holistically. In Chapter 9, we review the operational infrastructure required for these four functions to work effectively. Then, in Chapter 10: Putting It All Together, we review, step by step, how these functions can be put in place and how the overall organization can be built. At this point, we will have presented all the key tactics you need to create a functional PS business unit.

In Chapter 11: Customer Engagement Workflow, we address the day-to-day operations of the business by walking through the customer engagement workflow. This is the process of actually qualifying new service opportunities, bidding for business, and then delivering the service.

In Chapter 12: Four Phases of Building PS, we revisit the product-services wheel and review the maturity curve a typical PS firm lives through. Each phase has a distinct business model, specific objectives, and unique issues. By understanding this maturity life cycle, realistic expectations can be set for senior management regarding financial performance.

Finally, in Chapter 13: Unique Issues, we itemize the unique issues faced by a PS organization when it is seeded in a product company. These issues are significant and can be debilitating to the service business if not addressed.

▶ Secondary Audiences

While our primary audience is the service provider, there are other target audiences for this book, including the senior managers of product companies that interface with the new service organization. The more these individuals understand the new service entity, the more effectively they can utilize the service function. Marketing managers can better promote the companies' new services. Product managers can better align their go-to-market activities. Product engineering managers can mine valuable data amassed through customer engagements.

And finally, let's not forget the end customer. Almost every senior manager out there has employed a PS firm for one reason or another. More often than not, these professional services are now being offered and provided by product vendors. If senior managers are to be users of these burgeoning services, they should understand what is driving the service provider's business. This insight will assist in assessing the true capabilities of product-service companies that are being considered. Knowledge truly is power: The greater the knowledge of the product or service business, the greater the leverage when negotiating and engaging.

Ultimately, our goal is to provide insightful frameworks to all three audiences. These frameworks can serve as ballast through some of the rough waters ahead. And we believe the short-term forecast is for very rough seas. We believe the majority of product companies, both large and small, are really just beginning to understand the nuances of offering professional services.

So, regardless of whether you are a newly appointed services manager or a new services customer, go ahead, listen to that Sirens' song. Dive into the service waters. But don't forget to use these concepts to strap yourself to the mast. Otherwise, you are heading directly into the boulders of poor margins and operating loss.

▶ Chapter Overview Table

Table 1-2 provides a summary of the level of the business on which each chapter focuses: strategic, tactical, or operational. Chapters focused on strategy provide a high-level view (the 100,000-ft. view) of the PS business. Chapters focused on tactics provide more detailed frameworks on how to manage the business. Finally, chapters focused at the operational level provide very specific ground-level details on how to actually carry out specific processes.

Table 1–2   Chapter Overview.

Level of Business	Viewpoint	Overarching Framework(s)	Supporting Framework(s)	Chapters
	100,000 ft.	• Product-Services Wheel • 10 Key Parameters		Introduction Ch 1: Mapping the Voyage Ch 2: Setting the Parameters Ch 12: Four Phases of Building PS Ch 14: Summary of Key Concepts

Table 1–2   Chapter Overview. (cont.'d)

Level of Business	Viewpoint	Overarching Framework(s)	Supporting Framework(s)	Chapters
	50,000 ft.	• Profitability Triangle • PS Organizational Model	• Customer Engagement Model • Project Delivery Model • Solution Development Model • Go-to-Market Framework • Operational Infrastructure Framework • Aligning Core Competencies • Aligning Skills	Ch 3: Levers for Profitability Ch 4: Organizational Overview Ch 5: Selling Ch 6: Delivering Ch 7: Productizing Ch 8: Promoting Ch 9: Operational Infrastructure Ch 10: Putting It All Together Ch 13: Unique Issues Appendix E: Solution Portfolio Management
	Ground Level	Customer Engagement Model	Customer Engagement Workflow	Ch 11: Customer Engagement Workflow Appendix A: Customer Check List Appendix C: PS Business Review Appendix D: Sample Project Review Appendix F: Customer Request and Qualification Form

Setting the Parameters

Mission, business model, objectives, and guiding principles

When a product company first hears the call of professional services, the call may indeed sound very sweet. The potential for more revenue is seductive. The hope of high margins is uplifting. And, the benefit of greater customer account control is a soothing concept to nervous executives. But before a product company launches a new service endeavor, it must set clear parameters for that portion of the organization. If these parameters are not discussed at inception, the success of the new service business unit can be grossly inhibited. Specifically, the executive staff must discuss the mission, the strategic objectives, the guiding principles of operation, and, finally, the financial business model (or the level of performance) the new unit will be expected to execute. This chapter reviews each one of these parameters in detail and provides guidance on what to consider when setting them.

Sirens' Song: Offering high-margin professional services is a sound business move for most product companies.
Boulder Ahead: The truth is, like any business decision, the decision to offer professional services should first be reviewed and evaluated before being agreed to. Not all product companies are well positioned to offer professional services.

▶ Are You Sure? Four Qualifying Questions

Before we explore the parameters that need to be set for the new PS unit you're dying to launch, let's step back. Are you absolutely sure this is the right thing for your company? Should your company create a PS organization? These are fundamental questions. In the introduction, we highlighted many of the reasons product companies want to offer professional services, but *want* and *should* are entirely different things. We know you *want* to get into the PS game, but *should* you? Your answer to that question is probably driven by many complex variables. Here are four fundamental questions the executive team of any company should ask before plunging into the PS business:

1. **Can your management team articulate what would differentiate your professional services from everybody else's?** Typically, product companies possess some type of unique technical expertise. If you cannot identify any unique skills or solutions that will set you apart in the service world, perhaps partnering with another service provider is the better play.

2. **Do you intend to make fee-based professional expertise a core competency of your company?** The story goes that way back when, IBM made the fundamental decision that it was actually a service company, not a product company. Today, offering everything from technology-planning consulting services to full-scale outsourcing is core to IBM. Will your new services be core to who you are? Or are they just expensive window dressing you really can't afford?

3. **Is there a market for your services?** You may be able to articulate a unique set of new services that you feel is core to future success, but is there a viable market? Before diving in head first, make sure the water is deep enough. In other words, is the customer base actually there?

4. **Can you sell these new services to your existing customers through your existing channels?**[1] You have identified the service, you are committed to it, and it looks like there is a healthy market. All good. But there are two potential issues you must consider. What if the buyer of your new services is not your current

---

1. The insight on this issue is based on a conversation one of the authors had with Tom Pencek of Pencek and Associates. Tom highlighted how so many product companies struggle as they attempt to shove new services down a channel optimized to sell products.

product customer? Here is a simple example: Your company makes specialized design software for engineers in the auto industry. Your typical buyer is a departmental engineering manager. Over the years your company has accumulated in-depth expertise and knowledge about how various manufacturers design automobiles. Now, you intend to offer high-level consulting on the entire design process. But guess what? The departmental engineering manager does not sign $250,000 purchase orders for consulting services. The vice president of engineering does, but your company has never sold to this vice president. In fact, your company has very few contacts at that level. It will be very difficult to sell your new service through your current channels. Is this a showstopper? It depends on your business objectives and how much you are willing to invest to create new channels. The important checkpoint is to assess your current channels and know where you stand before forging ahead.

From this point forward, we will assume your company has discussed these four questions and has determined that starting a PS organization is a sound business decision. If your service opportunity failed to pass these qualification questions, but you intend to move forward anyway, please don't disregard the rest of this book. You will need the frameworks it offers more than ever to survive the journey ahead. Now, let's review the key parameters the executive team needs to set before launching this new business unit.

▶ Mission

Most business units or departments have a mission statement, and most business leaders have had to craft one or two in their career. The goal of a mission statement is to capture the overall purpose or aim of your organization, or to state the reason your organization exists. For example, Business Computing Solutions lists the following mission statement on its Web site:

> Our goal is to seamlessly integrate with our clients to provide I/T Business Solutions that empower our clients and its people to achieve its business missions.
>
> *Q. Moosavi, president*

In other words, the mission of Business Computing Solutions is to help customers use technology to achieve their mission.

In *Managing the Professional Service Firm*, David Maister reveals the following insight:

> One of the most interesting discoveries in my consulting work has been a fact that (apparently) every professional-service firm in the world has the same mission statement, regardless of the firm's size, specific profession, or country of operation. With varying refinements of language, the mission of most professional firms is:
>
> > To deliver outstanding client service; to provide the fulfilling careers and professional satisfaction for our employees; and to achieve financial success so that we can reward ourselves and grow.
>
> The commonality of this mission does not detract from its value. Simply put, each professional firm must satisfy these three goals of service, satisfaction, and success if it is to survive.[2]

In principle, we agree with this conclusion: The financial success of a PS business is based on meeting the needs of both customers and highly talented employees. However, when the PS firm is folded under the umbrella of a product company, the rules change. The previous mission statement will not serve a product-based PS firm well. In fact, this mission statement will lead the new service unit directly into horrible internal conflicts. So, let us build on what's there.

When crafting the mission statement for a PS organization that is part of a product company, there are three key items to consider: format, audience, and overarching objective.

Format

First, let's review the issue of format. Janel Radtke writes that mission statements should:[3]

2. David H. Maister, *Managing the Professional Service Firm*, New York: Simon and Schuster, 1993.

3. Janel M. Radtke, "Strategic Communications for Nonprofit Organizations: Seven Steps to Creating a Successful Plan," *The Grantsmanship Center Magazine*, Fall 1998.

- Express your organization's purpose in a way that inspires support and on-going commitment
- Motivate those who are connected to your organization
- Be articulated in a way that is convincing and easy to grasp
- Use proactive verbs to describe what your organization does
- Be free of jargon
- Be short enough so that anyone connected to your organization can readily repeat it

A mission statement for a PS organization should adhere to all the guidelines applied to crafting any good mission statement. If the mission statement your executive team crafts is not *crisp, compelling*, and *convincing*, it probably needs some work.

Audience

The second issue to consider is the audience for the mission statement. Is this mission statement to be viewed internally or externally? There is a story that states Nike has a very simple mission statement: Crush Reebok. However, if you review their corporate Web site, this mission statement is nowhere to be found. If this mission statement for Nike does indeed exist somewhere, we would call this an "internal" mission statement. In other words, the audience for this mission statement includes those within the walls of the company. An "external" mission statement, on the other hand, is one that would be shared with customers. At first, your focus should be on the internal mission statement and should address the new service entity's mission from a strictly company-oriented perspective. Later, an external mission statement can be developed that is targeted at your organization's customers.

Overarching Objective

The third, final, and most important issue when crafting a mission statement for a product-based PS firm is the main purpose of the service unit. Before finalizing the mission statement, the executive management team needs to agree on one key point: What is the overarching purpose of this new business unit? What is the purpose that overrides all other objectives? What is the fundamental reason this business unit has been created at the company? Let's look at some potential answers to this critical question. The overarching purpose of your new PS organization might be to:

- Drive/sell the product and service portfolio of the company, or
- Ensure high customer satisfaction, or
- Maximize profits (for its own P&L), or
- Assist in developing leading-edge solutions for key customers

In reality, your executive team may want to see the PS unit fulfill the entire list. But what is the *primary* objective? The executive team must call this out at the beginning. If not, conflicts will occur. Geoffrey Moore, the technology-marketing expert quoted earlier, addresses this issue of mission directly:[4]

> True, they (professional services) are also expected to generate revenue, and true, this revenue does count on the bottom line, but that is not their primary value-creating function. It is, instead, to contribute to the greater good.
>
> The challenge facing this organization's management team is to charter it correctly, to make absolutely clear what is core and what is context. For independent consulting firms, revenue is core; for professional-services organizations (that are part of a product company), revenue is context!

Let's review a simple example to drive the point home. A key customer is using your PS team to implement a new solution. During implementation, the customer determines that they are better off using a competitor's product in the solution as opposed to yours. What should your service unit do? If the prime mission of your service unit is to maximize its own profits, it should probably continue with implementation to get the service revenue. Also, if the prime mission is to ensure customer satisfaction, the service staff should not disengage. But what if the primary mission is to maximize the company portfolio? Why then would the service unit deploy a solution on someone else's platform? It wouldn't. Here is another quick example to highlight the point. What if the second largest customer for your company wants to engage the services team—at a hefty discount. Does the service unit comply or find

---

4. Geoffrey Moore, *Living on the Fault Line*, New York: Harper Business, 2000. © 2000 by Geoffrey A. Moore. Reprinted by permission of HarperCollins Publishers Inc.

more profitable pastures? Once again, the primary mission would guide that decision.

Mission and the SAR Factor

Now you can see how critical the issue of setting the overarching purpose has become. When a primary mission is put in place, it can effectively be used as a compass to navigate tricky seas. In the introduction, we discussed a variable called the service alignment risk factor, or the SAR factor. This concept comes into play when you are attempting to align your PS business unit as closely as possible to the rest of your company. Remember, professional services are the first services you are offering that are not directly and clearly linked to your core products. This phenomenon creates the potential for a dangerous gap between what professional services you offer and how well they fit into your overall product and service portfolio. This potential gap is demonstrated in Figure 2-1.

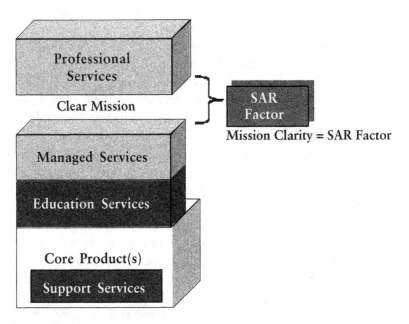

Figure 2–1 Mission and the SAR factor.

There are strategies you can employ to greatly reduce the risk of creating a PS unit that does not fit synergistically into your overall business portfolio. If you don't manage this risk factor, you can create a distanced PS unit that does little to drive forward your overall business objectives. A clear, agreed-upon mission statement is one of the tethers that will anchor your PS organization to the rest of the company portfolio. However, without it, you can expect many stormy conversations in the future—conversations where your VP of professional services must disagree with a sales executive regarding what should be done for customer so and so. Without the overarching mission in place for services, the VP of PS and the VP of sales will wrestle over the "right" thing to do. They both will have opinions, they both will have valid points, but they might never come to agreement. You can also expect the real possibility of a business unit that is profitable in its own right, but has alienated itself from other key business units.

▶ Business Model

Once the overarching mission for the new PS organization is determined by the executive management team, the target business model, or financial model, for the business unit can be discussed. If the mission is profitability, benchmarks against other profitable service firms can be used to determine the right financial model to put in place. If customer satisfaction is the overriding driver, perhaps a break-even business model is acceptable. In later chapters, we present sample business models, and in Appendix B: Key Financial Models, we offer several business models from the industry. The important point is that the executive management team *agrees* on the business model to which they are holding the PS management team accountable. If there is disagreement around this topic, or, worse yet, no discussion whatsoever, the newly appointed VP of professional services will be tilting at financial windmills. Does the executive management team want the new VP to chase top-line revenue growth or bottom-line profitability? What gross margins are acceptable for this business? Without agreed-upon answers, the potential for frustration is high. Put a first draft business model in place now. It can be validated and adjusted later, but this specific anchor is a critical prerequisite to success.

▶ Objectives

With the mission and target business model in place, the discussion surrounding strategic objectives can begin. On a strategic level, what does your new services organization need to achieve? You are looking at the two- to four-year time frame. Here, we'll take a play from David Maister's playbook. He recognized patterns in the mission statements of stand-alone PS firms. For service firms connected to product companies, we see greater potential for variability at the mission level and for commonality at the objectives level.

Every product-based PS organization must address the following strategic objectives sometime in its life span if it hopes to sustain itself as a viable business unit:

1. **Finalize your mission and business model**: As stated, these two items may need to be refined once the service organization is actually operating. The PS senior management team must validate it is executing a mission and a business plan that make sense for its parent product company.

2. **Achieve your financial objectives**: Regardless of what the financial objectives are (lose money, break even, make 5 percent operating profit), the new business unit must prove its ability to deliver results. If the management misses this objective, more often than not it will soon be the ex-management team of the PS unit.

3. **Teach your company to sell solutions**: If the new PS team cannot transition the company from selling products to selling solutions, the service business will wither on the vine with no effective channel. Incidentally, achieving this objective is the reason many CEOs create an internal PS unit.

4. **Align your capabilities and solutions**: A PS unit must offer skills and solutions that are in line with their corporate objectives. This topic is covered in greater detail later in the text. Suffice to say that failure in this objective will lead directly to poor profitability and internal friction.

5. **Implement your processes and infrastructure**: As a new business unit, there is a host of business processes to be implemented and infrastructure needs to be met to support the business. Typically, a product company will be missing much of the support infrastructure critical to its services business. Also, the sooner

the service team establishes common business practices across its workforce, the more efficient the service employees will become and the more consistent the delivery of services will be.

6. **Implement your customer satisfaction metrics**: References are the lifeblood of the services organization. This topic is discussed in more detail in Chapter 3.

7. **Create an employee development program**: Services can be differentiated by the unique skills you offer customers or the sophisticated solutions you deliver. Both solutions and skills require employee training and development. If the management team disregards this objective, it will find it extremely difficult to differentiate its service organization from others, now or later.

A new PS organization may have more than these seven objectives listed here. But these are the seven that simply won't go away. If they are not highlighted and addressed, the performance of the service organization will most likely not meet the expectations of this executive management team.

▶ Guiding Principles

We use the term "guiding principles" in the way many people use the term "policy." Guiding principles are the general rules that guide the decisions of your organization. They set the boundaries within which sound business decisions can be made. Authors Michael Lissack and Johan Roos provide a wonderful working definition for guiding principles:

> Guiding Principles: Simple rules interacting within a defined area starting with some goals.[5]

Lissack and Roos also provide insight to the problems with old rules:

> In the traditional "decision making is everything" business model, rules are used as a shortcut. In a complicated world, the trick was to cram more into less and to hide things that were uncomfort-

5. Michael Lissack and Johan Roos, *The Next Common Sense,* London, UK: Nicholas Brealey Publishing, 1999.

able. Rules provided a heuristic device so that thinking was less necessary and more time was available for deciding and acting. The intriguing thing about your rules of business is that we succeeded in creating vast corporate empires in spite of them.

Rules don't allow for autonomy or for a context-dependent reaction to each situation. They do not allow room for interaction.

Guiding principles are designed to allow managers to make context-dependent decisions based on the specific issue at hand. They also require interaction between managers to discuss and determine what action to take. Guiding principles are clearly more vague than traditional rules and procedures, but they are much more effective in complex and rapidly changing business environments. Also, they have a much longer life span than standard rules that must be updated for each new exception.

Now that you have the definition, let's work through an example. Let's say your new PS unit has started offering new integration services. When delivering these services, the PS team often implements third-party products (i.e., products from other vendors that complement your product). Now, customers are asking your company to support some of these third-party products. PS management sees these custom-support plans as a new revenue opportunity for the support-services organization. However, the support-services team sees this as a massive headache because they have no idea how to support the other products. How should these two management teams solve this issue? There are no current processes or rules for dealing with the scenario. If it is not addressed, customer satisfaction will be impacted and the relationship between the two service units will become strained. The answer: guiding principles. Before this issue becomes a problem, the senior management teams of both professional services and support services should establish a set of guiding principles on how the two service units will work together. A sample could look as follows:

1. Professional Services and Support Services will function as a global-services business unit.

2. Professional Services and Support Services are committed to providing support for the custom solutions the company develops and implements for customers.

3. All custom-solution support contracts will be held and managed by Support Services.

4. Support Services will define all custom-solutions support options.

5. Professional Services will engage Support Services as soon as possible in the opportunity to assure the support solution is provided, ideally in the requirements-definition phase.

6. Support Services is committed to a timely response to all Professional Service engagements throughout the bid process.

7. Professional Services proposals will not be sent to the customer without Support Services involvement, where appropriate.

8. Where possible Professional Services and Support Services agree to use existing processes, tools, and services in order to leverage existing investment, capabilities, and what is already working well in the environment.

9. The entry point for all delivered support will be Customer Support Centers (CSC). Delivery of services may be provided using partners or other third-party providers.

10. Both Professional Services and Support Services are committed to working together on all custom-solution support activities through agreed processes.

With this set of guiding principles in place, the professional-services unit and the support-services unit could work through almost any business issue that comes between them. With the birth of a new PS business unit, there are at least nine key areas where the company now needs firm guiding principles in place. Table 2-1 provides an overview of the topics around which guiding principles should be established when the senior managers of the various business units and functions sit down together. The table also provides insight on what the potential issues are and who should get involved when setting the principles.

If you successfully completed the objectives of this chapter, then you have successfully set the parameters for your new business. This is time well spent on the front end. As the saying goes, "garbage in, garbage out." If you slouch on the design, if you shortchange the parameter-setting process, you greatly increase the potential for failure. If you truly did need to skip some of the above issues, don't worry; you'll have a chance to address them at a later date—because these are issues that don't go away!

Table 2–1 Guiding Principles.

Topic	Description	Potential Issue(s)	Senior Management Involved	Comments
1. Account Management	How will the traditional product sales organization and the new PS sales organization work together to manage customer accounts?	Poor account planning. Uncoordinated sales efforts.	VP of Professional Services, Regional PS Directors, VP of Product Sales, Regional Product Sales Directors	
2. Business Development Funding	Who will fund business development investments with strategic customers?	Professional Services will be asked to perform services at low or negative margins for strategic customers. This activity will impact PS profitability.	VP of Professional Services, VP of Product Sales, VP of Marketing	

Table 2–1   Guiding Principles. (cont.'d)

Topic	Description	Potential Issue(s)	Senior Management Involved	Comments
3. Compensation	How will the organization compensate its staff?	Compensation plans do not drive needed results.	VP of Professional Services, VP of Human Resources	1. Establish a program that is consistent with the goals and objectives of the organization. 2. If the goals and objectives of the organization change, then change the program at the same time. 3. Pay for performance not seniority. 4. Link program to job type. Sales compensated with revenue targets, delivery based on project performance, and operations based on targeted deliverables. 5. Establish realistic expectations and strive to always beat them.
4. Internal Transfers	What will the policy be for transferring staff from other organizations into Professional Services?	With no guidelines in place, animosity can be created if PS "cherry picks" sales and delivery staff from other organizations.	VP of Professional Services, VP of Human Resources, VP of Product Sales	

Table 2–1   Guiding Principles. (cont.'d)

Topic	Description	Potential Issue(s)	Senior Management Involved	Comments
5. Intellectual Property (IP) Transition	How will new intellectual property be gathered and developed?	Failure to collect and develop new intellectual property will hinder new solution development.	VP of Professional Services, VP of Marketing, VP of Engineering	1. Senior management must demand that IP be captured and reviewed. 2. Staff should have incentives to capture IP. 3. Guidelines should be established that are globally and consistently applied throughout the organization. 4. A simple, well-thought-out process should be implemented that minimizes collection time. 5. IP must be captured as quickly as possible to avoid personnel changes and loss of information. 6. Existing IP should be periodically reviewed to ensure relevancy to business objectives.

Table 2–1 Guiding Principles. (cont.'d)

Topic	Description	Potential Issue(s)	Senior Management Involved	Comments
6. Partner Management	What process will the company follow when identifying, qualifying, negotiating, and signing new partners? What variables is the company trying to optimize when signing new partners?	Business units will sign up partners that create direct conflict with other business units within the company.	VP of Professional Services, VP of Marketing, VP of Product Sales, VP of Engineering	1. Find, qualify, contract, and manage a select group of partners to further expand the company's current offerings and opportunities. 2. Do business with the partner as a consulting customer. 3. Jointly develop and deliver new high-value services that generate incremental revenue. 4. Jointly develop and possibly cobrand new high-value services that enable customers to focus on their core business, instead of technology. 5. Through committed reciprocal business, highly leverage the scarce human resources, the comarketing funds, the equipment pool, the training capabilities, and the management time. 6. Supplement the company PS workforce with skill sets not yet available.

Table 2–1   Guiding Principles. (cont.'d)

Topic	Description	Potential Issue(s)	Senior Management Involved	Comments
7. Revenue Recognition	How will revenue be recognized between Professional Services and the other business units? For example, if PS sells product as part of a large engagement, does PS receive revenue recognition for this?	With unclear guidelines, it becomes difficult for PS to predict revenue if it is unclear what should be included in PS revenue.	VP of Professional Services, VP of Product Sales, VP of Marketing	

Table 2–1 Guiding Principles. (cont.'d)

Topic	Description	Potential Issue(s)	Senior Management Involved	Comments
8. Solution Development Funding	How will the overall company fund new solutions?	Failure to develop and invest in new solutions will inhibit progress through the four phases.	VP of Professional Services, VP of Marketing, VP of Product Engineering	1. Use incentives at all levels of the organization to bring ideas forward. 2. Create a simple way for new ideas to be articulated and include preliminary business case. 3. For ideas that could become solutions, develop a comprehensive business case. 4. Have executive team review, approve, and fund solution. 5. Establish accountability for solution back to the company. 6. After instituting solution, have period review to ensure solution is still in line with objectives. 7. Fund only those solutions that provide greatest return to the organization.
9. Support Contracts	How will the new Professional Services unit and the existing Support Services interact?	Professional Services implements third-party products that Support Services cannot support	VP of Professional Services, VP of Support Services	

Levers for Profitability

Revenue, references, and repeatability

Enough of missions and objectives—let's get to business. Let's make some money! So, how are you going to successfully sail this new services business through the narrow straights ahead? As in any P&L business, the ultimate strategy is quite straightforward: *Make more than you spend*. The PS business inside a product company is no different. There may be a spectrum of acceptable profitability based on how much product the services pull-through, but at the end of the day the PS business unit is usually required to carry its own water. Now, how best to do that? What are the key levers you can use to drive a profitable professional-services business?

There is an old business saying that there are only two ways to improve profitability in a business: either raise the bridge (increase prices) or lower the water level (reduce costs). This simple universal business law clearly applies to a PS organization. Specifically, the growth and success of a PS organization is driven by three critical variables. These three variables, as shown in Figure 3-1, are revenue, references, and repeatability. Revenue and references raise the bridge while repeatability helps lower the water. Every activity should be targeted at improving one of these three variables. If you are not improving in these three areas, you are probably not improving the health of your business. That is why we refer to this as the *Iron Triangle of PS Profit-*

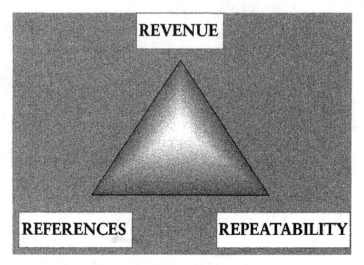

Figure 3–1 PS triangle of profitability.

ability. Without the concepts of this triangle firmly in place, it is very difficult for the PS business unit to be profitable. Break this iron triangle and you dramatically reduce your chance for success.

▶ Revenue

Revenue is obviously the first and foremost variable a consulting organization must manage. It may seem simple, but of course it is not. There are many components to the revenue variable that must be understood and managed. In Appendix B, there is a detailed discussion on financial metrics and reporting. For now, let's highlight some of the key points to revenue management.

Revenue Types

There are three types of revenue for a PS business: direct revenue, pass-through revenue, and reusable intellectual property (IP) revenue, as shown in Figure 3-2. Direct revenue comes from billing customers for your direct consulting resources. Pass-through revenue comes from

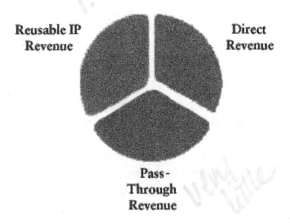

Figure 3–2 Revenue types.

passing through the products and services of other companies. For example, when the PS business unit subcontracts expertise it does not have from other consulting firms, the PS business unit is "passing through" revenue from the end customer to the subcontracted firm. Reusable intellectual-property (IP) revenue is generated whenever your service organization is able to take the deliverables (i.e., products and knowledge) from one engagement and reuse them again to generate revenue.

Direct revenue is more desirable than pass-through revenue, but revenue from reusable IP is the most attractive revenue of all. Direct revenue provides better gross margins (20 percent to 40 percent) than pass-through revenues provide (10 percent to 20 percent). Why? There is only so much "uplift" (or markup) end customers will allow you to charge them for managing other companies. Typically, you can't tack on more than 15 percent when selling someone else's services. With direct revenue, you are delivering the goods yourself and receive the entire margin associated with the service. There is another benefit of direct revenue. When you are receiving direct revenue, your employees are delivering solutions themselves and they are building valuable expertise for which customers pay a premium. These direct-revenue activities allow you to build valuable intellectual property and reuse it. Which leads to reusable IP revenue. With pass-through revenue, you are simply adding a fee as you pass on the expertise (product or service) that belongs to others. Reusable IP can bring gross margins any-where from 50 percent to 100 percent based on how much your service staff needs to fine-tune the deliverables from customer to customer.

Revenue Mix

Revenue mix refers to the mix of the three revenue types. The more direct revenue and reusable IP revenue you have in your mix, the better your gross margins. To prove this point, let's look at two firms that have different revenue mixes. Firm A has a revenue mix of 30/70/0 (i.e., 30 percent of their revenue comes from direct revenues, 70 per-cent comes from pass-through revenues, and 0 percent comes from any type of reusable IP). Firm B has a slightly different revenue mix of 60/30/10, (or 60 percent comes from direct revenue, 30 percent from pass-through revenues, and 10 percent comes from high-margin reusable IP). Now, look at Table 3-1 to see the impact this has on overall gross margins. Due to the healthier revenue mix, Firm B benefits with a gross margin 12.5 points better than Firm A's.

Table 3–1   Revenue Mix.

	Firm A	Firm B
Annual Revenue (millions)	$100	$100
Direct Revenue	$ 30	$ 60
Pass-Through Revenue	$ 70	$ 30
Reusable IP Revenue	$ 0	$ 10
Average Margin on Direct Services	25%	35%
Average Margin on Pass-Through Services	15%	15%
Average Margin on Reusable IP	60%	50%
Average Gross Margin Percentage	18%	30.5%

Revenue Growth Rate

Typically, revenue growth is a desirable objective. Almost every business has the objective to grow the top line. But with professional services, there is a cost associated with aggressive revenue growth. The faster you grow your revenue, the lower your profitability will be. This correlation occurs for two reasons. First of all, to grow direct revenue, you need to hire consultants. When you hire new employees, there is ramp-up time involved, because new employees need training, on-site mentoring, etc. With all this going on, your billable hours decline. This cuts into profitability. The second reason relates back to the revenue mix. Large growth rates in PS revenues are usually fueled by large amounts of pass-through revenues. As described in the previous paragraph, a revenue mix that is heavily loaded in pass-through will not result in high gross margins. Figure 3-3 demonstrates how profitability and revenue growth curves could look over a four-year time frame for a new PS firm. This curve is reviewed again in Chapter 12: Four Phases of Building PS.

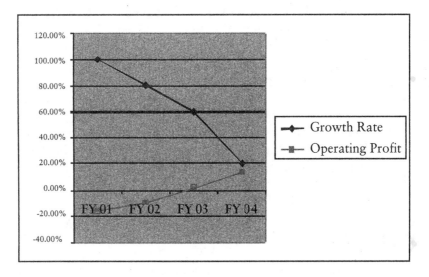

Figure 3–3   Growth versus profitability.

▶ References

As product companies well know, customer references are important to the acceptance of new products. When promoting cutting-edge technologies, references are often cited as the key to helping companies drive their new product into the mainstream. References are just as critical to a service business; they are the seal of approval for a consulting organization. Without them, you lack credibility. Without credibility, your customers become very price sensitive. There are four types of references a service organization should seek: product references, capability references, solution references, and industry references.

Product References

First and foremost, the PS organization of a product company should help develop product references. The goal of the service organization is to make a customer wildly successful at using the product. The entire product company benefits from this type of reference.

Capabilities References

Next, the service organization should build references that attest to the wonderful skills of the service employees. If the service organization claims to have the best Internet security experts in the industry, then past customers willing to validate that are important.

Solution References

Solution references establish your credibility in a specific solution area. If you want to be known as an expert Customer Relationship Management (CRM) system implementer, you need a customer that will raise his or her hand and state how much you know about installing CRM software. Regardless of the customer's industry, that reference has solution credibility.

Industry References

These references establish your credibility in a specific industry. If you want customers to believe you understand auto-manufacturing environments, you need an auto manufacturer to raise its hand and crow about how well you understand the specific business or technical environment.

▶ Repeatability

The equation is simple: Repeatability drives margin. This is a natural law from which you cannot run or hide. Repeatability means being able to use a solution more than once or transfer a solution to another situation. Repeatability helps your margins in two ways. First, the more direct revenue that comes from services you have rendered before, the greater margin you will see from those services. This is true for several reasons. The first time you implement a new solution, your employees are in learning mode. Learning involves making mistakes. Mistakes at customer sites must be corrected. This takes time and costs money. The PS unit may actually lose money on the project. The next time you deliver the same type of solution, your employees are much more effective. By the third time members of your staff deliver the solution, they should be experts. Not only are they delivering the solution in an optimal fashion, the customer is willing to pay a premium price for their expertise (which reduces the overall risk of the project failing). Figure 3-4 illustrates how this effect can play out over several implementations of a target solution.

The second way repeatability helps margins is in the area of reusable IP. Recall that reusable IP represents deliverables that are generated for one customer and can be used for another. If you target specific solutions to deliver again and again, you begin to identify these reusable components. You begin to capture and improve them until, ideally, you are redeploying the IP throughout your global organization to generate high-margin engagements.

The equation is simple, but the implementation is difficult. It requires discipline. Strategies on productizing your hard-won intellectual property are provided in Chapter 7: Productizing.

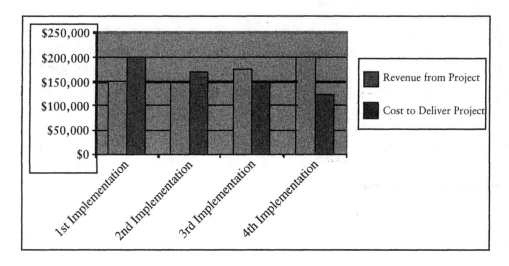

Figure 3–4 Growth versus profitability.

▶ Tale of Two Business Units

Let's compare two different consulting businesses. Both are part of technology product companies and were created with the following parameters:

- Each is a separate, stand-alone business unit with its own profit and loss (P&L) statements.
- Each is chartered to maximize company revenues, not just service revenues (i.e., pull product).
- Each is required to be profitable (carry its own water).

Both target the same industries. They even have the same exact revenue, as you can see in Table 3-2.

Table 3–2 Two Business Units with Equal Revenue.

	Solutions R Us	We B Solutions
Annual Revenue (millions)	$100	$100

But these two organizations are dramatically different. To highlight the differences, we will refer to the concept of the *balanced scorecard* developed by Robert S. Kaplan and David P. Norton. In their 1996 book, these gentlemen promoted the concept that there is more than just financial metrics that can be used to assess the health of an organization. In fact, there are four key areas that need to be measured and managed:[1]

Financial: ROI, revenue growth, revenue mix

Customer: Customer satisfaction, retention, account share

Internal: Quality, time-to-market

Learning and Growth: Employee satisfaction, training, development

In this chapter, we have introduced items that would be included in this balanced scorecard for a PS organization (PSO). Financial metrics would include revenue mix and gross margin. Customer metrics would include the attainment of product, capability, solution, and industry references. And finally, a learning and growth metric could be the number of repeatable solutions the company has in its service portfolio. So, with this "balanced" scorecard in mind, one that considers all four areas in the preceding list, we can now take a more comprehensive look at the two organizations in Table 3-3.

Table 3–3 Balanced Scorecard Review.

Area to Measure and Manage	Specific Metric	Solutions R Us	We B Solutions
Financial	Annual Revenue (millions)	$100	$100
	Direct Revenue	$ 30	$ 60
	Pass-Through	$ 70	$ 30
	Reusable IP Revenue	$ —	$ 10

1. Robert S. Kaplan and David P. Norton, *The Balanced Scorecard,* Cambridge, MA: Harvard Business School Press, 1996.

Table 3–3 Balanced Scorecard Review. (cont.'d)

Area to Measure and Manage	Specific Metric	Solutions R Us	We B Solutions
	Average Margin on Pass-Through Services	15%	15%
	Average Margin on Direct Services	25%	35%
	Average Margin on Reusable IP	60%	50%
	Average Gross Margin Percentage	18%	30.5%
Customer	Number of Product References	20	20
	Number of Capabilities References	10	15
	Number of Industry References	4	8
	Number of Solution References	0	6
Learning & Growth	Number of Repeatable Solutions	0	3

Who has the healthier business? Based on a balanced scorecard that's focused on expanded financial, customer, and employee metrics it becomes clear We B Solutions has a stronger business with healthier margins.

In summary, here are the key correlations to understand regarding the professional services triangle of profitability. First, you must constantly be managing and improving the three main levers for profitability: revenue, repeatability, and reference. Specifically, you should work on improving your revenue mix to include more direct revenue. You should instill discipline and processes to capture valuable intellectual property that can be reused again and again. And finally, you should

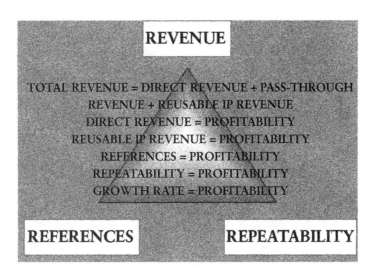

Figure 3–5 Growth versus profitability.

strategically identify customers that will provide the most powerful references for your target industries. Figure 3-5 summarizes these and the other key points made in this chapter regarding profitability levers. If you acknowledge and manage these levers, you can dramatically increase your ability to run a profitable PS organization.

Organizational Overview

Selling, delivering, productizing, and promoting

At the strategic level, you understand you need to drive direct revenue, relevant references, and high-margin repeatable services. You are ready to weigh anchor and begin your services odyssey. But to begin any successful journey, you need a map. The map for your new world is the Professional Services Functional Map seen in Figure 4-1. This is a diagram of the four key functional units in the professional-services organization. This map will guide you through the new landscape.

▶ Professional Services Functional Map

To successfully complete the professional services journey, you must create a new organization that can perform four key tasks: selling, delivering, productizing, and promoting. And of course, the new business must execute general operations activities.

51

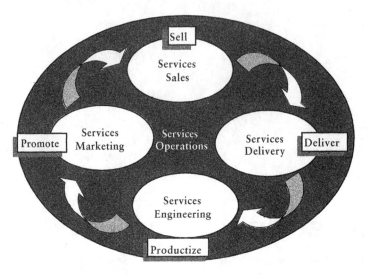

Figure 4–1   Professional services functional map.

Selling

There is an ocean of opportunity awaiting your new service organization. However, someone needs to navigate these waters, search out the most hospitable locations, and help you establish yourself in those locations. This part of your organization needs to be truly expert in positioning and selling complex services. Otherwise, it will lead you into rough waters or bring you to shore on forbidding terrain. This is why you need a distinct *Services Sales* element in your organization that can identify and close service opportunities.

Delivering

Once your services organization has identified territory that can be settled, you need to actually execute and build your solution. You need a *Services Delivery* element in your organization that will assign resources, manage their implementation, and collect the money when you are done. These are the folks that actually settle the new territories and build the deliverables that will generate revenue.

Chapter **4** I Organizational Overview

Productizing

As you settle more and more terrain, you should experience efficiencies. Once again, revenue, references, and repeatability are the key to profitability. The notion of repeatability requires you to capture your intellectual property from each engagement, evaluate it, and determine what you can leverage in future customer engagements. In this way, you are not creating new blueprints every time you need to build a new structure. To achieve this leverage, you need a *Services Engineering* team dedicated to managing this critical function.

Promoting

And of course, every business needs to position and promote its services. You need an organization that will wave your flag—an organization that will let the world know how much you have accomplished, how many islands you now inhabit. This is your *Services Marketing* department. They will be focused on differentiating and evangelizing your service offerings.

Operations

Finally, there are other general operational activities that need to be managed for the benefit of all the departments. There are tasks such as the documentation of standard business procedures and the management of core infrastructure. The *Services Operations* team is the group that manages any infrastructure that cuts across all departments or is mission critical to manage the business.

These five functions work together to manage the engagement life cycle for service offerings. This life cycle is pictured in Figure 4-2. Together, these service functions work together to identify new service opportunities, qualify those opportunities, generate proposals, negotiate those proposals, and get those deals signed. They then work to deliver those services and support those customers. Also, your organization must analyze how to deliver services more effectively and how to best market your successes. Together, these five functions represent the core components of a profitable PS organization. In the next five chapters, we will review each function in great detail. By the end of Chapter 9:

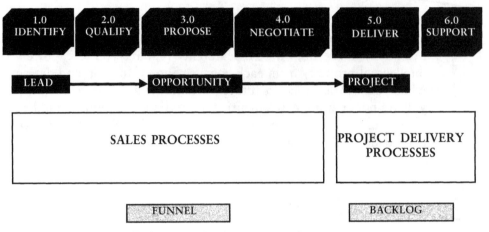

Figure 4–2   Engagement life cycle.

Operational Infrastructure, you will have a sound understanding of how to organize, measure, and compensate each one of these core functions.

▶ Professional Services O-Map

The second map that can help guide your understanding of the PS organization is an O-Map. An O-Map, short for organizational map, is a tool created by the authors to help demonstrate key organizational interfaces from a functional perspective. Instead of fumbling through organizational charts to decipher who needs to work together, an O-Map provides that information directly. It is very similar to comparing logical system diagrams to physical system diagrams in the world of IT. If you are reviewing a computer system and you want to know where a specific cable is plugged in, you look at the physical diagram. If you want to know what data the system acquires and how it manipulates the data, you would refer to the logical system diagram. The same applies to organizational charts versus O-Maps. If you want to know who to call in a specific department to resolve an issue, pull out an organizational chart. However, if you want to understand how one organization must interface with another, what they need to accomplish together, and who else is involved—you need an O-Map.

General PS Interfaces

At the highest level, the PSO within a product company must interface with at least four key functions in that environment:

Product Sales: This is the existing sales force that is responsible for selling the products of the company.

Product Marketing: This typically represents the bulk of the product company's marketing resources. This is the team responsible for positioning the product portfolio of the company.

Product Engineering: This is the team that actually builds the products (comprising the folks who really understand how it works).

Customer Service: This is the team that provides support services for the core product portfolio.

Putting the new PS organization in the center, a view of the organization and its functions would look like Figure 4-3. The challenge for PS management is to determine exactly how to interface into these existing functions on the product side. Figure 4-3 does not provide much insight on this front. That is where the O-Map comes into play.

Figure 4–3   General interfaces for PS.

O-Map Interfaces

Taking a more functional perspective, we can create a much more insightful view of how the PS team truly fits into the product company environment. First, let's start with the four key PS functions defined earlier in the chapter. Figure 4-4 maps those functions.

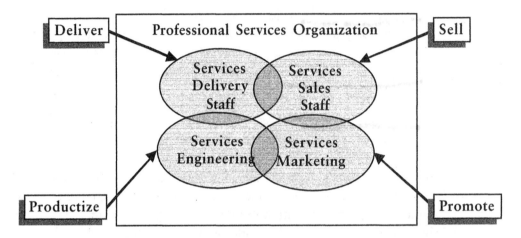

Figure 4–4   Functions of PS.

Now, let's add the product sales force, as shown in Figure 4-5.

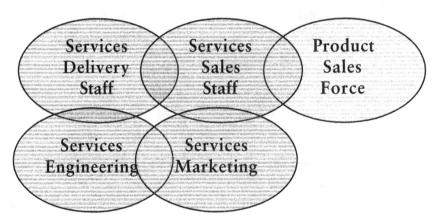

Figure 4–5   Product sales interface to PS.

Add product marketing staff, as shown in Figure 4-6.

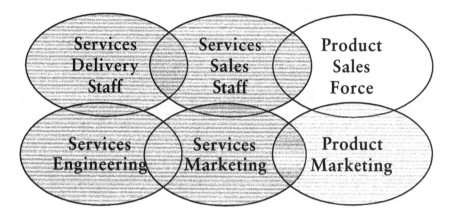

Figure 4–6   Product marketing interface to PS.

Next, we can place product engineering on the map, as shown in Figure 4-7.

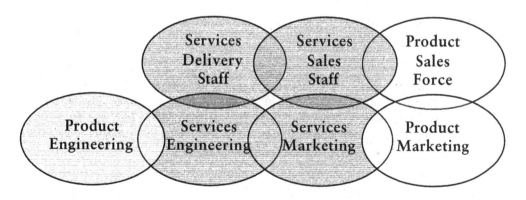

Figure 4–7   Product engineering interface to PS.

And last but not least, there is the traditional service-support team in the field, as shown in Figure 4-8.

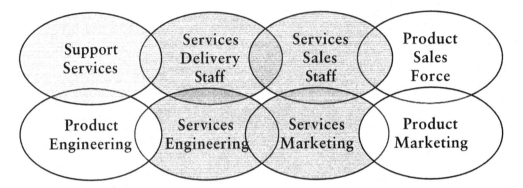

Figure 4–8 Support services interface into PS.

Now we can take this basic map and layer on the following additional information:

- Customer interfaces
- Partner interfaces
- Field versus corporate departments
- Technical versus sales roles

By adding this information, we arrive at our O-Map. Figure 4-9 shows the completed O-Map for the PS organization. In the next five chapters, as we review each PS function in more detail, we will review the key interfaces captured in this O-Map. For each interface, we will discuss key inputs, outputs, and potential issues. Isn't this much more insightful than pages of organization charts?

So now you are prepared for the journey ahead. You have a map of the four key PS functions and how they fit into the product-company environment. Our next objective is to dive deep into each one of the four functions.

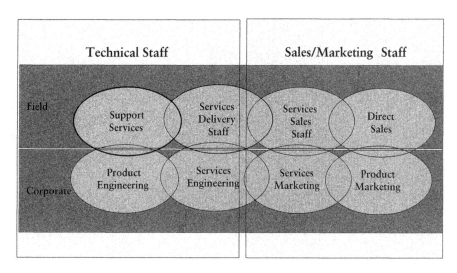

Figure 4–9 O-Map for professional services.

5

Selling

Building demand

As with all good design challenges, there are trade-offs between the competing variables you want to optimize.

In this chapter we will explore the process of designing the Services Sales function (highlighted in Figure 5-1). To survive the odyssey of turning the product-services wheel, you need to build a ship that is strong yet fast, a ship that is well provisioned but not overstocked. Generating demand and maintaining supply is one of those precarious equations. On the service side of the business, just like on the product side, too much demand and not enough supply equates to lost revenue and lower customer satisfaction. Too much inventory and not enough demand equates to overhead expenses and poor financial performance. The difference on the service side of the business is that the supply curve is not as elastic: If demand is high, you can't simply add a third shift to crank out consultants with the expertise you need. You risk frustrating key customers that need and expect to receive your services. But worse still, if your demand goes soft, you are burdened with an inventory of very expensive people that you can't just place on a markdown shelf. Suddenly, your prospects of being profitable look bleak.

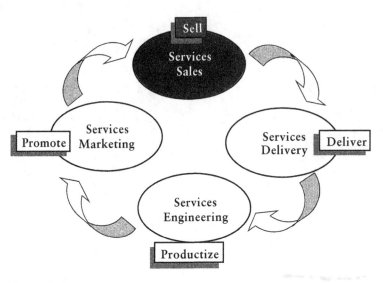

Figure 5–1 Services sales.

▶ Supply and Demand in Professional Services

To illustrate this critical relationship between demand for your services (D) and your ability to fulfill (or supply) that demand (S), we will employ that standard supply-and-demand curve used in all economics 101 classes. Figure 5-2 shows our starting point: a simple supply-and-demand curve for your PS business. This supply curve you are managing is composed of human beings—consultants who need to be hired and properly trained to increase supply. On the flip side, these are employees who need to be reallocated or laid off when you need to decrease supply. In other words, these facts make this supply curve inelastic and challenging to move. So, let's review how these two curves can interact.

First, what happens if you dramatically increase the demand for your professional services? Figure 5-3 illustrates demand improving from D level to D' level. The good news is that you should expect billable utilization to increase and profitability to increase. However, if you cannot fulfill this demand in a timely manner, you can create a customer satisfaction issue. The greater the gap between the demand for your serv-

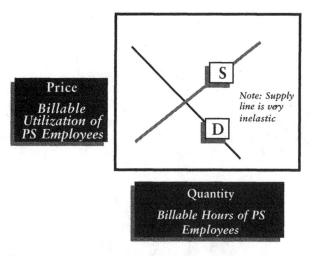

Figure 5–2 Professional services supply and demand.

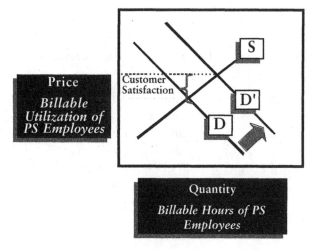

Figure 5–3 An increasing demand for services.

ices (D') and your actual ability to deliver those services (S), the greater the customer satisfaction issue becomes.

Now, let's look at the reverse scenario. Let's say you have invested heavily to ensure you have enough consultants to deal with forecasted demand. But what if that increased demand doesn't pan out? What if

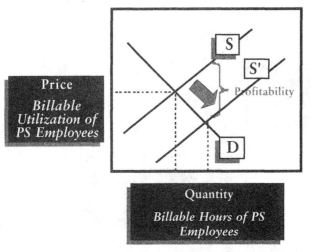

Figure 5–4 An increasing demand for services.

your sales organization dramatically misses its forecasts and does not book business at the level you expected? Now you are left with excess supply. This overhead will go directly to the bottom line. This loss of profitability is shown in Figure 5-4 by the difference between supply curve S and supply curve S'.

From this discussion, you can see how imperative it is to effectively manage the relationship between supply and demand. In this chapter, we will be focusing on managing the Services Sales function, which is responsible for predicting and managing the demand curve. In the next chapter, we will focus on the Services Delivery function, which manages that inelastic supply curve for the organization.

▶ Warning!

Now, I know what you are thinking: "Why do I need to worry about the sales function? We already have one at my company." Before you skip ahead to the next chapter, there is a cold reality of which you need to be aware.[1]

---

1. "Training Fish to Fly? Seven Tips to Convert a Product Sales Force to Solutions Selling," June 2001, *www.itsma.com.*

This statistic is based on research reported by the Information Technology Services Marketing Advisors Association (ITSMA). Why do so few product sales people learn to sell services effectively? Lots of reasons. Fundamentally, product-sales cycles are different than Services Sales cycles. The Services Sales cycle is longer and more complex. Services Sales cycles last longer because negotiations and deliverables are complex. And the sales process doesn't end when the purchase order is cut. The customer often needs to be managed throughout the potentially lengthy delivery cycle. Also, the value proposition for services is more intangible. Your Services Sales reps are selling ideas like "reduced risk" and "technical expertise." These are not black and white concepts like performance benchmarks and price/performance statistics. Finally, the services buyer may be a different person in the account altogether. Your sales reps may need to strike new relationships at new levels.

The bottom line: teaching expert product-sales staff to effectively sell services is a hard conversion. Many product companies have failed to execute this transition or are currently struggling at the task. For this reason, it is wise to begin your new endeavor with an overlay sales force dedicated to selling services. This chapter overviews that overlay Services Sales function.

▶ Function Overview

The Services Sales function must manage the first four steps in the engagement life cycle that was introduced in the previous chapter. Looking at an expanded version of the engagement life cycle, in Figure 5-5, the highlighted boxes represent the steps for which the Services Sales team has primary ownership. The sales team must effectively identify new service leads, qualify those leads, and then drive them to close. Figure 5-5 also highlights the extensive overlap between Services Sales and Services Delivery in the phases of proposing and negotiating new deals.

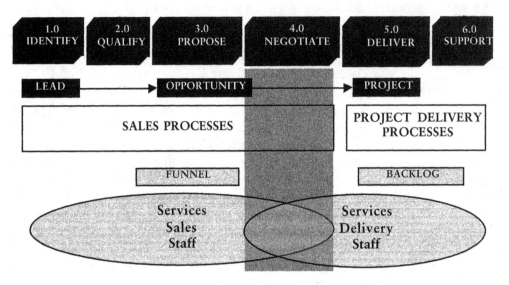

Figure 5–5 Responsibilities of the Services Sales team.

◗ Critical Success Factors

When designing the Services Sales function, always keep in mind that you must build effective channels for selling complex professional services. This objective drives several of your critical success factors. First, you must design an organization that can *manage longer sales cycles.* Typically, a product-sales organization is optimized to manage shorter sales cycles focused on placing specific products relatively quickly. Selling professional services moves you higher up in the value proposition. Now, you are talking to customers about larger business problems they want to solve. Unfortunately, it takes longer for customers to make strategic investments than it does for them to make tactical technical purchases.

To help quantify this difference, let's use the example of a computer-hardware vendor selling to a large auto manufacturer. If the computer-hardware vendor simply provides product, the vendor is brought in late in the sales cycle, when the project's ROI has already been approved, the software packages have been selected, and the company is serious about implementation. This sales cycle may last a few weeks. However, if the product vendor is positioning a "solution" that involves hardware product, third-party software, and professional services, the timetable is obviously much longer. It may take months to gain approval and funding before the purchase order is ever issued.

This new sales function must be designed with the stamina to last these longer sales discussions. This is accomplished in the organizational design, hiring profiles, and compensation systems.

Second, you must create a Services Sales function that, as tightly and cleanly as possible, *integrates into the existing product-sales organization*. If you design an overlay sales force that operates as a stovepipe organization (i.e., without integration into the existing organization), you inherently create stress and conflict in the system. This integration includes having your new Services Sales staff educate the existing product-sales staff on selling services. Remember from Chapter 2, one of the key strategic objectives of a PSO is to educate the company on selling solutions.

Next, you must *implement business processes that help identify and qualify the right service opportunities for your company*. The right service opportunities are engagements that are aligned with the strategic objectives that have been outlined for your new professional services organization. If you do not implement some type of qualification process, your new sales organization will pursue revenue opportunities that do not coincide with your overall business objectives.

Finally, it is critical that you populate your new organization with the right employees. This sounds childishly simplistic, but it remains a critical success factor. You must identify sales managers and sales representatives who are experts at positioning services. To accomplish this, we recommend you *design and implement a disciplined process for qualifying new sales hires*.

So there are the critical success factors. You must design a sales organization that can address these needs. To accomplish this task, we will start at the top and work down to the detail. So let's begin with the charter of this new function.

▶ Services Sales Charter

The charter of the Services Sales function is as follows: *Identify, Close, Forecast.*

- Identify new service opportunities in the existing product install base
- Identify new service opportunities with new customers
- Manage pricing and positioning of service proposals made to the customer
- Close business
- Forecast the demand for delivery resources

▶ Identify and Close

To begin our discussion on sales processes, we need to review each phase of the engagement life cycle that the Services Sales function must manage.

Identify

In this first step (shown in Figure 5-6), the Services Sales organization is simply identifying new service opportunities. These leads can come from the following sources, typically in the percentages presented in Figure 5-7.

In reality, the greatest revenue streams for professional services will come from the existing customer base with products installed (often called the product install base). This is as it should be. Also, the old 80/20 rule will most likely apply: 80 percent of the professional services

Figure 5–6   Identify service opportunities.

Source of Leads for Professional Services

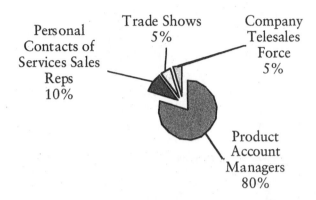

Personal Contacts of Services Sales Reps 10%

Trade Shows 5%

Company Telesales Force 5%

Product Account Managers 80%

Figure 5–7   Sources of leads.

revenues will come from 20 percent of the current customer accounts. There will be a small yet lucrative set of accounts PS should work to partner with. A majority of the leads, identifying customers that will be most receptive to the services of the company, will come from the existing product-sales force that understands the install base.

Qualify

As Figure 5-8 illustrates, the qualification process is second in the engagement life cycle. Once the opportunity is on the radar screen, it needs to be reviewed and qualified. Standard qualification criteria include the following:

| 1.0 IDENTIFY | 2.0 QUALIFY | 3.0 PROPOSE | 4.0 NEGOTIATE | 5.0 DELIVER | 6.0 SUPPORT |

Figure 5–8   Qualify service opportunities.

Funding: Does the customer have budget for the proposed project?

Expertise: Have you delivered this type of solution before? Does your company have the resources required to deliver the project?

Timing: When does the customer need to start?

Competition: How is your company well positioned? How many competitors are you bidding against?

If the opportunity is qualified (i.e., it looks like it has real potential), the sales organization must determine if it actually wants to bid the opportunity.

SIRENS' SONG: The more business that's bid, the more business will be won and the more profit there will be.

BOULDER AHEAD: The truth is bidding service contracts that have a low probability of being won can be the most expensive mistake a service-sales organization can make.

If completing a product bid is intensive and resource consuming, completing a service proposal is at least twice the effort. More detail on this complexity in Chapter 11: Customer Engagement Workflow. For now, understand that it's critical to make sure your company *really* wants to bid this business *before* the investment is made in the proposal. If there is not at least a 50 percent chance of securing the business, then you should walk away! The best way to assure you are not pursuing unlikely business is to implement a rigorous Bid/No Bid evaluation process. This process must be followed with great discipline to be effective. The filtering criteria must also be fine enough to catch the often-unrealistic optimism of your sales team. Sample criteria for a Bid/No Bid process include:

- Number of competitive bidders
- Estimated effort to complete proposal
- Estimated total revenue from project
- Estimated gross margin from project
- Estimated probability of winning the project
- Estimated start date

If it is unlikely you will win the project, if the effort to bid the project is much greater than other opportunities, or if the project does not help you meet your financial objectives, walk away! Carry your kicking and screaming sales person with you.

Propose

The third step in the engagement life cycle is to generate a formal proposal (see Figure 5-9). If the opportunity makes it past the Bid/No Bid gauntlet, it is time for the sales person to roll up his or her sleeves and create an actual proposal. In this activity, the sales person will need to engage several resources from within and without the services organization. Table 5-1 shows what each of these resources need to offer the proposal process.

The proposal is then submitted for internal review and approval. Details of this process are provided in Chapter 11: The Customer Engagement Workflow.

Figure 5–9   Propose service solution.

Table 5–1   Resources and Their Inputs to the Proposal.

Resource	Input(s) to the Proposal
Services Sales Rep	Overall proposal document. Final pricing and positioning.
Product Sales Rep	Product pricing. Product technical specifications.
Services Delivery: Solution Architect	Effort estimates. Technical viability review of solution.
Services Delivery: Project Manager	Proposed project plan.

Negotiate

Negotiation is the fourth stage of the engagement life cycle. Once the proposal is approved internally, it is submitted to the customer. Then the fun begins. It costs too much, it takes too long, etc., etc. You know the drill. The key during the negotiation phase is to always understand where the floor is for an acceptable project margin. At some point in the negotiations you may lose so much ground that the deal is no longer financially attractive. Don't let your salesperson forget where that walking point is.

Figure 5–10 Negotiate the contract.

▶ Forecast

Besides managing the engagement life cycle to identify and close business, the Services Sales function must also forecast demand. This is critical to your ability to manage those treacherous supply-and-demand curves. Poor forecasting can lead to a deep and expensive hole or, at the minimum, a lost revenue opportunity.

The process of forecasting involves the Services Sales team successfully predicting and tracking the following information concerning sales opportunities:

Service Type: What skills are being requested by the customer? What solution is the customer asking for?

Dollar Amount: What revenue can the company expect from this opportunity? This should include projections for product revenues as well as professional-service and support-service revenues.

Timing: When will this project begin? How long will it take to get a signed contract?

Probability: What is the realistic probability that the above projections regarding dollar amount and timing will actually be accepted?

You can see how critical this information is to managing the precarious balance between demand for services and the supply of consulting staff. The more accurate the Services Sales team is with its forecasting, the greater chance for profitability.

There are two keys to creating a successful forecasting process: (1) accurate methodology for assessing probabilities, and (2) consistent implementation of the forecasting process. First, the professional services senior management team needs to create an accurate scale for assessing opportunities and the likelihood they will result in real revenue. A sample probability table shown in Table 5-2 could look as follows.

Table 5–2 Probabilities for Forecasting Revenue.

Probability (that revenue will be realized as originally forecasted)	Description of Situation	Phase in Engagement Life Cycle
0%	New opportunity is brought to Services Sales staff.	Identify
20%	Opportunity has passed initial qualification process.	Qualify
40%	Professional Services has decided to bid the opportunity and the proposal is being generated.	Propose
50%	Proposal has been submitted to customer.	Propose
80%	Proposal has been verbally accepted by customer but final negotiations are not complete.	Negotiate
100%	Signed contract in hand. Work scheduled to begin.	Deliver

The above percentages are applied to all opportunities being tracked by the Services Sales team in order to calculate what revenue professional services can forecast. Figure 5-11, the Sample Forecasting Work-

Customer	Solution Type	PS Revenue	Product Revenue	Support Service Revenue	TOTAL REVENUE	Probability	TOTAL Forecasted Revenue	Estimated Start Date	Comments
Lighthouse One	Custom Architecture & Implementation	$ 100,000	$ 200,000	$ 20,000	$ 320,000	20%	$ 64,000	Q3	Jim Smith is reviewing lead
Big C	Oinsight Facility Assessment	$ 40,000	$ -	$ -	$ 40,000	100%	$ 40,000	Q1	Consultant starts Monday
Very Imp	System Tuning	$ 60,000	$ 100,000	$ -	$ 160,000	50%	$ 80,000	Q2	Proposal submitted last week.

TOTAL Forecasted Revenue	$ 184,000
Q1	$ 40,000
Q2	$ 80,000
Q3	$ 64,000
Q4	0
Professional Services	
Support Services	
Product	

Figure 5–11   Sample forecast worksheet.

sheet, provides an example of a very simplified worksheet that tracks three opportunities worth $520,000 to the company. The probabilities table is applied to create a forecast of $184,000 in revenue, spread over three quarters. Once again, agreeing to these probabilities and verifying their accuracy are key to creating accurate forecasts.

The second tactic for creating accurate forecasts is to drive consistent implementation of the forecasting process throughout the global organization. If the process is not followed consistently, you will be comparing apples to oranges when assessing forecasts from different Services Sales representatives or from different sales geographies.

It is important to note that the forecasting process actually creates two critical business reports for the PS management team:

- The funnel report
- The backlog report

Both of these reports are reviewed in Chapter 7: Operational Infrastructure. Please refer to that chapter for additional information on forecasting.

Roles and Responsibilities

Identify, close, forecast. These are the activities being managed by the sales function. Now, to accomplish this, here are the players you need in place. The first role you need to fill is that of the Services Sales representative. This person is your feet on the street, the person who will aggressively sell your capabilities and close business. This person must be well versed in consultative selling. The sales cycle has become much more complex these days. The old 1,2,3 approach of identifying a need, making a presentation, and then closing the business just doesn't play these days.[2] Customers need help navigating complex business decisions. They need help learning and understanding various options. The Services Sales rep is there to guide the customer through that longer sales cycle.

Your reps will need management. The second key role in the service-sales function is the sales director. This is the manager responsible for the overall sales targets. This person will also have financial responsibility for sales expenses.

Finally, you may need to hire a director of business development. This person will be responsible for identifying new capabilities and solutions your professional services organization can develop and profit from.

The complete overview of these positions is provided in Table 5-3.

Key Interfaces for Sales

The Services Sales force must manage four key interfaces, as shown in Figure 5-12. First, sales must interact with the Services Delivery team when bidding and negotiating new business. Next, the Services Sales force must play nice with the direct sales force that is in place. From the service-marketing team, the Services Sales force must get critical sales IP, which will be discussed in Chapter 8: Promoting. Finally, the Services Sales force provides the face to the customer.

Key inputs and outputs between these entities are shown in Table 5-4.

---

2. Ken Davis, *Getting into Your Customer's Head*, New York: Random House, 1996.

Table 5–3 Roles and Responsibilities of the Services Sales Team.

Role	Purpose	Responsibilities			Requirements		
		General	Managerial	Financial	Experience	Education and Training	Technical
Services Sales Rep	• Identify and qualify opportunities • Generate proposals • Close business • Forecast demand for their territory	• Manage accounts • Manage proposals • Provide weekly sales forecasts	Manage virtual teams assigned to proposals	• Meet booking targets • Meet expense objectives	• 4+ years general sales experience • 2+ years selling services	4-year degree	• Understand companies' product line • Understand customers' use of technology in their business
Sales Director	• Assist in closing business • Forecast demand for their region • Upsell existing programs	• Provide weekly sales forecasts • Manage customer escalations • Prospect for new business	Manage sales reps	• Meet booking and revenue targets for region • Meet expense objectives • Ensure collection of A/R	• 8+ years general sales experience • 4+ years selling services • 2+ years managerial experience	4-year degree	• Understand companies' product line • Understand customers' use of technology in their business
Business Development Manager	• Build relationships w/ prospects • Educate customers on company offerings	• Generate leads • Qualify prospects	• Educate sales force • Advise staff	Meet booking and revenue targets for target solution areas	• 4+ years general sales experience • 2+ years selling services	4-year degree	Understand customers' use of technology in their business

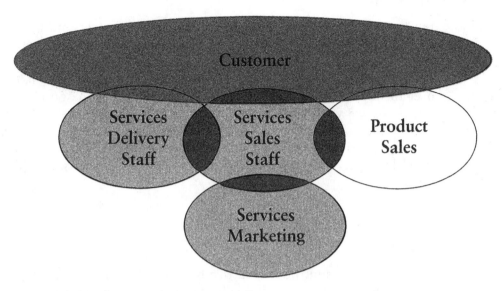

Figure 5–12   Key interfaces for serious sales.

Table 5–4   Interface Inputs and Outputs for the Services Sales Function.

Services Sales Force	Customer	Direct Sales Force	Services Delivery	Services Marketing
Outputs To	• Pricing • Proposal	• Pricing • Proposal	• Customer requirements	• Customer requirements
Inputs From	• Customer requirements	• Customer requirements • Account landscape • Service opportunities	• Project schedules • Cost estimations	• Solution positioning • Reference customers
Comments		• Potential conflict over account ownership and opportunity management		

▶ Compensation for Sales

In Chapter 1, we highlighted ten key parameters managers must define to run their business. Employee compensation is one of those ten key areas. The literature on compensation strategies is deep and wide. Economists, psychologists, and sociologists continue to fight it out over theories of equity, motivation, and behavior. For the purpose of this book, we will keep it simple. First, we will identify the primary variables for which a PS organization should compensate. We will then map these variables to the role in the organization that should be measured by them. Finally, we will provide a sample compensation plan table.

Key Variables

All of the metrics introduced in this book can be used for compensation purposes. However, especially when the organization is young, simpler is always better. The PSO must manage the five M's: money, margin, mix, milestones, and minutes. The details behind these are shown in Table 5-5.

Table 5–5   Services Sales Compensation Metrics.

Area	Variable	Description	Calculation
Money	Total services revenue	Measure of total revenues recognized by Professional Services, composed of the different types of revenue by consulting, solutions, and third-party pass-through.	Total Services Revenue = Direct Revenue + Third-Party Revenue + Reusable Solution Component Revenue
	Bookings	Dollar value of engagements that customers have agreed to, or projects that have been "booked" and purchase order generated by the customer, but no revenue has necessarily started to flow.	Total Service Revenues expected from signed proposals

Table 5–5   Services Sales Compensation Metrics. (cont.'d)

Margin	Gross margin %	Gross profit generated per dollar of service delivered. Gross margin = total services revenue − cost of services delivered (COS), traditionally called costs of goods sold (COGS).	Gross Margin Dollars per Total Services Revenue
	Target project margin	Estimated gross profit generated per dollar of services delivered in a specific project.	Target Project Margin = Estimated Service Revenues per project − Estimated COS per project.
	Actual project Margin	Actual gross profit generated per dollar of services delivered in a specific project.	Actual Project Margin = Actual Service Revenues from project − Actual COS to deliver project.
Mix	Revenue mix	Breakdown of revenue sources for Professional Services. Revenue sources include direct revenue, third-party revenue, and reusable-solution component revenue. For example: 30% of total service revenues comes from direct consulting.	
Milestones	Project completion ratio	Measures the degree of completion against project milestones.	Number of milestones accomplished on schedule per total milestones targeted.
Minutes	Billable utilization	Measures the organization's ability to maximize its billable resources.	Total number of hours billed / (number of working hours in a year * number of billable employees)

The sales organization has direct control over the following variables:

- Bookings
- Mix
- Target project margins

Compensation plans for the sales organization could look like the one shown in Table 5-6.

Table 5-6 Services Sales Compensation.

POSITION	PLAN TYPE	MONEY			MARGIN			MIX	MILE-STONES	MINUTES	TOTAL VARIABLE COMPEN-SATION
		Bookings	Revenue	Gross Margin	Target Project Margin	Actual Project Margin		Revenue Mix	Project Completion Ratio	Billable Utilization Rate	
Sales Director	70/30	10%			10%			10%			30%
Business Development Director	70/30	10%			10%			10%			30%
Services Sales Rep	60/40	20%			10%			10%			40%

Key Metrics for Sales

As you will recall from Chapter 1, the subject of metrics used to judge the health of the business is another one of the ten key areas a manager must understand. The beauty of sales is the simplicity of their metrics. That is why many folks gravitate to this profession; success is very black and white. However, there are other metrics that can be employed that are subtle but helpful. In addition to the metrics used for compensation, Table 5-7 provides a list of metrics that can be used to measure the effectiveness of your sales organization.

Table 5–7   Services Sales Metrics.

Metric	Sample Target	Person Responsible
Bookings	1.5 of revenue target	Sales Director and Services Sales Representative
Gross Margin for Sales Area	> 30%	Sales Director
Target Project Margin	> 35%	Services Sales Representative
Revenue Mix	Meet mix objectives of the business	Sales Director and Services Sales Representative
Bid and Proposal Costs	Within parameters set by management, for example, <2% of projected revenue from engagement	Services Sales Representative
Hit Ratio	> 50%	Sales Director and Services Sales Representative
Revenue Growth	> 20%	Sales Director
Sales Costs	< 8%	Sales Director

Organizational Structure and Sizing

Now you know the type of activities this selling function needs to manage and you know the key roles involved. Next, you have to create an organizational structure and size it for your new business. When creating the first draft structure, there are three questions you need to answer:

1. What revenue am I targeting?
2. What quota do I expect my reps to carry?
3. Will the sales function be geography focused or industry focused?

Target Revenue

Your initial target revenue can be sized by several techniques. Two common ones are:

Percentage of Product Sales: Using this technique, you anticipate your service-revenue opportunities to be a percentage of your product sales. A product-centric company should be able to capture 6 percent of product sales in consulting sales. Anything less than that begs the question of why your company is investing in creating the services.

Pipeline Analysis: Using this technique, you would analyze your current product install base and survey to determine what customers require consulting services from your company.

In our example, to keep things simple, we are targeting $100 million dollars in revenue.

Rep Quotas

The next question you need to answer is what will be the quota for each of your consulting sales representatives? This is greatly influenced by how experienced your reps are and how healthy your pipeline is. To give you a sense of the range, see Figure 5-13.

		Annual Revenue Quota						
$2M						$8M		
Inexperienced Rep					Experienced Rep		
Limited Pipeline					Strong, Well-Qualified Pipeline		

Figure 5–13   Range of quotas (in millions).

For our new consulting organization, we will be targeting quotas of $4 million per representative. This means we will need approximately 25 reps.

Geography versus Industry Based

Finally, you need to address one of the toughest issues: How will your sales force be focused? There are two common choices. The first and traditional choice is to go with geographical boundaries. The second choice is to segment by expertise, or industry. The pros and cons are shown in Table 5-8.

Table 5–8   Geography versus Industry.

	Geography Focus	Industry Focus
PROS	• Faster implementation • Tight territories, lower travel costs • Clearer coverage model • Faster response times • Easier to find reps with "general" skills	• Increased credibility with the customer • Clear understanding of customer needs • Cross-reference between industry customers
CONS	• Reps may not understand unique customer requirements • Limited credibility with the customer	• Longer to implement • Harder to find skill sets • Wider territories, higher travel costs

In the infancy of a consulting services business, it is often wise to start with a geography-based sales organization. This may help to kick-start your pipeline because it's the easiest model to hire for, implement, and integrate into the product-sales team.

For our case study, we will be using a geography-based sales force.

▶ Sample Organizational Structure

You are now ready to get something on paper. To review, you are working with the following parameters, shown in Figure 5-14.

Target revenue	$100M
Target Quota per Rep	$4M
Focus	Geography

Figure 5–14 Services Sales parameters.

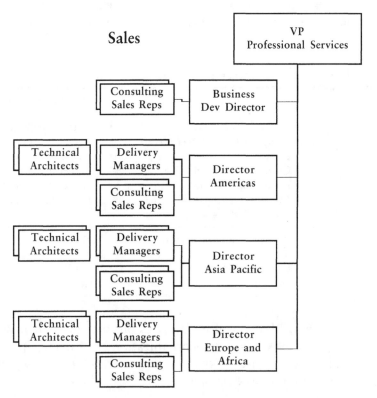

Figure 5–15 Services Sales organization chart.

An organizational chart illustrating how the staff will be assigned is provided in Figure 5-15. Reporting to your new VP of professional services, there will be three regional sales directors, each with consulting sales reps reporting to him or her. The number of reps is based on the quota the geography will carry. In this case, each geographical area is carrying a quota of $28M and there will be seven reps assigned to each geographical area.

There will also be a director of business development. This person will carry the remaining revenue quota of $16M and will be focused on target solutions that cut across all geographies. There will be four consulting sales reps in this function. Each will have quotas attached to target-solution areas. By creating this small business development group, you offset some of the cons of having a geography-based sales force.

▶ Sample Budget

The budget to support these 29 employees assigned to the sales function could look as shown in Figure 5-16.

The line items for the sample budget are as straightforward as possible. The Salaries and Benefits line includes the base salary of all employees plus the costs to pay the employees' benefits (typically 40 percent of each employee's base salary). Occupancy includes the facility expenses associated with employees. Outside Services includes temporary labor, contractors, etc. Finally, Depreciation contains costs for employees' laptops and other office equipment.

As can be seen, human resources represent the greatest expenses in the sales budget.

▶ Issues to Watch

So, there you have it—the basics of the Services Sales function. What it does, how to measure its success, how to compensate its staff, and how to organize its structure. As your service business grows and matures, this function will change over time. That metamorphosis is described in Chapter 12: Four Phases of Building PS.

Creating an overlay sales function is inherently a risky task. Nevertheless, we advocate taking this risk. Otherwise, your ability to drive the demand of complex services is extremely limited in a typical product-centric company. If your executive staff wants to swim the service

Services Sales		
Number of Employees 29		
Salaries and Benefits	$2,600,000	52%
Commissions and Bonuses	$1,000,000	20%
Occupancy	$ 145,000	3%
Travel	$1,055,000	21%
Outside Services	$ 55,000	1%
Depreciation	$ 145,000	3%
TOTAL	$5,000,000	

Figure 5–16 Services Sales sample budget.

waters, they need to be practiced swimmers with a map of the eddies, hidden rocks, and undertows.

First, **closely manage the relationship between product sales and Services Sales**. Address conflicts and tensions sooner than later. Make sure the compensation packages are similar in nature and are fair. Make sure the management teams and account reps are working together to plan their territory strategies. Verify that opportunities are effectively being managed between the two sales groups.

The majority of the time, the product-sales force will own the customer accounts. For new customers, a Services Sales rep may actually establish and manage the account. Regardless of who owns the customers, **make sure there is always one primary sales contact assigned to each key customer account**. Don't let the Services Sales and product-sales reps trip over each other in front of customers.

Next, **verify you are closing business that meets your qualification criteria**. Spot check the outstanding proposals or recently won deals. Boxing the sales force into pursuing business you care about is critical to long-term profitability.

Finally, **look for success within the product-sales force**. Check to see how many product-sales reps are actually selling services. At first, this percentage will be low. But over time, you should see an increase in this area. If not, then your Service Sales staff is not fulfilling its obligation to educate the product-sales staff on how to sell services.

So, that is the Services Sales function. What if you implement this new sales function and your staff actually sells your services? What happens then? That is the story of the next chapter.

6

Delivering

Supplying your services

Supply and demand, supply and demand. In the last chapter, we reviewed how you manage the demand side of the equation. This chapter focuses on the supply side. We are now discussing the meat of your organization—where most of your resources will be allocated. This is the Services Delivery organization as highlighted in Figure 6-1. To use a military analogy, these are your ground troops. Without them, you can never win. Poor construction here leads to an organization that leaks away profits and eventually sinks from the burden of its own weight. This chapter will help you understand the concepts of constructing a sound delivery function.

▶ Function Overview

The Services Delivery function must assist in proposing new business; then it must manage the final two phases of the engagement life cycle, often called the project delivery process (see Figure 6-2). First, Services Delivery team members must have the expertise to assist the sales team in the process of bidding and closing business. Specifically, they must provide technical expertise to validate customer proposals and to estimate what it will take to implement those proposals. Next, Serv-

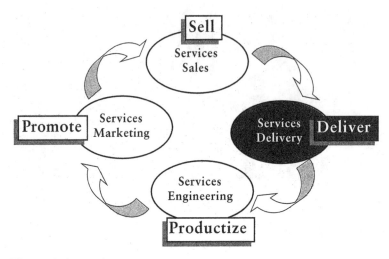

Figure 6–1   Services Delivery.

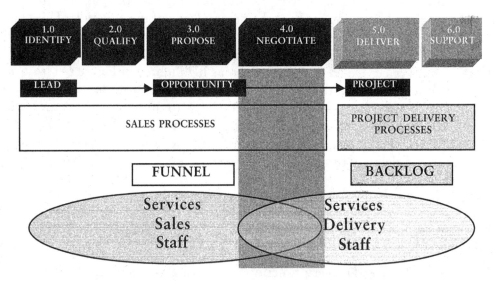

Figure 6–2   Responsibilities of the Services Delivery function.

ices Delivery must successfully manage the project delivery process. This means keeping projects on time and on budget as much as possible. Finally, the Services Delivery team must manage the transition of each customer engagement from a PS project to an ongoing installed customer linked into the support-services organization for ongoing maintenance.

▶ Critical Success Factors

The Services Delivery function must have discipline: discipline to manage projects effectively on a day-in and day-out basis, and discipline to stay on top of critical project issues and keep customers satisfied. To maintain this discipline, there are several critical success factors to keep in mind when designing your Services Delivery organization.

First, you must include in your design **a risk-assessment process for new proposals.** This is the process of formally reviewing customer proposals of any significant size and making sure the proposal team has minimized the risk to your company. This process includes reviewing the technical feasibility of the new project, the timing constraints, and the projected margins. It must all make sense and the proposal objectives must be reasonably achievable.

Next, your delivery organization must implement a **standard delivery methodology.** This is the process the delivery organization follows when implementing a project. By defining a delivery methodology, training staff on that methodology, and adhering to that methodology, the Services Delivery function can greatly reduce project risks and increase potential for profitability.

In addition to the standard delivery methodology, your organization must maintain **consistent use of project metrics.** For the senior-management team members of professional services to clearly understand the health of the business, they must have some basic insights into customer projects. These insights can be gained only by consistently measuring different elements of project success.

The Services Delivery organization must be designed to provide a **single point of contact for each customer engagement** (i.e., a point person who feels ownership for the account and will manage it appropriately). Typically, this will be the project manager assigned to the engagement. Whatever you do, don't implement a convoluted matrixed organizational structure that provides unclear ownership for the customer, especially for revenue-generating activities.

Next to last, you must design your organization to **aggressively manage utilization**. Utilization is the number of hours your delivery staff is actually billing to paying customers. If your delivery team does not have a firm understanding of its current utilization rates, your team really doesn't have a firm understanding of its business.

The last critical success factor concerns the type of people you hire. **Hire delivery staff that can sell your business.** Customer-oriented delivery employees will be one of your most effective sales channels. Make sure you are hiring staff with the consultative skills required to drive the business.

▶ Services Delivery Charter

The charter of the Services Delivery function has three elements: **estimate, execute, and educate**.

- **Estimate** the effort required to deliver customer engagements.
- **Execute** customer engagements on time and on budget.
- Continually **educate** delivery staff on new technologies and techniques.

▶ Estimate

Before an engagement is actually delivered, it had to be bid. The activities of proposing and negotiating are reviewed in the previous chapter. During the proposal process, the delivery function plays a critical role in estimating the effort required to deliver the solution. This estimation is critical in establishing price.

> **SIRENS' SONG:** Project effort estimations are relatively accurate.
> **BOULDER AHEAD:** The truth is 50 percent of consulting engagements are delivered late and over budget.[a]

a. Based on numerous reports and articles on the topic of IT project estimation. Seasoned project managers often double effort estimations provided by technical staff when planning a first-time implementation.

Unfortunately, delivery teams have a very difficult time accurately estimating efforts. This is especially true when bidding a solution for the first time. Management can expect its delivery experts to be off by a factor of two. There are many issues that create this phenomenon; unclear customer requirements, unforeseen technical difficulties, and outright optimism are the most common.

One of the key techniques to improving the estimation process is managing intellectual property from past engagements. Data from past engagements can prove to be an invaluable resource when estimating the effort for new customer projects.. This is covered in the next chapter.

▶ Execute

Once the customer accepts the proposal, the delivery team must implement it. Thus begins execution and the start of the delivery life cycle. The amazing thing about the delivery life cycle is how complex PS firms have made it. Every PS firm touts its own, very unique, very special delivery methodology. And they all have great names like the p4d methodology from Blue Diesel web developers, or the 4-E methodology from Mobilocity. Each one of these methodologies has a noble goal: to improve the delivery process. Some methodologies are great at adjusting to changing customer requirements. Some methodologies manage risk well and help contain cost overruns. Some methodologies just look cool. But every delivery methodology must somehow manage the basic process implementing the project: review the customer requirements, create an implementation plan, design the new solution, and implement the new solution.

SIRENS' SONG: Once the proposal is signed, the delivery team can begin execution.

BOULDER AHEAD: The truth is, you can expect at least 30 percent of the customer's requirements to change after the initial proposal is signed.

Requirements Review

During the sale cycle, a proposal was made to the customer. That proposal typically includes a summary of the customer requirements, a project plan, and target deliverables. This is only the starting point.

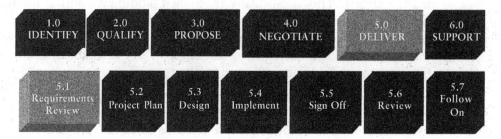

Figure 6–3   Requirements review.

Rarely does the proposal the customer signs accurately describe the solution that is actually implemented.

In the requirements review activity (Figure 6-3), the newly assigned delivery team meets with the customer to validate the requirements of the new solution.

Plan

Once the requirements have been thoroughly reviewed and crystallized, the delivery team can create an updated project plan (Figure 6-4) and statement of work. There is a host of literature regarding the process of creating exceptional project plans. The important point for service organizations is that the project plan and statement of work (SOW) clearly articulate deliverables and milestones. These two items should be crystal clear or you can expect delays in receiving precious revenue for your work. If anyone on your management team reads the project plan and SOW and is still unclear about what your company has committed to deliver, rework the plan.

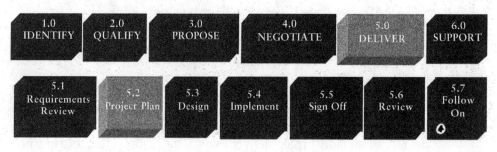

Figure 6–4   Project plan.

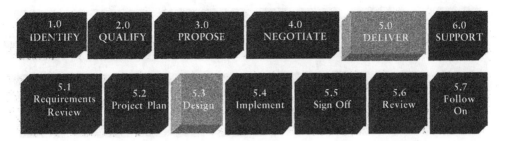

Figure 6–5 Design and develop.

Design and Develop

Once the new project plan and SOW are in place, the design process begins (Figure 6-5). Hopefully, the delivery team is not starting with a blank page. At its disposal should be examples of designs they have employed in previous engagements. Once again, there is a host of literature that describes the proper development of physical and logical system diagrams. And once again, the mantra is clarity, clarity, clarity. Design documents should leave little wiggle room for the customer's imagination to run wild. The design documents should explicitly demonstrate what would be implemented at the customer site.

Once the customer has agreed to the final design documentation, development can begin. Often, much of the technical development can be done at your corporate office rather than on site at the customer location.

Implement

It's time to actually install the customer's solution (Figure 6-6). The delivery team works to meet the clear deliverables articulated in the SOW. The challenge in this phase is to stay focused on the original statement of work. If the customer wants to increase the scope of the project, the delivery team must diplomatically yet effectively manage requests for additional work. Requests must be documented, priced, and then approved by the customer. Lack of discipline in this phase will always lead to unfavorable project metrics: late delivery, cost overruns, and lower customer satisfaction.

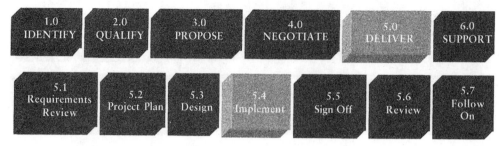

Figure 6–6   Implement.

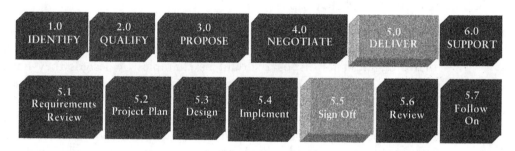

Figure 6–7   Sign-off.

Sign–Off

And now, for the moment of truth. If the SOW was clear and the delivery team executed well, the customer sign-off (Figure 6-7) should be a formality. If, however, customer requirements shifted or customer expectations were not clear, this can be the most harrowing step in the process for your project manager. Customer sign-off means invoicing and revenue recognition.

Review

This is the process of reviewing (Figure 6-8) the project that has just been completed. The details of this process are provided in Chapter 11:

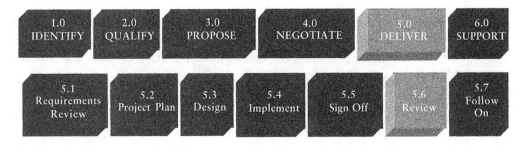

Figure 6–8   Review.

The Customer Engagement Workflow and in Appendix D: Sample Project Review. For now, understand that the Services Delivery team needs to make this review, or debriefing, a mandatory step in the delivery process.

Follow-On

Every good delivery team should always be on the lookout for additional service opportunities. As highlighted earlier in this chapter, your delivery staff can and should be one of your most effective channels for selling your services. In the follow-on step (Figure 6-9), the delivery team works with the Services Sales staff to identify and qualify additional service opportunities that can now be pursued in the account.

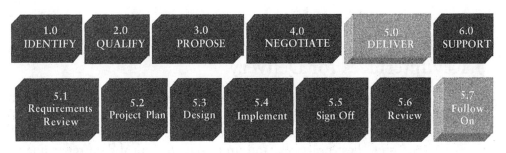

Figure 6–9   Follow-on.

Educate

Beyond managing the delivery phase of the engagement life cycle, the Services Delivery function must effectively develop and grow its staff. By investing in this area, the delivery organization ensures the ongoing market value of the delivery staff.

Creating an education roadmap can be an effective tool to manage the development of your delivery staff. Table 6-1 provides an example of such a tool. The important point is that the Services Delivery management team consciously reviews the educational needs of its staff and articulates what the education process should be.

Roles and Responsibilities

There are four key roles in the Services Delivery organization. At the management level, there is a delivery manager responsible for the care and feeding of the delivery employees. Next, there are project managers responsible for managing the virtual teams that are assigned to customer engagements. We cannot emphasize enough how critical the project manager role is. Next, there are senior technical consultants, who are the technically oriented staff members who also spend a significant amount of time creating and pitching customer proposals. Much of your organization's technical credibility will come from these individuals. Finally, there are technical consultants, who are the more junior but still expert consultants in the areas on which you are focused. They will do much of the hands-on integration required to make your customers successful. Table 6-2 provides an overview of the roles and responsibilities of the delivery staff.

Key Interfaces for Delivery

The Services Delivery team must manage four key interfaces (see Figure 6-10). First, the delivery team must interact with the Services Engineering team. This interaction will provide key information on delivery techniques, best practices, and up-to-date technical data regarding target solutions. Second, the interface with the field-engineering team will

Table 6–1   Training Roadmap for PS Staff.

Professional Services Position	Certifications		Internal Courses						External Courses	
	Project Management Certification	Company Product Certification	Leadership Training	New Hire Training	Consulting Skills Development	Linux Training	Product Training Courses	Customer Skills	Microsoft Office	Other
Delivery Managers			Required		Required					
Project Managers	Required				Required					
Senior Technical Consultant				Required	Required			Required		
Technical Consultant				Required	Required					
Services Sales Reps				Required	Required					
Regional Directors			Required		Required					
Operations Staff			Required							

LEGEND:

Ready to Go	Under Development	To Be Developed

Table 6-2 Roles and Responsibilities of Delivery Staff.

Role	Purpose	Responsibilities			Requirements		
		General	Managerial	Financial	Experience	Education and Training	Technical
Delivery Manager	Manage delivery staff	• Schedule resources • Manage staff development	• Manage delivery staff • Evaluate employees • Train or oversee training for employees	• Meet overall expense objectives • Meet project expense objectives	• 4+ years general management experience • 2+ years delivery manager	4-year degree	• Understand technical skills being requested by customers • Understand project life cycle
Project Manager	Manage customer projects	• Create project plans • Manage project • Provide weekly project updates	• Manage virtual project teams • Manage sub-contractors	Meet project expense objectives	• 8+ years general work experience • 2+ years project management experience	2-year degree	• Understand project life cycle • Understand how customers are using technology in their business
Senior Technical Consultant	• Create system architectures • Implement solution	• Create system architectures • Provide effort estimations • Implement solution • Assist in closing business	Manage and mentor technical consultants	Meet project expense objectives	• 10+ years general work experience • 4+ years technical consultant	4-year degree	Deep understanding of technologies being deployed
Technical Consultant	Implement solution	• Provide effort estimations • Implement solution	None	Meet project expense objectives	4+ years work experience	4-year degree	Thorough understanding of technologies being deployed

provide key input on product capabilities. Third, the delivery team must work with the Services Sales staff to provide estimations for the proposal process. Fourth and final, the Services Delivery team must interact with the customer as the solution is delivered.

Key inputs and outputs between these entities are illustrated in Table 6-3.

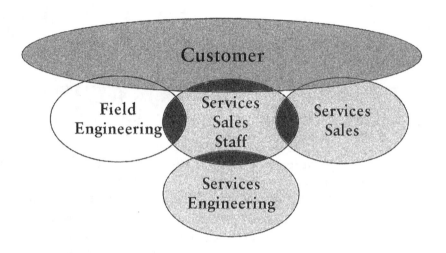

Figure 6–10   Key interfaces for the Services Delivery function.

Table 6–3   Key Interfaces for the Services Delivery Function.

Delivery	Customer	Field Engineering	Services Sales	Services Engineering
Outputs To	• Project reports • Project deliverables	• Proposed architectures	• Project schedules • Cost estimations	• Customer requirements
Inputs From	• Customer requirements • Sign-offs	• Product specifications and capabilities • Technical landscape of customer site	• Customer requirements	• Sample solution architectures • Delivery methodologies

Table 6–3 Key Interfaces for the Services Delivery Function. (cont.'d)

Delivery	Customer	Field Engineering	Services Sales	Services Engineering
Comments		Domain-expertise friction		Tension between the Services Delivery and Services Engineering teams. Classic friction that exists between staff (Services Engineering) and line (Services Delivery) functions.

There are three areas of friction that occur naturally in this model.

- The first is the tension between sales and delivery. Sales people want to sell and close. They may agree to unreasonable customer requirements and requests as part of closing the deal. Delivery people actually have to make the commitments real.

- The second is the classic staff-versus-line friction that will occur between the Services Engineering team and the field-delivery team. The Services Engineering team will pontificate with best practices while the field team will gravitate to what they know best (even if that is not the optimal solution to the customer's problem). To alleviate this natural schism, it is helpful to have the Services Engineering team actually spend time on field engagements.

- The third area of friction will occur between the delivery staff and the field-engineering team. This is an issue of turf. To have a service consultant waltz in and tell the account team what the customer needs is more than most competent and proud field engineers can bear. If the Services Delivery team does not learn how to engage the field engineers in an inclusive manner, bad blood is sure to occur.

▶ Compensation for the Delivery Function

The delivery function has little control over when engagements are booked. However, the delivery function has immense influence over when revenue is recognized from engagements and how profitable the engagements actually are. The mantra of the delivery organization must be "billable hours." The math is very simple. If the delivery function does not achieve its target number of billable hours, the overall service function will not be profitable. A compensation plan for the delivery organization might resemble that shown in Table 6-4.

Key Metrics

There are numerous metrics that can be applied to the delivery organization. Revenue, project, and utilization metrics are the most critical. Table 6-5 illustrates the key metrics for the Services Delivery team.

Organizational Structure and Sizing

The key parameters to consider when sizing the delivery function are as follows:

1. What is the overall revenue objective for the PS business unit?
2. What will the revenue mix be (i.e., what percentage of revenue will come directly from billable delivery staff)?
3. What utilization rate is expected from the billable delivery staff?
4. What average rate will be charged for the billable delivery staff?

Revenue Mix

Our target revenue was determined earlier to be $100 million. How much of that revenue will come from selling other companies' products and services? How much of that revenue will come from selling your own consultants? Before you answer, there are some pros and cons you should consider. They are outlined here in Table 6-6.

For our new services function, we will be targeting a 60/40 revenue mix. That is, 60 percent of our revenue will be direct revenue and 40 percent will come from reselling the products and services of other companies.

Table 6–4 Compensation for Services Delivery Staff.

POSITION	PLAN TYPE	MONEY			MARGIN		MIX	MILE-STONES	MINUTES	TOTAL VARIABLE COMPEN-SATION
		Bookings	Revenue	Gross Margin	Target Project Margin	Actual Project Margin	Revenue Mix	Project Completion Ratio	Billable Utilization Rate	
Delivery Manager	80/20					10%			10%	20%
Project Manager	80/20				5%			5%	10%	20%
Senior Technical Consultant	80/20	20%			10%		10%		20%	20%
Technical Consultant	80/20								20%	20%

Table 6–5   Key Metrics for Services Delivery.

Metric	Description	Calculation	Sample Target	Person Responsible
Project Completion Ratio	Measures the degree of completion against project milestones.	Number of milestones accomplished on schedule divided by total milestones targeted	> 80%	Project Manager
Project Overruns	Measures the accuracy with which project costs are forecasted.	Total project costs incurred divided by total estimated project costs	10%	Project Manager
Billable Utilization Rate	Measures the organization's ability to maximize its billing resources.	Total number of hours billed divided by number of working hours in a year per number of total employees	> 65%	Delivery Managers
Project Actual Margin	The actual gross margin achieved by a project.	Revenue from project minus costs to deliver that project (including employee salaries, subcontractors, and travel expenses)	Depends on what type of services you are providing, but target >35% for high-end consulting services	Project Manager
Revenue per Head	The average revenue generated per full-time employee. If subcontractor or third-party's work is counted in revenue, then include their expenses.	Total services revenue divided by number full-time employees	$300k per year	Regional Director
Turnover Rate	The percentage of delivery staff that leave the organization. Typically measured on an annual basis.	Number of employees that left divided by total number of employees	< 15%	Delivery Manager

Table 6–5 Key Metrics for Services Delivery. (cont.'d)

Account Expansion	The ability of a vendor to expand its account penetration and volume of business.	Additional revenue divided by revenue from initial project	>20%	Project Manager
Training Days	Average number of working days spent in training.	Number of employee working days spent training divided by total number of employee working days	10%	Delivery Manager

Table 6–6 Pros and Cons of Indirect Revenue.

	Indirect Revenue (other Companies' Products and Services)	Direct Revenue
PROS	• Easy money • Minimal investment • Quickly grows the top line • Can use best of breed	• High margin • Clear value add • Builds company Intellectual Property (IP)
CONS	• Low margin • Less of your own value add • Potential Channel conflict • Potential Strategic conflict	• Harder to grow • Dependent on your ability to hire and train

Billable Utilization Rate

This is the percentage of time your delivery staff is actually charging the customer. To someone new to the service business, the target rate seems obvious: 100 percent. However, this is not realistic. First, consultants are human beings. They take vacation and get sick. Second, your staff constantly needs to be retooled; they need downtime for process training and technical education. Finally, your demand might not support the high utilization rate you desire.

World-class consulting firms target 65 percent to 85 percent billable utilization rates for their consultants. Product-centric consulting firms often are happy with 50 percent to 75 percent billable utilization rates. This is because of the large number of presales activities that the delivery staff is brought into by the Product Sales teams. Often, a senior technical consultant will be critical in closing a product sale even though no services were sold by him or her.

For all these reasons, our new delivery function will target a 65 percent billable utilization rate.

Billable Rate

How much will people pay? There are two techniques you can employ to determine how much you should charge for your delivery talent.

- **Market analysis:** With this technique, you assess what customers are currently paying for similar talent. If you have technical skills that are hard to find, you can get top dollar. Unfortunately, you will also pay top dollar to acquire and retain staff with those skills.
- **Cost analysis:** With this technique, you access what it actually costs you to employ your delivery staff. Once you have accurate cost figures, you add a target margin on top to arrive at your target billable rate.

There is one other factor that needs mentioning regarding billable rates. Remember, if your staff members possess hard-to-find technical skills or unique solution knowledge, you will be able to charge higher rates. More on this in Chapter 7: Productizing.

The new delivery function will be billing out staff at an average rate of $200 dollars an hour.

Sample Organizational Structure

We are now ready to create the first draft of the delivery organization.

Table 6–7   Services Delivery Planning Parameters.

Description	Parameter
Target revenue	$100M
Revenue mix	60/40

Table 6–7   Services Delivery Planning Parameters. (cont.'d)

Target billable utilization	65%
Target billable rate	$200/hr

Using the parameters in Table 6-7, we can easily understand the existing situation and plan for the remaining parameters. A sizing worksheet is presented in Table 6-8.

Table 6–8   Services Delivery Parameter.

Parameter Description	Value
Target revenue	$60,000,000
Yearly hours	2080
Target utilization	65%
Billable hours	1352
Avg. billable rate	$200
Total delivery staff	222
Revenue generated	$60,028,800
Number of geographies	3
Delivery staff per geo	74

An organizational chart illustrating how the staff will be assigned is provided in Figure 6-11. From the beginning, it has been assumed that each geographical area has the same level of revenue potential. This means each geographical area needs the ability to deliver one-third of the total revenue objective. Roughly, each geographical area will need 74 delivery personnel that generate 91,520 billable hours per year at a rate of no less than $200 dollars per hour.

Currently, we have three regional sales directors in place. To minimize management overhead, we will have one director in charge of each geographical area. That director will be responsible for both the sales and the new delivery function. The regional directors will have delivery managers reporting to them. Each delivery manager will have 20 or more staff reporting directly to him or her. At first glance, this may

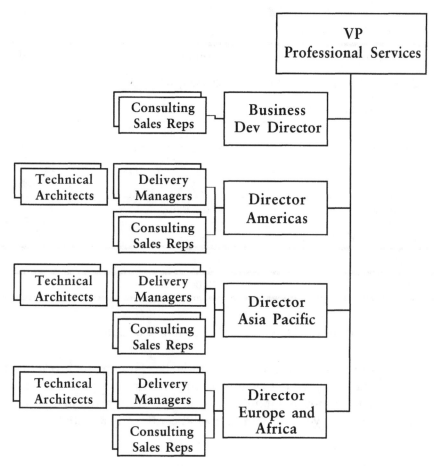

Figure 6–11 Services Delivery organization chart.

seem excessive. However, this is not a classic employee-manager relationship. These employees will spend a majority of their time on-site with their clients. Based on this ratio, each regional director will need approximately four delivery managers.

▶ Sample Budget

A sample budget for the Services Delivery function is provided in Figure 6-12. As can be seen, the current revenue mix of 60/40 means that

Services Delivery		
Number of Employees: 234		
Cost	Amount	Percent of Total
Salaries and Benefits	$24,528,000	35%
Commissions and Bonuses	$ 6,132,000	9%
Occupancy	$ 1,170,000	2%
Travel	$ 2,910,000	4%
Outside Services	$ 90,000	0%
Depreciation	$ 1,170,000	2%
Third-Party COGS	$34,000,000	49%
TOTAL	$70,000,000	

Figure 6–12   Services Delivery sample budget.

third-party COGS represents the largest expense line item. This makes managing your delivery partners critical to your financial success. If you cannot maintain at least a 15 percent gross margin on third-party services, your bottom line will be adversely affected.

▶ Issues to Watch

Once again, the delivery function is the heart and soul of the new consulting organization being constructed. If this function estimates, executes, and educates well, the overall service organization will be profitable. If estimates are poor, execution lax, and education nonexistent, the service organization will die a costly death.

As you develop the delivery function in your service organization, there are several items to keep your eye on. First of all, you must **constantly monitor the relationship between demand and supply**. If you overstaff your delivery function and outpace demand, your service organization will undoubtedly be unprofitable. Beyond macrolevel supply and demand, you also must monitor **how well the skills of your delivery staff are aligned with the skills and solutions that are important to the company.** If you grow skills that are not core to the future success of the company, you will be missing the mark and setting yourself up for failure. The company will be marketing and selling skills that you should but don't have—this disconnect will be costly to your bottom line.

SIRENS' SONG: The more delivery staff the organization has, the more money the organization will make.

BOULDER AHEAD: The truth is poorly aligned hiring leads to low utilization and unprofitability.

The issue to watch is growth. Every time a delivery resource is added, there is potential for incremental revenue. If demand is strong, you have just added the potential for $208,000 in revenue. However, you have just added fixed costs as well. The fully burdened cost of that employee is probably $150,000 a year. It will take time for this new employee to be trained and reach his or her target utilization rate. Worse, if he or she is hired without the right skills and he or she rides the bench, you just put yourself $150,000 in the hole. Making poor hires is more likely to happen when you are hiring fast and furiously. **Understand that the faster you grow your delivery function, the worse your profitability will be!**

7

Productizing

Building your portfolio

It is clear why you need a sales function. It is clear why you need a delivery function. But productizing? What is this all about? Productizing is the business of treating your services as products. To be clear, the discipline of managing the intellectual property (IP) that makes up those services is not optional for a successful consulting business. Ask any industry leader such as Price Waterhouse, Accenture, or IBM. That is what this chapter is all about: managing your valuable and hard-won intellectual property. By investing in this function, you create leverage—leverage you need to drive margin. This is why repeatability is part of the profitability triangle. Productizing your services encourages repeatability. Repeatability drives margin. How? By reducing risks and costs associated with delivering fledgling services. Each time you deliver a service, you get better at it. Fewer surprises. Greater efficiency. Figure 7-2 maps this effect.

SIRENS' SONG: Managing IP costs too much. We don't need unique IP to make money.
BOULDER AHEAD: The truth is it will be difficult to maintain gross margins greater than 25 percent without some level of IP management.

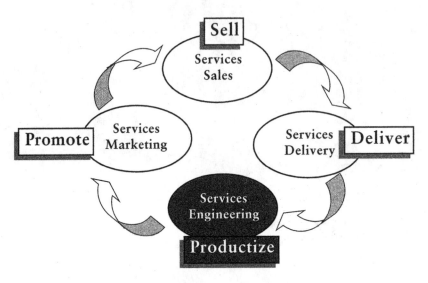

Figure 7–1 Services Engineering.

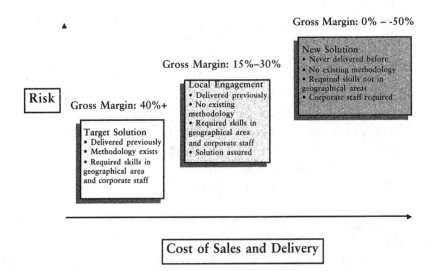

Figure 7–2 Engagement types and risk levels.

The first time a consulting team tackles a solution, there is great risk. The cost of delivery is always higher than anticipated. In fact, when working with project managers and technical architects, it is not uncommon to see the most senior of these people grossly miscalculate the effort required to complete a new solution, often by a factor of two. However, the next time that same team estimates what it takes to deliver that same type of solution, the risk goes down. The team has a better understanding of what it really takes. The estimation is much more accurate. The cost to deliver also goes down. But the real trick is to take that final step, that is, to productize your service. When you treat your solutions, or your services, with clear methodologies (as you would if they were tangible products), you drive consistent, efficient delivery and minimize risk. This is the holy grail of a product-based professional services business. This correlation between increasing project margins and decreasing project risks is captured in Figure 7-2. The graph maps three types of professional services engagements: a new solution engagement, a local engagement, and a target solution engagement. New solution engagements occur when a professional services firm delivers a solution for the first time. As the graph maps, the risk during this type of engagement is high and the costs can exceed the revenue. A local engagement occurs when the local PS team delivers a solution they have delivered before. There is less risk in this scenario, and based on team experience, the cost to sell and deliver the solution should be less than the revenue received. As you can see, we are moving in the right direction. But the real win occurs when PS delivers a target solution that is well documented and well understood. In this type of engagement, the PS firm often can command a premium price due to expertise that is documented and easily articulated. The risk to deliver a well-understood solution is lower and the mature delivery methodology drives down costs and improves margins.

So, it becomes clear that delivering target solutions has financial benefits. However, successfully productizing intellectual property to generate target solutions can be the most challenging function any PS firm can face. It is even more challenging for PS organizations that are part of product-centric companies. Why? Because product-centric companies inherently believe their intellectual capital is represented in their products. They often fail to recognize the intellectual capital locked in their service capabilities. Thomas Stewart, in his book *Intellectual Capital*,[1] highlights three areas where valuable intellectual capital exists:

1. Thomas Stewart, *Intellectual Capital*, New York, Doubleday, 1997.

- Your employees
- Your processes
- Your customer relationships

Product companies have a tough time looking beyond the widget to these other categories. This creates an Achilles' heel they can't afford. Yet, to drive the service margins they anticipate, product companies must look beyond their products. In this chapter, we will provide a framework on how you can do that within your service function.

▶ Function Overview

The Services Engineering function is designed to help take solution knowledge full circle from the first successful implementation of a solution, into captured intellectual property, to the next successful implementation of the solution. (see Figure 7-3). The department does this by first getting heavily involved in the tail end of the project delivery life cycle we have been using in the last two chapters. Specifically, Service Engineering works closely with Services Delivery in conducting the actual project-review step. Intellectual property from project reviews is evaluated by the Services Engineering team and the Services Marketing team. Solutions that have potential are taken into development by the Services Engineering team and then rolled back out to the field by the Services Marketing team.

▶ Critical Success Factors

For this corporate-based, non-revenue-generating organization to be worthwhile, several issues must be addressed. First, your organization **must generate deliverables that are valuable to the sales and delivery functions of your PS organization.** If Services Engineering does not create intellectual property that drives more revenue at better margins, then it is missing the mark.

Second, whatever **solutions your organization invests in should be aligned with overall company objectives.** The Services Engineering team should not be developing solutions that are not core to the future

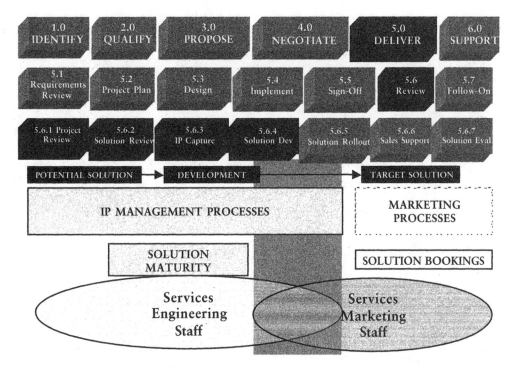

Figure 7–3 Services Engineering responsibilities.

success of the company, regardless of the revenue potential for services. As Geoffrey Moore states, the professional services organization must "focus its talents on serving the shareholder–value-creation opportunity of getting its own company's technologies across the chasm." Services Engineering leads the charge to keep service offerings aligned.

Next, you must **shield this team from becoming an extension of the Services Delivery team.** In the process of taking new solutions to market, the Services Engineering team will be involved in various aspects of delivery. This is different, however, than being a delivery group. If Services Engineering become focused on short-term revenues, the ability of professional services to capture future revenues will be compromised.

Finally, you must create and staff a team that **has true credibility with internal and external departments.** The Services Engineering team must know how to bring value to Services Sales and to Services Delivery. Also, Services Engineering must be credible with Product Marketing and Product Engineering. These two external groups will be bringing multiple solution opportunities to your PS organization that need to be evaluated. The Services Engineering team will be heavily involved in these discussions. If there is friction here, the team may lose potential leverage it can receive by being aligned with other company efforts.

▶ Services Engineering Charter

The charter of the Services Engineering function is as follows: **capture, improve, leverage.**

- **Capture** valuable intellectual property generated from your customer engagements.

- **Improve** your intellectual property.

- **Leverage** intellectual property throughout your global organization.

▶ Capture

To capture, improve, and leverage intellectual property, the Services Engineering function must manage the solution development life cycle. This cycle is a subset of the project delivery life cycle. The solution development life cycle begins when valuable intellectual property has been captured from a customer engagement.[2] This occurs in the review step of the project delivery life cycle (see Figure 7-4).

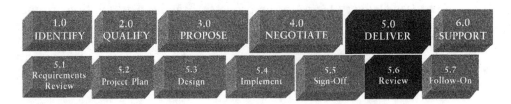

Figure 7–4   Review.

2. The solution development life cycle can also be initiated when Product Marketing has a specific solution it would like to take to market. For this chapter, we will focus on the first scenario, which is driven by customer needs and known success.

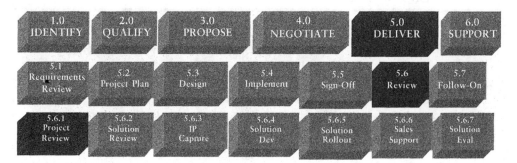

| 1.0 IDENTIFY | 2.0 QUALIFY | 3.0 PROPOSE | 4.0 NEGOTIATE | 5.0 DELIVER | 6.0 SUPPORT |

| 5.1 Requirements Review | 5.2 Project Plan | 5.3 Design | 5.4 Implement | 5.5 Sign-Off | 5.6 Review | 5.7 Follow-On |

| 5.6.1 Project Review | 5.6.2 Solution Review | 5.6.3 IP Capture | 5.6.4 Solution Dev | 5.6.5 Solution Rollout | 5.6.6 Sales Support | 5.6.7 Solution Eval |

Figure 7–5 Project review.

Project Review

At the end of each significant consulting engagement, a project review should be performed (see Figure 7-5). What defines a significant project? Several helpful parameters are shown in Figure 7-6.

Significant Project Criterion	Sample Range
Dollar Value	> $100k, largest project to date
Time Frame	> 4 weeks of work
Solution Type	Completed work in target solution area

Figure 7–6 Parameters of a significant project.

The first two parameters are obvious. This last parameter, Solution Type, will be covered in more detail later in this chapter.

Once you determine that a project review should occur, you need to determine what information should be captured in this review. A sample project review is provided in Appendix C. Basic information that needs to be captured is listed in Table 7-1.

Each one of these items contains valuable insight into your business and provides kernels of wisdom that can be used to improve profitability and differentiate your offerings. We cannot stress enough the criticality of performing project reviews on a consistent and ongoing basis.

Table 7–1 Solution IP.

Element to Capture	Description
Solution Description	Two or three paragraphs describing what was implemented for the customer
Planned Deliverables	The deliverables specified in the initial project plan
Actual Deliverables	A list of what was actually delivered to the customer
Planned Expenses	Original budget (staff hours, third-party services, third-party products, travel, etc.)
Actual Expenses	The actual expenses incurred to complete the project
Planned Effort	Original hours estimated to complete project
Actual Effort	Actual hours required to complete project
Resource Profiles	List of skills required on the project team to deliver the solution
Reusable Components	A list of any components that other customers might ask for
Lessons Learned	A list of gotchas, or surprises, with brief description of what happened and how each can be avoided next time

This little act of discipline, which could require less than a day or two of effort after each project, will reap bushels of benefit. If you chose to ignore this step, you will be unable to answer many questions. What was your most profitable project last quarter? Last year? What is your project completion ratio? What critical skills are required to deliver your most important solutions? Without solid project review data, not even the oracle of Delphi can answer these questions for you.

Solution Review

After the project review is completed, a solution review (Figure 7-7) should occur. This is the activity used to determine if there is any "gold in them hills." Each engagement is analyzed to determine if there is knowledge that is marketable and can be reused with other customers. If there is, the solution that was delivered becomes a target solution to be used in the future.

Figure 7–7 Solution review.

IP Capture

If it is determined in the solution review that the there might be gold there (i.e., there are marketable knowledge, revenue, and identifiable customers), then all the existing IP for that solution should be captured and quantified. There are two types of solution IP lying around from completed projects:

> **Sales IP:** Sales IP identifies why customers bought this solution and how it was sold. Examples of sales IP include:
> - Past proposals
> - Customer presentations

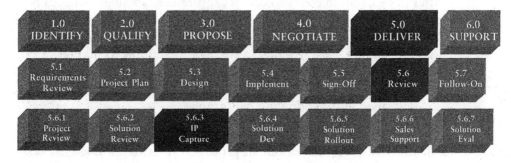

Figure 7–8 IP capture.

Technical (Delivery) IP: Technical IP identifies how the solution was actually delivered. Examples of technical IP include:

- Actual project plans
- Project review
- List of people and skills required to implement
- List of partners required to implement
- Any unexpected risk factors or solutions

This raw project IP needs to be cleaned, generalized, augmented, and stored in a central repository for easy access by your Services Engineering team and Services Delivery teams.

▶ Improve

Once intellectual property is captured from field engagements, the Services Engineering team needs to generalize and improve that knowledge. The next step, solution development, addresses this.

Solution Development

After IP from completed projects is captured, a gap analysis needs to be performed between what IP is available and what is required to sell this solution to multiple customers, that is, to develop a more universal solution (Figure 7-9). To effectively take a solution to market, a core set of information that describes and documents the solution must be created. A sample list of solution components is provided in Table 7-2 and described in the following paragraphs.

The Services Marketing team owns several of these components. Its role in the solution-development process is discussed in the next chapter. The relationship between Services Engineering and Services Marketing regarding solution portfolio management is discussed in Appendix E. For now, let's focus on the specific deliverables required from Services Engineering.

Figure 7–9   Solution development.

Table 7–2   Components of a Solution.

Area	Component	Description	Owner Services Engineering	Services Marketing
Executive Overview	Executive Overview*	A high-level overview that describes what the solution is and the business problem it addresses		✓
Sales and Marketing	Customer Presentation*			✓
	Datasheets*			✓
	Whitepapers			✓
	Demos		✓	
	Sales Tips			✓
	Customer References*			✓
	Competitive Analysis*	Information on comparative solutions available from other companies		✓
	Target Customer List/Profile	A list of customers the Services Sales organization should be targeting with this solution		✓

Table 7–2   Components of a Solution. (cont.'d)

Delivery Methodology	Partner Profiles*	A list of partners that are used to deliver components of the overall solution	✓	
	Resource Profiles*	Descriptions of the skills required to implement the solution	✓	
	Engagement Framework*	Implementation strategy and steps	✓	
	Engagement Activity Forms*	Detailed instructions on implementation activities	✓	
	Software Source Code (as req.'d)		✓	
Sample Engagement Documentation	SOW*		✓	
	Proposal*		✓	
	Project Plan*		✓	
	Sample Architecture*		✓	
Training	Sales Training Materials*			✓
	Delivery Resource Training Materials*		✓	
Support	Sample Customer Support Agreement*		✓	
	Support Staff Training*		✓	
	*required elements			

Sample Architecture

A sample architecture is simply a diagram depicting what the solution physically and logically looks like. It would identify XYZ computer hardware running the PDQ version of software, etc., etc. The real value is to document configurations that are known to work and have been tested to some level.

Sample Project Plan

Every IT director worth his or her salt will ask for a project plan. By providing a sample project plan that can be modified per engagement, the Services Engineering team provides the following benefits to the local delivery teams:

- Reduces the hassle of creating a project-plan document from scratch.
- Reduces the risk of local team omitting key steps or tasks.

Sample Proposal

Like the sample project plan, a sample proposal saves time and reduces risk.

Engagement Framework and Engagement Activity Forms

First and foremost, the Services Engineering team must develop engagement frameworks for any solution it wishes to implement globally and consistently. An engagement framework is simply a document describing your game plan. Regarding any new solution, the engagement framework illustrates how you are going to get the customer from point A to point B and what the steps are that you need to follow. Now, how you document your engagement framework is up to you. You can make this document as textual or graphical as you like. Personally, we find that the more visual it is in nature, the better. You may find the following design principles helpful when you are working to create an engagement framework format:

Visual: Use pictures to tell the story. Customers and others quickly get lost in heavy text.

Layered: Take a top down, high-level overview to low-level detail approach in your documentation. At the highest level, you should be able to overview your engagement framework on one page. Details are revealed in lower layers.

Modular: Make each component of your engagement framework as modular as possible. Creating a decent engagement framework is a lot like writing durable and reusable software. You want your functional modules to be as self-inclusive as possible so they can be ripped out and plugged in various places with ease.

Linear: The engagement framework should display some sense of time so customers can understand progress and critical path deliverables.

The object here is not to make you an expert on documentation techniques. The key point is that you must employ some mechanism to document your delivery strategies. Without some type of engagement framework, you prevent yourself from successfully capturing rich project information and reusing it consistently.

Figure 7-10 provides a sample of the highest level, or overview level, engagement framework for the implementation of a new software product. In this overview level, several of the modules can be exploded to provide submodels. For example, Module 7.0 Risk Analysis may have two submodules named 7.1 Technical Risk Analysis and 7.2 Operational Risk Analysis. As you can see, this version of an engagement framework is closely related to the Program Evaluation Review Technique (PERT) charts, a methodology developed by the U.S. Navy in the 1950s to manage the Polaris submarine missile program, you see generated from project plans. The difference is that the engagement framework here is the primary deliverable, not the by-product of a project plan. Appendix D contains a sample project review. In this review, you can see how this graphical engagement framework can be used to quickly summarize the rough spots of a specific implementation.

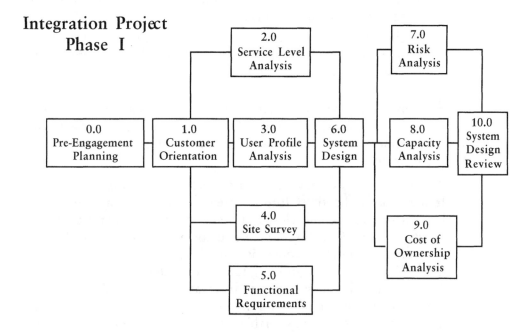

Figure 7–10   Sample engagement framework.

Engagement activity forms are the more textual summaries that back up the higher-level engagement framework. Specific activities required to execute the engagement framework are documented on these forms. Each activity has the following information documented on an engagement activity form:

Purpose: A statement of the business objective achieved by performing this activity.

Description: A brief summary of the activity, written so that any business layperson should be able to grasp what is being done.

Prerequisites: A list of the tasks that need to be performed before this activity can be performed—specifically, any inputs that are required.

Deliverables: A list of the hard deliverables that this activity produces, for example, a report, a piece of code.

Required Skills: A list of the specific technical and business skills required to complete this activity.

Task Listing: A list of each task required to complete the activity with as much detail as possible describing how to complete the task.

By combining visual engagement frameworks with detailed engagement activity forms, the Services Engineering team can create a powerful documentation set that can be used by field delivery staff for future engagements.

A critical point to make here is the iterative nature of engagement frameworks and activity forms. Often, corporate departments love to lock themselves behind closed doors to create the "perfect product." However, by disregarding valuable customer and field input, the corporate team might deliver something that is late, over budget, and off the mark. The Services Engineering team faces the same precarious fate if it is not careful. The goal is not to create perfect engagement frameworks that result in the flawless implementation of a solution. The goal is to quickly disseminate valuable information. The first version of any engagement framework released to the field will most likely be 50 percent adequate at best. But that's 50 percent more knowledge than the field delivery team had at its disposal when they began. As the documentation is used in actual engagements, it should be updated as part of each project review process. After the fourth or fifth update from project reviews, the framework will be fairly complete.

Resource Profiles

Resource profiles are simply descriptions of what skills must exist on the delivery team for successful implementation to occur. A resource profile may look like the one presented in Table 7-3.

Partner Profiles

In these days of open system architectures and virtual organizations, it is very unlikely that a solution will be delivered solely by one company. Thus, your target solutions will almost always contain critical

Table 7–3   Resource Profiles.

Role	Required Technical Skill(s)	Required Business Skill(s)	Estimated Project Effort
Solution Architect	• Skills in networking, scalable server architectures • Solution 123 architectures	• Customer ready (able to work directly with customers) • Manage technical staff of 3	45 hours
Project Manager	Skills in MS Project, Microsoft Office, and Solution 123 engagement methodology	Customer presentation skills	155 hours
Technical Consultant	Skills in C++, Unix, Software Package XYZ		255 hours

components from other companies. These can be product components or service components. When the Services Engineering team documents a solution, it should identify what partners are required to ultimately deliver the solution. Also, the documentation should indicate whether multiple partners can potentially deliver one component. The Services Engineering team should provide some insight into how partners have performed on past engagements. This partner report card can help local delivery teams engage the most responsive and competent partners first.

Source Code

As stated earlier, the PS organization in a product company is often engaged to create the glue required to make a solution real for the customer. This glue often comes in the form of custom software or source code. Ideally, this software can be leveraged from customer site to customer site with minimal modifications. If this type of intellectual property pops out of customer engagements, it makes great business sense to have this software managed centrally by the Services Engineering team.

Training Materials

Sample architectures, resource profiles, and engagement frameworks created by the Services Engineering team are all great enablers for the field. However, none of these can completely replace face-to-face knowledge transfer. Training materials and classes need to be organized. The Services Engineering team works to assure the intellectual property they are creating is actually being assimilated by the Services Delivery teams.

Demonstrations

Not all solutions require demos. You couldn't demonstrate some solutions if your life depended on it. But for the solutions that are more easily sold when demonstrated, the Services Engineering team should orchestrate those efforts. Otherwise, you may end up with multiple demonstrations created by various field staff and no confidence in the ability to duplicate a given demo on a given day.

▶ Leverage

Once IP is captured, then scrubbed and improved, it needs to be leveraged. Unless the solution is rolled out, that is, IP is actually used by the field to secure and deliver future engagements, the exercise has been wasted.

Solution Rollout

After the gaps are filled in the development phase, the solution can be rolled out (Figure 7-11). More on this in Chapter 8, where we cover in detail the process of deploying target solutions.

Sales Support

Once the solution is out there, how will you support (Figure 7-12) the ongoing sale and delivery of the solution? To illustrate how the newly created IP will assist in the sales process, let's review the workflow in Figure 7-13:

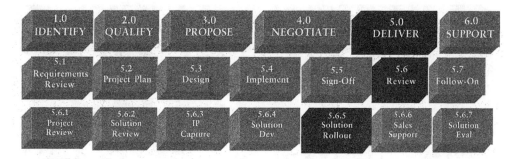

Figure 7–11 Solution rollout.

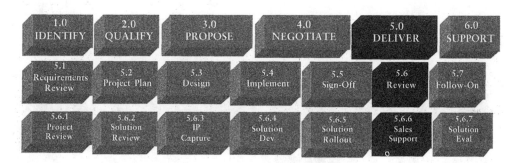

Figure 7–12 Sales support.

Qualification Support: If the field delivery team has never delivered a specific solution before, the Services Engineering team can assist in the qualification process.

Proposal Support: When the Services Sales and Services Delivery teams determine they actually want to bid the business and create a proposal, they should start by accessing IP available from the Services Engineering team. Figure 7-14 lists the documentation available from the Services Engineering team that will aid the proposal process.

Delivery Support: Once the proposal is accepted, the engagement framework, or delivery documentation (Figure 7-15), created by the Services Engineering team should be the guiding light for the field delivery team.

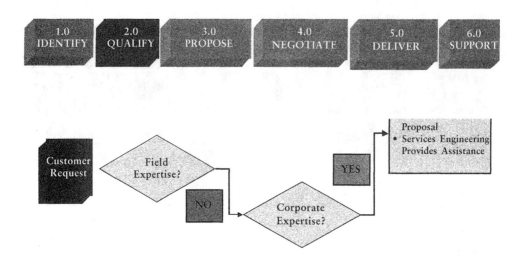

Figure 7–13 Sales support from the Servicee Engineering team.

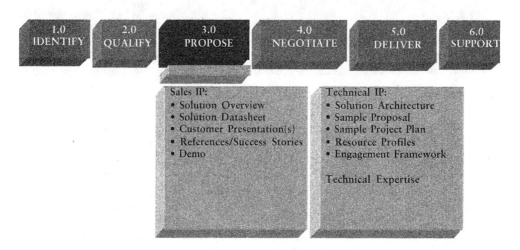

Figure 7–14 Proposal documentation.

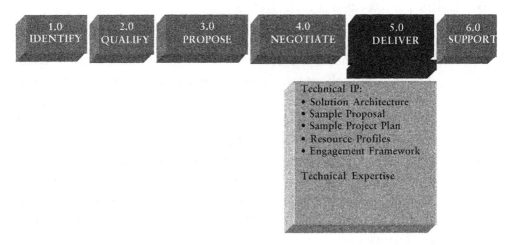

Figure 7–15 Delivery documentation.

Solution Evaluation

Was it all worth it? This solution and your overall solution portfolio must be reviewed and pruned. The solution evaluation step (Figure 7-16) should tell you what solutions are bringing in the best margins. This topic is covered in Appendix E.

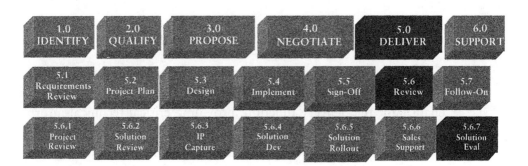

Figure 7–16 Solution evaluation.

Roles and Responsibilities

The Services Engineering organization is staffed by some existing roles and by some new roles. The function will be managed by a director. This director will ultimately be responsible for managing the maturity level of the solution portfolio. The director, like any good manager, should be evaluated on meeting development milestones, on time and on budget. To achieve this objective, the Services Engineering team will employ senior technical architects and project managers. These individuals will be on the core development teams, driving the deliverables of Services Engineering. The Services Engineering function will also employ a business analyst. This analyst is responsible for developing the financial business case for projects in development. For example, the business analyst will work with marketing and sales staff to generate revenue forecasts for new solutions. These revenue forecasts will be played against expense estimations that are provided by the Services Engineering project managers. The business analyst will verify that development efforts have an acceptable ROI.

The overview of all the roles and responsibilities for the Services Engineering staff is provided in Table 7-4.

Key Interfaces for Services Engineering

The Services Engineering function is not a front line corporate function but has many interfaces (Figure 7-17). Its primary objective is to be an enabler for the delivery function, providing critical technical information and delivery methodologies. A secondary objective is working with the Services Marketing function to provide marketing the data it needs to establish solution credibility. Another secondary objective is to maintain a bridge into Product Engineering. Finally, Services Engineering must work with external partners to merge outside technologies and capabilities that complete a target solution.

Inputs and outputs for these key interfaces are documented in Table 7-5.

Table 7–4 Roles and Responsibilities of the Services Engineering Staff.

Role	Purpose	Responsibilities			Experience	Requirements	
		General	Managerial	Financial		Education and Training	Technical
Services Engineering Director	Manage the Services Engineering function	• Assure the successful capture of project IP • Assure on-time delivery of new solution IP	Manage Services Engineering staff	• Manage Services Engineering expense budget • Help consulting BU hit target bookings and margin targets	• 10+ years management experience • Prior experience managing budgets • Prior experience managing technical staff • Prior experience managing large development projects	• 4-year degree • Master's preferred	Previous background in programming helpful
Project Manager	Manage the solution development life cycle for target solution(s)	• Create project plans • Manage project • Provide weekly project updates	• Manage virtual project teams • Manage subcontractors	Meet project expense objectives	• 8+ years general work experience • 2+ years project management experience	2-year degree	• Understanding of project life cycle • Understanding of how customers are using technology in their business

Role	Purpose	Responsibilities			Requirements		
		General	Managerial	Financial	Experience	Education and Training	Technical
Senior Technical Consultant	Manage the technical development for target solutions	• Create system architectures • Provide effort estimations • Implement solution • Assist in closing business	Manage and mentor technical consultants	Meet project expense objectives	• 10+ years general work experience • 4+ years technical consultant	4-year degree	Deep understanding of technologies being deployed
Business Analyst	Perform financial and business analysis of solution opportunities	• Create ROI estimations for solution development efforts • Present business analysis to senior management		Track financial performance of solution portfolio	• 6+ years experience • 2+ years performing ROI analysis	4-year degree in accounting or finance MBA preferred	

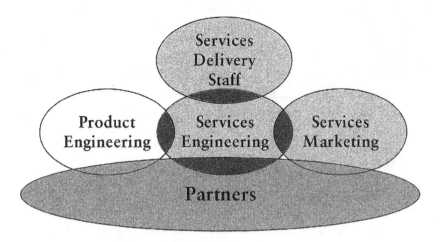

Figure 7–17 Key interfaces for Services Engineering function.

Table 7–5 Services Engineering Inputs and Outputs.

Services Engineering Type of Interface	Partners	Product Engineering	Delivery	Marketing
Outputs To	• Technical requirements (for partner's products) • Resource	• Technical requirements (for target solutions)	• Sample architectures • Sample project plans • Delivery methodology • Demos • Resource profiles • Technical expertise	• Solution roadmap • Sample architectures • Solution capabilities
Inputs From	• Technical requirements • Resource requirements	• Technical capabilities of product • Product roadmaps	• Technical requirements (from customers) • Engagement IP	• Solution positioning • Reference customers

Table 7–5   Services Engineering Inputs and Outputs. (cont.'d)

Services Engineering Type of Interface	Partners	Product Engineering	Delivery	Marketing
Comments	PS engineering staff must be careful not to reveal the protected technical information of one partner to another partner.			

Compensation for Services Engineering Staff

The Services Engineering team does not have direct control over when deals are booked; that's a sales function. The engineering team also does not have direct control over when revenue is recognized or how cost-effective the project team was. Despite all that, the success of the overall service business depends on bookings and margins. The Services Engineering team needs to be directly linked into this reality. By being compensated on bookings and target margins, this team is motivated to help the field teams succeed.

The Services Engineering team does have direct control over hitting development milestones and keeping staff marketable and utilized.

A sample compensation matrix for Services Engineering staff is shown in Table 7-6.

Key Metrics for Services Engineering

Often, research and development efforts are poorly evaluated. It is sometimes difficult to clearly measure the impact of R&D investments. As an R&D function, Services Engineering faces the danger of being poorly measured. However, there are clear metrics that can be applied to this function, as documented in Table 7-7.

Table 7-6 Compensation for Services Engineering Staff.

POSITION	PLAN TYPE	MONEY			MARGIN		MIX	MILE-STONES	MINUTES	TOTAL VARIABLE COMPEN-SATION
		Bookings	Revenue	Gross Margin	Target Project Margin	Actual Project Margin	Reve-nue Mix	Project Comple-tion Ratio	Billable Utilization Rate	
Direct or Services Engineering	80/20				10%	10%		10%		20%
Solution Manager	80/20		10%		10%					20%
Solution Architect	80/20							10%	10%	20%

Table 7–7 Services Engineering Metrics.

Metric	Description	Calculation	Sample Target	Person Responsible
Research and Development Expenses	Measures the degree of investment made to enhance the firm's tools, products, and methodologies. Total R&D costs equals infrastructure plus sales tools plus delivery tools.	R&D costs divided by total services revenue.	2% of service revenues	Services Engineering director
Project Completion Ratio	Measures the degree of completion against project milestones.	Number of milestones accomplished on schedule divided by total milestones targeted	80% or better	Services Engineering project manager
Project Overruns	Measures the accuracy with which project costs are forecasted.	Total project costs incurred divided by total estimated project costs	Less than 10%	Services Engineering project manager

▶ Organizational Structure and Sizing

The key parameters to consider when sizing your Services Engineering function are as follows:

1. What is your target mix? That is, what percentage of your revenue will come from target solutions?
2. How many solutions will you have in your portfolio?

Target Mix

As stated before, the more of your direct revenue that comes from delivering target solutions, the better your margins. However, you will and must continue to provide various services to your customers that are not directly related to a target solution. There is no one right answer for what your target mix should be. You should, however, have a sense of what you want it to be so you can hire the correct number of staff.

In our example, we will take the middle ground and size to be 50/50. Fifty percent of our $100 million in revenues will come from target solutions and 50 percent will come from new solutions deployed for the first time at customer requests.

Number of Solutions

How many solutions are required to drive that $50M in revenue? It depends on how big your solutions are. Do you have $50K solutions or $5M solutions? Or both. When you are building the PS function from the ground up, it is almost impossible to estimate how many solutions will be in your portfolio. Also, it is wise to walk before you crawl. Overinvesting in the Services Engineering function too early can be one of those expensive lessons learned.

For our case study, we will target the creation of three new target solutions the first fiscal year.

▶ Sample Organizational Structure

Working with the parameters summarized in Table 7-8, we are ready to seed the Services Engineering function.

Table 7–8   Services Engineering Planning Parameters.

Description	Parameter
Target revenue	$100M
Revenue from target solutions	$ 40M
Number of target solutions	3

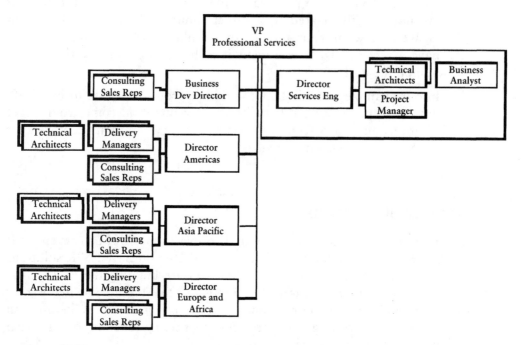

Figure 7–18 Services Engineering organizational chart.

Reporting to our VP of professional services will be the director of Services Engineering. This director will have five direct reports: three solution architects, one project manager, and one business analyst. There will be no solution managers the first year. They will be hired as solutions gain momentum and require more management attention. During the first fiscal year, with no historical revenue data in place, the director will be measured mostly on hitting development milestones. The structure for the Services Engineering organization is shown in Figure 7-18.

▶ Sample Budget

A sample budget for the Services Engineering department is shown in Figure 7-19. After human resource expenses, depreciation is the main investment. This represents the creation and support of lab environments where new solution architectures can be tested before being implemented at customer sites.

Services Delivery		
Number of Employees 234		
Cost	Amount	Percent of Total
Salaries and Benefits	$950,000	48%
Commissions and Bonuses	$120,000	6%
Occupancy	$ 30,000	2%
Travel	$200,000	10%
Outside Services	$300,000	15%
Depreciation	$400,000	20%
TOTAL	$2,000,000	

Figure 7–19 Services Engineering sample budget.

▶ Issues to Watch

There are several points to manage regarding the Services Engineering function. This function must stay aligned to the objectives of your company. **If the Services Engineering function does not build strong bridges into the Product Engineering function, services will run the risk of developing solutions that do not complement the company's product portfolio.** Make sure the Services Engineering function is a bridge builder and not a bridge burner.

Next, **make sure this function is extremely disciplined in its development efforts.** Just as the Services Delivery organization must be disciplined in delivering customer projects, the Services Engineering function must be disciplined in delivering valuable intellectual property to the field. If the Services Engineering team is permitted to miss deadlines, overspend, or pursue pet solutions, credibility will be lost with the field and long-term profitability will suffer.

Finally, **make sure this function does not become the business-development arm of the company.** The Services Engineering area is a natural place for highly skilled, customer-ready technical staff to congregate. These valuable resources should be leveraged with customers. However, if business development becomes its full-time concern, who is doing the actual solution development?

8

Promoting

Air cover

Let's assess where you are. To continue with the military analogy, you have assembled your infantry (Services Delivery) and you have an armored cavalry division (Services Engineering) that can sweep in for support. As highlighted in Figure 8-1, you are now ready to assemble the air forces (Services Marketing). The stronger the air cover you can provide your troops, the more likely they will succeed. In the world of professional services, marketing is the required air cover. Effective Services Marketing is not about general bombing runs. The objective is not to alter entire landscapes. Marketing services is all about strategic targeting. In this chapter, we will discuss the specific deliverables required from this support unit.

SIRENS' SONG: Existing Product Marketing managers can also market services.
BOULDER AHEAD: The truth is, Product Marketing managers will market their products. If you don't invest in Services Marketing, no one will be marketing your services.

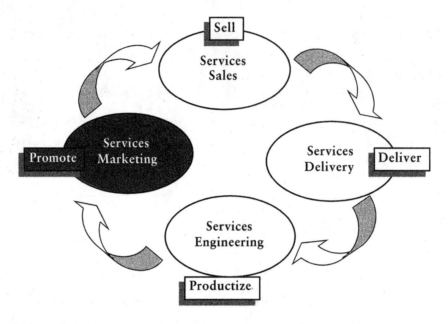

Figure 8–1 Services Marketing.

▶ Function Overview

The primary function of Services Marketing is to manage the final three phases of the Solution Development Life Cycle that was introduced in Chapter 7 (see Figure 8-2). The Services Marketing team assists the Services Engineering team in the development of marketing and sales IP for target solutions. Once Services Engineering has the solution documented, packaged, and ready to go, Services Marketing steps in and takes primary ownership of rolling the solution out to the field. This includes supporting the Services Sales team as they work to sell the solution. The Services Marketing team must also keep track of how solutions are performing in the field and where the PS organization is really making its money. Finally, the Services Marketing team is the mouthpiece for the entire organization—the voice to the external customers and to the other internal company departments. Without the Services Marketing function in place, you will struggle to tell your

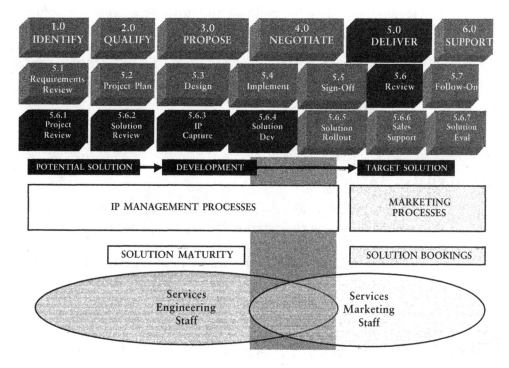

Figure 8–2 Service Marketing responsibilities.

professional-services story in a compelling and concise manner. Without it, you delegate the task of marketing to overbooked sales and delivery staff or to dry and technical Services Engineering employees. None of these other functions will excel at marketing or positioning your services to the level required. None of these other functions will provide you the proper air cover to launch and win market campaigns.

▶ Critical Success Factors

To market your new services, **you need to hire marketing staff that understands your organization's channels.** They need to understand the state of all current product sales channels and their inherent limitations, understand the current partner channel strategy your product company is employing, and build strategies for creating new channels!

Second, you need to implement metrics that hold the Services Marketing team accountable for building and growing a profitable solutions portfolio (see Appendix D for details on accountability for the Services Marketing function). Finally, you need to create an organizational design that couples the Services Marketing function to the Services Sales and Product Marketing functions. It must be linked tightly with both organizations if it is truly to bring value.

▶ Services Marketing Charter

To provide effective air cover, the Services Marketing function must achieve the following charter: **differentiate, validate, evangelize.**

- **Differentiate** the capabilities and solutions being offered by your service organization.
- **Validate** your competitive differences.
- **Evangelize** those differences to customers and partners.

▶ Differentiate

The first Services Marketing task is to differentiate what your company does from what all the other consulting organizations on the planet do. This is especially true of the target solutions you want to take to market. When your company launches into the PS arena, you are facing two issues regarding positioning: decreasing credibility and increasing competition. Figure 8-3 demonstrates the relationship between credibility, competition, and the various services a product company can offer.

First, the further your service offerings move from the core products of the company, the less initial credibility you will enjoy. Customers should not question your ability to deliver support services or education services centered on your products. But implementation services? The automatic credibility is not there; it has to be earned. Second, the further you move upstream in the services game by providing more value add services, the more competition you draw. Suddenly, you find

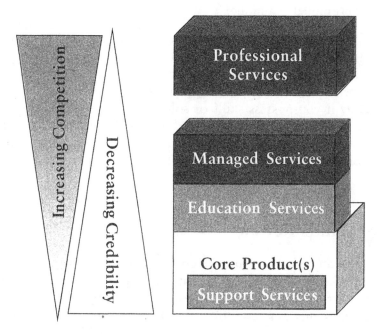

Figure 8–3 Marketing Services.

your new PS organization competing with the likes of EDS and Accenture! Now you can see why it is so important for the Services Marketing function to craft and broadcast the story that differentiates your professional services from everyone else's.

At the most general level, differentiation for product-centric PS firms can be positioned in two ways:

1. Capability differentiation
2. Solution differentiation

Capability differentiation is based on the unique technical skills possessed by your delivery consultants. Usually, these skills are closely associated with deep knowledge of your company's product line. *Solution differentiation* is based on your ability to deliver a business solution on time, on budget, and with minimal surprises (minimal risk). Each time a customer engagement is successfully completed, you have the opportunity to assess what specific skills allowed you to successfully deliver the solution and whether you delivered a solution that can be promoted as unique.

If there are no unique capabilities or differentiated solutions to articulate, you are simply a body shop operation. You will be providing general skills to the customer, skills they can acquire elsewhere. This generic positioning places you in a very price-sensitive environment. Only if you possess skills or solution knowledge not widely available can you hope to sustain higher margins for your services. It is the job of the marketing team to help identify those unique skills and solutions, then to promote those differences.

The Solution Review

Solution reviews (Figure 8-4) offer your marketing organization insight into the key differentiators that can be promoted. Each review is like a sieve, filtering out pieces of gold. During an actual solution review, a business analysis is performed by both the Services Engineering and the Services Marketing teams. The former provides estimates on exactly what development costs are. The latter determines if there is enough potential revenue from a solution concept to offset estimated solution development costs. At this point, we are assuming a solution concept has successfully passed the review phase and a promising business case has been established. Now, the Services Marketing team needs to help pick that money up and put it in your pocket. They must manage a successful solution rollout.

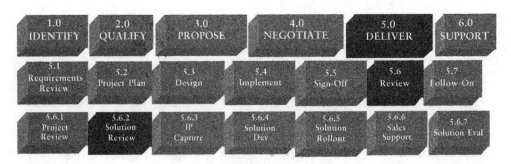

Figure 8–4 Solution review.

Solution Rollout

There are six steps in the solution-rollout process that the Services Marketing team must manage. Not all six steps make sense for every solution. However, all six areas should at least be reviewed when a new solution is being released for the field teams to sell and deliver.

Campaign Development

The first step in the solution-rollout process is campaign development (Figure 8-5). In this step, the Services Marketing team verifies the availability of all components developed by the Services Engineering team and by the product marketing team in the solution development phase. Specifically, the Services Marketing team is accountable for creating the following sales and marketing deliverables:

- **Executive overview:** A summary describing the solution, benefits, and advantages of using your company to implement this solution.

- **Customer presentation:** A complete presentation positioning the solution with end customers. This presentation will be used by Services Sales representatives and channel partners.

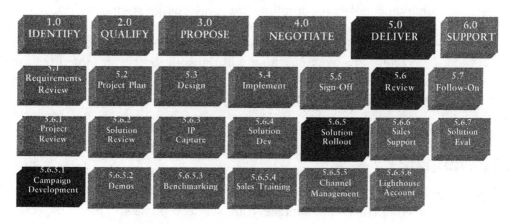

Figure 8–5 Campaign development.

- **Solution datasheet:** A one-page glossy overview of the solution, designed to be left on the desks of potential customers or handed out at trade shows.
- **Solution white paper:** An in-depth review of the technical components of the solution. This review provides insight on technical strategies employed and should be written in conjunction with the Services Engineering team.
- **Competitive analysis matrix:** A summary of what competition exists for the solution. Competitive analysis should include information on pricing of competitors' offerings, credibility of the competitors, and an analysis of strengths, weaknesses, opportunities, and threats (i.e., SWOT analysis) of your solution.
- **Sales tips:** An itemized list of pointers on how best to position this solution with customers. This should be written for Services Sales representatives and channel partners.
- **Customer references:** A documented list of customers to whom your company has successfully delivered the solution.

Each one of these documents should articulate the compelling advantages of the solution. The more complete and articulate they are, the more helpful they will be in selling the solution. It is important to note that during the creation of these materials, the Services Marketing team should be in constant contact with the Services Sales team. After all, it is the Services Sales staff that must find these marketing materials usable and effective with end customers.

Simultaneous with compiling the previous go-to-market documents, the Services Marketing team must define thoroughly which customers will be targeted. Then, a strategy for promoting the new solution can be created. For example, how will the solution be promoted (e.g., by direct mail, trade show booths, direct contact)? The overall campaign needs to be defined and funded at this point.

▶ Validate

The second component of the Services Marketing charter is to validate the competitive advantages your services possess. This is especially important as it relates to target solutions you're taking to market. There are two tangible deliverables the Services Marketing team can provide to help validate how great your solutions really are.

Demos

The first tangible deliverable that helps validate a solution is the creation of a working demo (Figure 8-6). Not all solutions lend themselves to demonstration. But for solutions that can be demonstrated, the Services Marketing team should coordinate the creation of a compelling customer demo that sales representatives can use to impress customers. It makes great economic sense to have this activity managed centrally. Often, regional sales staff will work with local delivery staff to bolt together a working demo for customers; this grass roots effort is commendable, but probably not efficient. The Services Marketing staff needs to work with regional teams, Services Engineering and Product Marketing teams, and whoever else might have input, to create a demo that can be consistently duplicated by all regional sales teams. This allows you to invent the wheel just once and it allows a consistent customer experience.

Figure 8–6 Demos.

Figure 8–7 Benchmarking.

Benchmarking

The second tangible deliverable that helps clearly differentiate a solution is benchmark data (Figure 8-7). Benchmark data compares the performance factors of your solution against a similar solution from competing companies. Benchmark data could include number of transactions processed per second, average response time to queries, or total cost of system ownership. Like solution demos, benchmarking may not apply to every solution. However, if benchmarking makes sense, the Services Marketing team should own the process for all the same reasons it should own the demo creation process.

▶ Evangelize

The final piece of the Services Marketing charter centers on evangelizing, that is, telling the story of your PS organization and making sure the sales channels understand exactly how to position your specific capabilities and solutions.

Figure 8–8 Sales training.

Sales Training

The first converts need to be the sales representatives of the company, both product and Services Sales reps. This is accomplished by providing thorough sales training for these individuals. Once again, the sales force should have been engaged during the creation of the marketing materials. Now, it is time to deploy these materials throughout the entire sales force. During this training, any newly created sales and marketing tools are presented to the reps. Reps must walk away from target-solution training understanding (and holding the support materials regarding) at least six key items:

1. What am I selling (solution description)?

2. Why would the customer want to buy from us (sample customer presentation)?

3. What supports our positioning (white papers, demos, benchmarks, references)?

4. Who, specifically, should I go call on (target customer list)?

5. Who is my competition (competitive analysis)?

6. Any final pointers on how to close this business (sales tips)?

Figure 8–9 Channel management.

Channel Management

After helping the direct-sales force see the light, the Services Marketing team must convert the other sales channels of the company (Figure 8-9). It must work with legacy channels from the product-centric days to educate them on the new services being offered. Then, the marketing team must identify and educate any new partner channels that may now make sense for the company to leverage.

Lighthouse Accounts

Finally, the Services Marketing team must identify, help capture, and then nurture key customer accounts. Remember, customer references are one of the key levers to ongoing profitability for professional services. Lighthouse accounts (Figure 8-10) are accounts that will serve, in the future, either as solution or industry references. The marketing team must determine which customers would provide the biggest impact on other potential customers. These newly identified lighthouse accounts must be pursued with a vengeance. Once sold on the idea, they must be wined, dined, and codified to guarantee they will serve as positive references.

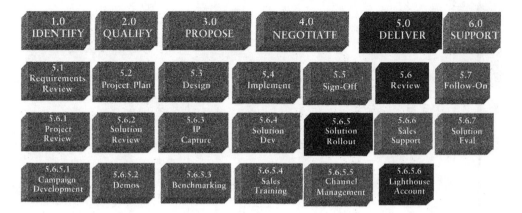

Figure 8–10 Lighthouse accounts.

Roles and Responsibilities

To be successful, the Services Marketing team must employ staff in three new positions not previously defined (see Table 8-1). The heart and soul of this team will be the Services Marketing manager. This is the person who is given direct responsibility for managing target solutions and making them successful in the marketplace. He or she is the "product manager of professional services." A marketing specialist, who supports the marketing manager, will provide general assistance in creating data sheets, presentations, etc. Finally, there will be the Services Marketing director. This individual must sit as an equal at the table with the other marketing directors of the company. He or she will provide much-needed leadership on how to position services to the existing product-oriented marketing team.

▶ Key Interfaces for the Services Marketing Function

The Services Marketing function, like the Services Engineering function, is a back line corporate organization; that is, it is not on the front

Table 8–1 Services Marketing Responsibilities.

Role	Purpose	Responsibilities			Requirements		
		General	Managerial	Financial	Experience	Education and Training	Technical
Services Marketing Director	Manage the Services Marketing function	• Assure the successful rollout of target solutions • Assure the availability of sales IP	Manage Services Marketing staff	• Manage Services Marketing expense budget • Help consulting business unit hit target bookings and margin targets	• 10+ years management experience • Prior experience managing budgets • Prior experience managing marketing staff	• 4-year degree • MBA preferred	
Marketing Manager	Manage the solution-rollout process	• Develop go-to-market plans for target solutions • Manage the development of marketing materials • Train sales staff	Manage marketing specialists and sub-contractors	Track bookings of target solutions	• 6+ years marketing experience • 2+ years experience developing sales channels	• 4-year degree • MBA preferred	Understand how customers use technology to solve their business problems

Table 8-1 Services Marketing Responsibilities.(cont.'d)

| Role | Purpose | Responsibilities | | | | Requirements | | |
		General	Managerial	Financial	Experience	Education and Training	Technical
Marketing Specialist	Coordinate the development of marketing materials	Manage day-to-day activities required to publish and distribute marketing materials				2-year degree	

line with the sales staff (see Figure 8-11). The primary objective on the back line is to be an enabler for the sales function, providing critical sales IP. This is accomplished by working closely with the Services Engineering function. A secondary objective is to maintain a bridge into the other marketing organizations that exist in the company. This bridge assures the services messages are aligned with the overall company messages. Finally, the Services Marketing team must work with external partners to review go-to-market strategies.

Inputs and outputs for these key interfaces are shown in Table 8-2.

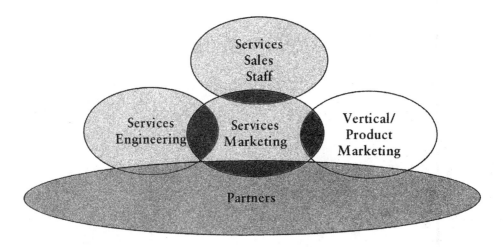

Figure 8–11   Key interfaces for the Services Marketing function.

Table 8–2   Services Marketing Inputs and Outputs.

Services Marketing	Partners	Product/ Vertical Marketing	Services Sales	Services Engineering
Outputs To	• Customer requirements (for partner's products) • Marketing and Sales literature on the service offerings of the company	• Services portfolio • Service datasheets • Customer presentations	• Services portfolio • Service datasheets • Customer presentations • References • Sales tips/scripts	• Solution Roadmap • Solution requirements

Table 8–2 Services Marketing Inputs and Outputs. (cont.'d)

Inputs From	• Customer Requirements • Marketing and sales literature	• Product Roadmaps • Product positioning literature • Target markets • Marketing Campaign strategies	• Customer requirements • Sales pipeline	• Solution maturity • Solution Capabilities
Comments	Services Marketing should map capabilities of internal PS staff with partner capabilities to satisfy complex customer needs.	Services Marketing and Product Marketing should align efforts to attack target markets and customers.	Services Marketing must create tools that enable the sales force to successfully position the services portfolio.	

Compensation for Services Marketing

The compensation strategy for the Services Marketing team is the same as the one for the Services Engineering team. While the Services Marketing team does have direct control over hitting delivery milestones for the development of the marketing materials defined earlier in this chapter, it does not have direct control over when deals are completed, when revenue is recognized, or how profitable specific projects might be. Yet, once again, the success of the overall services business depends on bookings and margins. The Services Marketing team also needs to be directly linked into this reality. By being compensated for bookings and target margins, this team is motivated to help the field staff succeed.

A sample compensation matrix for Services Marketing staff is shown in Table 8-3.

Key Metrics for Services Marketing

Every marketing organization is measured by its ability to drive revenue. But the true effectiveness of Services Marketing can be assessed through other metrics as well. Beyond solution revenues, Table 8-4 lists two of those additional metrics: solution margins and total marketing costs.

Table 8–3 Compensation for Services Marketing Staff.

POSITION	PLAN TYPE	MONEY		MARGIN			MIX	MILE-STONES	MINUTES	TOTAL VARIABLE COMPENSATION
		Bookings	Revenue	Gross Margin	Target Project Margin	Actual Project Margin	Revenue Mix	Project Completion Ratio	Billable Utilization Rate	
Director Services Marketing	80/20		10%					10%		20%
Marketing Manager	80/20	10%						10%		20%

Table 8–4 Services Marketing Metrics.

Metric	Description	Calculation	Sample Target	Person Responsible
Solution Revenues	Company revenues that can be attributed to implementing a specific solution for a customer			Services Marketing manager
Solution Margins		Revenue from solution engagement minus cost to deliver solution	+30%	Services Marketing manager
Total Marketing Costs	The investment made by professional services to provide Services Marketing where marketing costs equals advertising costs plus collateral material plus consultant and media relations plus alliance and partnering costs plus market research	Marketing costs divided by total service revenue	2% to total service revenues	Services Marketing director

▶ Organizational Structure and Sizing

The key parameters to consider when sizing the Services Marketing function are as follows:

1. How many unique regions does your organization have?

2. How many target solutions will you have in your solution portfolio?

Unique Regions

Different parts of the world may have different requirements for promotional materials. There must be individuals with local marketing expertise who can modify promotional materials to account for the local language, culture, and competitors.

In our organization, we have three geographical regions: the Americas, Europe and Africa, and Asia Pacific. Each of these regions has multiple languages, cultural differences, and competitors.

Number of Solutions

The more solutions you are taking to market, the more marketing cycles you need to complete the sales IP. Each target solution has its own set of required marketing materials and related staff training concerning those materials. Based on the complexity and customer volume for a target solution, it may be difficult for one marketing employee to effectively manage more than two or three solutions in the marketing portfolio.

For our case study, we will target the creation of three new target solutions during the first fiscal year.

▶ Sample Organizational Structure

Working with the parameters shown in Table 8-5, we are ready to seed the Services Marketing function.

Table 8–5 Services Marketing Planning Parameters.

Description	Parameter
Target revenue	$100M
Global regions	3
Number of target solutions	3

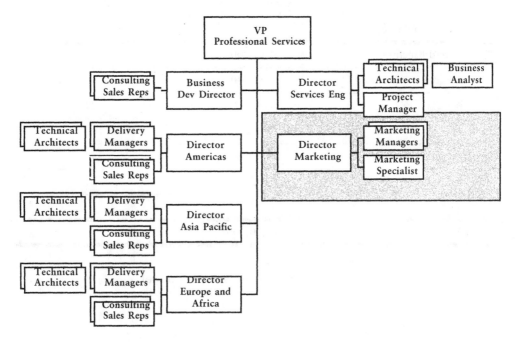

Figure 8–12 Services Marketing organizational structure.

Reporting to our VP of professional services will be a director of Services Marketing. This director will have five direct reports: four marketing managers and one marketing specialist. One marketing manager will be dedicated to target-solution marketing. The remaining three marketing managers will be allocated to the three global regions. Finally, the marketing specialist will provide assistance to all the marketing managers.

▶ Sample Budget

The budget for Services Marketing is human-resource intensive and outside-services intensive. The high-level Services Marketing team will be leveraging multiple outside contractors to execute go-to-market campaigns.

Services Marketing		
Number of Employees 6		
Salaries and Benefits	$950,000	48%
Commissions and Bonuses	$120,000	6%
Occupancy	$ 30,000	2%
Travel	$200,000	10%
Outside Services	$670,000	34%
Depreciation	$30,000	2%
TOTAL	$2,000,000	

Figure 8–13 Services Engineering sample budget.

▶ Issues to Watch

The Services Marketing function is born as a bastard child within a product-centric company. There is no sensitive way to state that sad fact. From inception, the Services Marketing function will be fighting an uphill battle to gain mindshare with product-focused sales and marketing staff. **Don't let your Services Marketing staff get discouraged.** If they do not have confidence or the ability to evangelize your services, no one will. Next, **verify your team is being treated with respect by the other marketing departments** in the company. If the Services Marketing team is not truly considered a peer organization by the Product Marketing team, it will struggle and wither on the vine. Finally, **hold your new team accountable to objective criteria.** Just like the Services Engineering team, the Services Marketing team has the potential to become disconnected from the real issues being faced by Services Sales and Delivery. Make sure the Services Marketing function is benefiting your organization by holding it accountable to hard measures of marketing-tool delivery and solution-portfolio management.

Operational Infrastructure

Enabling your business

▶ The Framework

Think of the operational infrastructure as the rigging and all the miscellaneous equipment you need to sail your vessel. Without it, you can't manage and maneuver the ship.

This operational infrastructure really has two parts, operational processes and operational reports. Operational processes include procedures and methods that are meant to help sell, deliver, productize, and promote your business. Operational reports provide you with information about your business and guide you in making decisions going forward. Together they form the infrastructure you need to run your organization. There are many different processes and reports used throughout the organization, and they are usually targeted at one of three areas: those areas that support the general business, those that support the projects, and those that support the staff of the organization. Figure 9-2 illustrates these three areas and their relative scope, starting in the center with processes and reports that are focused on the individual employee and moving outward to processes and reports that support the general business. In the pages to follow, we will review the processes and reports necessary to support these areas and identify

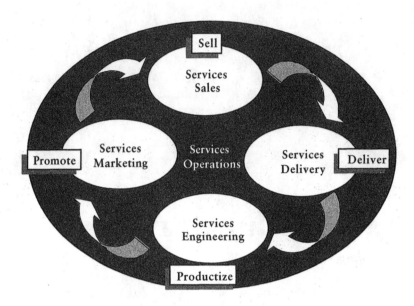

Figure 9–1 Services Operations.

Figure 9–2 Levels of operational infrastructure.

Chapter **9** | Operational Infrastructure

Figure 9–3　Levels of operating reports and processes.

some of the issues you should consider as you design your infrastructure. Figure 9-3 overlays the concept of processes and reports on the three focus areas.

▶ Critical Success Factors

When designing your infrastructure, keep in mind that you are designing an infrastructure that should be efficient and should add value to your organization. First, **make sure that the infrastructure the Services Operations team is creating is in line with the goals and objectives of the overall service organization.** If the Services Operations team focuses on infrastructure that is not aligned with the priorities of the business, you risk wasting valuable resources that could take away from the organization's overall profitability.

Second, **implement an infrastructure that delivers consistent, global, processes and reports.** If every geographical territory operates differently, then it will be difficult to centralize your processes and gain the economies of scale that you need to ensure profitability. Reporting will also break down because you will not be comparing like information throughout the organization; you, therefore, run the risk of making poor decisions. Imagine a rowing crew, where everyone had a different type of oar. The crew could still paddle ahead but not nearly as smoothly and effectively.

Third, **design an infrastructure that is consistent with the phase of business**. In Chapter 12, we will be reviewing in detail the four phases of building a PS organization, but for now you should consider whether you are in the implementation, integration, consulting, or productized services phase. The implementation phase will require an infrastructure more targeted at the general business processes and reports, while the integration phase will require a more project-focused infrastructure. The consulting phase will require a strong focus on the staff, and the productizing phase will require a fairly robust infrastructure that addresses all three of the previously mentioned areas: business, project, and staff. Fourth, add only infrastructure that adds value, not overhead. It's easy to fall into a trap of thinking you must have everything right away, but instituting complicated processes and reports may not really make sense for where you are in the life of the business, and they could take focus and energy away from where you need your teams. Remember, you want your salespeople spending their time with the customers, not filling out forms or trying to print reports. Likewise, you need your delivery force performing their duties, not spending a lot of time filling out time cards.

Next, **start by building infrastructure focused at the business level**. After this infrastructure is in place, you can then focus on project-level and staff-level infrastructure. This ensures that you have the basics in place to run and understand your business. Then, as your business moves through the four phases of PS, you can add more complex and focused processes and reports.

Be willing to invest in infrastructure. To really gain efficiencies and meet the demands of your growing business, you will need to spend some money. New tools are coming on the market every day that can significantly help PS organizations manage their businesses better but, like other new tools, they come with a price. As your business grows and becomes more complex, using a spreadsheet to manage the business will not be practical or efficient.

Finally, **include your operations person on the senior management staff.** It is important that operations be a part of the senior management decision-making process so that the infrastructure can keep up with the changes in the rest of the organization. Let us now review the specific processes and reports that will make up your operational infrastructure.

▶ Operational Process

We will start our review of key operational processes and reports at the business level. The following are processes focused on managing the overall PS business.

Legal Support

Protecting the interests of the company is the primary purpose of any legal staff, advice, or process. In professional services, there are often multiple contractual arrangements that are entered into between the company and its customers, suppliers, and outside contractors. Strong legal support is necessary to ensure that the company minimizes the risks associated with these contracts and that all terms and conditions are clearly understood by all parties. Legal support may be brought in before, during, or after contract negotiations depending on the complexity and timing of the engagement.

PS Automation

There are hundreds of different tools and applications available for running a business, but researching and implementing all these different applications takes time and resources that could be better spent on other aspects of the business. Also, many applications are more suited to product-oriented companies and do not address the needs of the PS organization. It is for these reasons that some companies today are marketing applications called professional services automation (PSA) tools. These applications take customer resource management (CRM), resource management, time reporting, project accounting, knowledge management warehouses, and financial reporting and combine them all into one integrated application. PS organizations are then able to purchase one application and transact their business through the entire PS lifecycle. Be aware though that PSA tools are expensive and require well-defined processes to be used effectively. A PS organization that is just starting out may not be able to afford such an integrated system, but as the business grows, it may make sense to invest in one.

▶ Operational Reports

These are the reports focused on managing the overall PS business.

Funnel Reports

Salespeople use a variety of sources to gather leads on potential customers. Some leads are sourced directly by the company's product salespeople, some are discovered through tradeshows and product launches, while others are people who approach the business directly. Regardless of how the leads are generated, the salesperson needs to keep track of the potential sales and the likelihood of turning them into revenue. This information is usually tracked in a database or spreadsheet and is called the funnel report. The funnel report details the customers who are being called upon, the potential revenue to be earned, the probability for winning the engagement, and the date the engagement could begin. Because you are a PS organization within a product company, it is also a good idea to track the amount of potential revenue that could be earned on product sales as well. Most fledgling PS organizations will begin by capturing this information manually on a spreadsheet. The problem with manual tracking is that it is prone to errors and cannot be linked easily to other applications within the company. Key metrics such as win/loss ratios must be manually calculated, and it can be difficult to record the reasons an engagement was not successful. Accordingly, as the organization grows, it may make sense to invest in or take advantage of the CRM system, if one exists, on the product side of the organization. CRM applications are available from a variety of vendors and range from very simple databases to highly complex systems. Most CRM products can be interfaced with other financial or Enterprise Resource Planning (ERP) systems, and all provide basic metrics such as win/loss ratios.

Bookings Reports

Bookings represent the new business that is brought into the organization and is recognized once a purchase order or contract has been established with the customer and a sales order entered into the order management system. Bookings are closely watched by management in order to assure a continual flow of new engagements into the business. Low bookings indicate that future revenue targets are at risk because no new business is in the pipeline to be delivered. On the other hand, very high bookings signal the need for delivery resources to be added.

Billings Reports

Billings represent the amounts that have been invoiced to the customer. Billings may or may not represent revenue depending on the revenue-recognition policies of the company. It is possible that the customer may be invoiced up front and the revenue recognized in a later period, usually upon completion and acceptance of the engagement. However, in most cases, the number and amounts of billings give management a strong indication of the company's ability to generate revenue. Companies with low billings may not be able to reach their revenue targets and may be overstaffed while companies with high billings will have more to invest in the business.

Backlog Reports

A backlog is an unfilled obligation to the customer. Those engagements that have been booked but not invoiced represent backlog. A declining backlog indicates that new business is not being brought in and the sales force needs to close more deals. An increasing backlog could indicate that the delivery force is understaffed and is having trouble completing engagements. For PS businesses just starting out, backlog will develop over time and then level out as new business is continually brought in while solutions are consistently being delivered.

Web Sites

In today's market, when the Internet is a part of everyone's daily life, it is important to have information readily available for your customers, suppliers, and outside consultants. Web sites can offer just such an opportunity. An effective Web site for a PS organization should provide an overview of the types of services offered, a listing of key contacts, and a few success stories from prior engagements. It is also helpful to make sure that your PS Web site is linked to the company's Product Sales Web site.

Electronic Newsletters

Electronic newsletters allow both internal and external audiences to stay up to date on the latest developments in professional services. They can be particularly helpful for organizations with global reach where different types of engagements are occurring and information flows are fragmented. Electronic newsletters are usually less expensive to produce and disseminate than traditional newsletters, and they can be more easily timed to specific events or situations.

Internal Distribution Lists

It is important that members of a PS organization keep up to date with what is happening throughout the organization. Encouraging individuals to share success stories and trade ideas and new knowledge can have extensive payoffs down the road. Many PS organizations use internal email distribution lists to ensure that everyone in the organization is kept properly informed.

Financial Reporting

Every business needs financial reports to summarize the fiscal health and performance of the organization; PS organizations are no different. Two of the most common financial reports are the balance sheet and income statement. Although, these reports are usually prepared by the finance team and are intended for the most senior management of the company, they are also used heavily by the PS management team. These reports tell a lot about how the business is doing and show comparisons of performance from period to period. In addition to the balance sheet and income statement, additional financial reports such as quarterly review packages provide more specific detail on the results obtained by the PS organization.

Executive Dashboard

An executive dashboard is an electronic management tool that provides summarized information to the senior management of the organization. Executive dashboards often include summaries of bookings and billings by geographical territory, key metrics such as utilization rates and revenue per salesperson, and the largest engagements currently being delivered. While this information is presented as a summary, it can be elaborated upon to provide more detailed information as necessary. Dashboards may be computer spreadsheets linked together, Web sites with regularly updated content, or separate reporting applications. Regardless of the type of dashboard implemented, the information must be timely, accurate, and meaningful to senior management.

Metrics Reporting

The reports that are most critical to the success of a PS organization are those that summarize the metrics of the organization. Metrics are the measurements of the health of the business. They help all levels of the organization better understand how the business is functioning and allow senior management to hold others accountable to specified aspects of the business. They can be compared against prior period metrics, industry benchmarks, or internally established goals. Their primary purpose is to provide a quantitative measurement of the quality of the business and to determine if the business is improving and becoming more efficient. PS metrics will generally fall into one of the following four groups.

Financial Metrics. Financial metrics provide information about the fiscal condition of the business. They summarize the results of the business and are usually provided for the current period and a prior period. In addition to being used by the internal PS staff, they are often provided to other teams within the company such as the finance and marketing teams. Some of the more common financial metrics are:

- Bookings, revenue, and gross margin by geography
- Bookings and revenue per employee
- Average gross margin percentages on consulting revenue and on third-party revenue
- Average engagement value
- Total product pull-through from PS engagements
- Operating cost ratios

Operational Metrics. Operational metrics provide information about how efficiently and effectively the business is being run. Operational targets are assigned by senior management in an effort to meet certain objectives, then compared to industry benchmarks to show the business is performing at a level consistent with other similar businesses. They are more often used internally within PS and to show trends and analyze improvement. Some of the more common operational metrics are:

- Billable utilization percentages: the number of staff hours that can be billed to the customer for services rendered divided by total staff time
- Target billable hours: the desired number of staff hours billed to the customer
- Head count metrics: key measurements about the company's employees and productivity
- Win ratio: the number of successful bids divided by total bids submitted to customers
- Walk ratio: the number of times customers choose to use another consulting company divided by total number of bids
- Turnover rate: the frequency with which staff leave the company

Customer Satisfaction Metrics. Customer satisfaction is one of the more difficult elements to measure because it's an attempt to quantify the customer's opinion or discretion and cannot be generated internally. Some companies develop their own survey that is provided to customers at the end of each engagement as part of the workflow. This survey process needs to be administered in a timely and consistent manner in order to provide meaningful data. The advantage to developing your own survey is that it can be tailored to your PS business. The disadvantage is that survey development can be expensive and time-consuming and can take the focus away from delivering solutions to your customers. Some PS organizations choose, instead, to participate in the annual company survey performed by the overall product organization. The advantage is that minimal resources are invested; the disadvantage is that the survey may include only a limited number of questions specific to PS and therefore may not provide significant feedback.

Employee Satisfaction Metrics. Unlike the product organization that turns inventory into goods to be sold to customers, the inventory for PS is in the heads of the sales and delivery people who design and implement solutions. If employees are unhappy and unfulfilled, they could leave the organization and take much of the business with them. Therefore, it is critical to understand how those people feel about the organization and its performance. Important information can be gathered from employees, but they have to be asked and sometimes even prodded to speak up. An internal survey is one way to gauge the health of the organization. Monthly or quarterly all-staff meetings for general business updates is another way of seeking input. Regardless of how you do it, it's important that management create an environment where people can be heard and management reacts appropriately to the concerns of staff.

▶ Project Processes

These are the processes that support specific projects.

Partner Management

The purpose of a partnership program is to create, enhance, and leverage a select group of global, strategic, and committed business relationships. These other consultants, system integrators, and developers should help expand your company's business opportunities and secure your company's leadership position in target industry segments and competency focus areas.

The philosophy of a partnership program is to seek out a few highly skilled companies that complement the existing capabilities of your PS organization. With larger firms, it is preferable to develop a tight relationship with a specific practice or portion of the partner firm; this sort of relationship is easier to attain and to manage than is a strategic alliance with the entire firm. Those partnerships that allow for reciprocal business offer the best chance for long-term success because both companies benefit from the relationship. It is also important that the number of partners not become so large that the partnership becomes difficult or costly to manage. The scope of each relationship should be kept fairly narrow to ensure that the partners complement instead of compete with each other. Any partnership that is not enhancing the company's industry stature, skill set, or capabilities should not be pursued.

As we discussed in Chapter 1, a major portion of the revenue mix may be composed of third-party products and services. Partners can be instrumental in meeting the objectives of increasing revenue and developing repeatable solution templates that add significantly to the solution portfolios of your PS organization.

The plan for a partner program describes the general approach your company will pursue in establishing partnerships. This plan is based on the preceding philosophy and objectives.

Here are some general guidelines and approaches to partnering:

1. Find, qualify, contract, and manage a select group of partners to further expand your company's current services. The current offerings fundamentally assume that the customer wants to own and operate a company-based solution but needs the PS organization to help to assess, design, develop, implement, place into production, train, and provide future consulting on a turnkey company-based solution.

2. Treat the partner as a consulting customer.

3. Jointly develop and deliver new high-value services that generate incremental revenue in new high-growth markets and in target-application areas where your company has had difficulty winning business with its traditional capital-intensive product-oriented model. This incremental business may consist of customers who like the solution your company offers, but do not want to purchase and own the products required to have the solution. Instead, these customers would like to rent the solution as an ongoing service.

4. Jointly develop and possibly co-brand new high-value services that enable customers to focus on their core businesses, instead of on technology.

5. Through committed, reciprocal business, leverage your scarce human resources, co-marketing funds, equipment pool, training capabilities, and management time.

6. Add individuals with skills not currently available in your company's workforce, including:
   a. Process redesign consultants
   b. Application developers
   c. Product-specific experts
   d. Industry experts
   e. Other service providers that rely on third parties to develop and deliver services

Resource Management

In order to successfully deliver solutions to your customers, it's important to have the appropriate delivery personnel on every engagement. Knowing who is available and what skills they offer is invaluable information to both the resource and project managers. Résumés are often collected from each delivery person and summarized into some kind of document or database. Again, fledgling PS organizations may track skills and availability on a spreadsheet, while mature organizations may choose to invest in computerized resource management tools. Such tools specifically designed to help industries like professional services manage their workforces better have recently come on the market. A resource management database usually collects the skills of each delivery person, the engagements on which the delivery person has worked, the times the person is currently booked or available. It then cross-references the needs of current/future engagements with available skill sets. A good resource management system can help avoid double-booking delivery staff and can help maximize your chances of winning bids by determining that the appropriate delivery personnel will be available for the engagement.

Solutions Assurance Review

As your PS business grows, more and more engagements will be undertaken. But should you be taking on all the business that comes your way? Are these engagements technologically and financially feasible for you to tackle? Is the customer seeing your best proposal? These are a few of the questions that the solutions assurance review function answers. PS organizations can benefit from a solution assurance review because it acts like a quality control function. The solution assurance review function usually resides in the operations group and should have no loyalties to either the sales or delivery function. Once the salesperson has prepared the customer proposal, it should be passed to the solution assurance review manager for review. The solution assurance review manager reviews the proposal to ensure that it meets the organization's financial goals and can be delivered to the customer. At the end of the engagement the solution assurance review manager should also initiate the project review process outlined in Chapter 8. This review brings together all the various participants in the engagement in order to capture lessons learned and to ensure that knowledge gained during the engagement isn't lost.

Project Accounting

Remember in Chapter 3, when we discussed the fact that not all engagements return a profit and that it is acceptable to turn down business that does not meet your organization's profitability goals? So, how do you know when an engagement is profitable? How do you ensure that you don't repeat engagements that lose money? A system of project accounting will help answer these questions. A project accounting system is typically a database that has hooks into other applications to capture the revenue and costs unique to a specific project or customer engagement. It pulls revenue transactions from the accounts receivable and order management systems, and it collects costing transactions from the accounts payable, purchasing, payroll, time reporting, financial reporting, and inventory systems. Once captured the individual profitability of each engagement can be reviewed and understood by all the functions of the business. Certain project accounting systems are certified by the U.S. government, and their use allows PS businesses to participate in the bidding for certain types of government contracts. Project accounting systems are usually complex in nature and require well-thought-out business processes and procedures to correctly gather the project data. However, once gathered and analyzed this information becomes invaluable to both the general staff and management staff.

▶ Project Reports

These are the reports that support specific projects.

Knowledge Management

In today's highly competitive environment, it is not enough for a PS organization to merely offer its customers quality services. PS organizations must continually be developing and offering new ideas and solutions. These ideas and solutions often come from the collective knowledge of the organization's employees. The benefits of managing this knowledge are many and varied. First, in today's marketplace, many companies have been forced to downsize and have lost much of their workforce. With that loss comes the loss of valuable knowledge, which is often costly if not impossible to replicate. Second, there are many more tools available today, such as intranets, video conferencing, and databases, that make knowledge capture much more viable. Third, the current marketplace demands shorter time-to-market solutions, and companies must be ready with a variety of solutions for their customers. Managing your organization's knowledge not only leverages existing solutions but also expands idea boundaries and allows for accelerated innovation.

As discussed in Chapter 7, one of the charters of the Services Engineering function is to capture valuable intellectual property. This process of capturing, organizing, displaying, and accessing the knowledge of the organization is called knowledge management (KM). Knowledge is created in many ways. It can be stored in databases, printed on paper, or stored in someone's head. Knowledge is captured by identifying and recording information that has specific value to the organization. A process should be implemented that requires each step of the engagement to be documented. The information is best organized in a KM warehouse, which is usually a large database set up to store documents that are critical to understanding solutions delivered to customers. Usually, one or two people who are familiar with the engagement flow will set up the file structure. Inputting and retrieving information from the warehouse should be simple and should include some kind of search capabilities that allow easy access to documents associated with engagements. Use of this warehouse is usually restricted to PS personnel because it may contain sensitive customer information, but only minimally restricted within PS personnel to ensure knowledge sharing across geographical territories.

Implementing a KM process may be met initially with a fair amount of resistance from staff members. The KM process can be perceived to be a time-consuming process that takes away valuable time and resources from the customer. However, once a reasonable process is in place, it will become a routine part of the engagement and the benefits will outweigh the costs. It is also possible that some employees will resist KM because it appears to diminish their individual value to the organization. Therefore, it is important to emphasize the importance of knowledge sharing (as another form of knowledge acquisition) and appropriately reward and/or acknowledge those who share information.

▶ Staff Processes

These are the processes that support the staff.

Commission Payments

Once a salesperson has successfully signed the customer, it won't be long until he or she expects to see a commission check. Commissions are one (if not the most important) driving force for a salesperson. You do not want to discourage a salesperson from closing future sales by not paying for the deals he or she has closed. If your sales force is small, you can begin by calculating and tracking commission payments on a spreadsheet, usually by a financial person or business analyst. As the business grows, and hopefully the need for salespeople increases, you may want to invest in or use the established commission system of the larger Product Sales organization. These systems are typically linked to the company's payroll system and work best if all salespeople are on similar compensation plans.

Proposal Generation

To be competitive in today's constantly changing environment, it is important for the PS salesperson to outline the potential solution and benefits for the customer as soon as possible. Generating proposals can be laborious, but companies that are slow to get proposals to their customers will lose to competitors who get there first. Some larger Product Sales organizations have proposal generation groups who generate proposals and put them in front of customers quickly. PS organizations that are part of product companies would be wise to take advantage of this type of support structure. Whether or not there is a proposal generation group, proposal templates (as discussed in Chapter 7) should be developed that already have standard solution information incorporated within.

Professional Development

In a PS organization, the consultants, solution architects, and technical staff are the boards that keep our ship together. Accordingly, it is important that they be given opportunities to strengthen their skills and develop beyond their initial capabilities. PS organizations that offer their employees various types of professional development programs differentiate themselves from their competitors and stand a better chance of maintaining their talented staff and keeping their boat together.

Project Management Certification

One way to help develop PS employees is to sponsor them in obtaining certifications. The Project Management Institute (PMI) sponsors a project management certification program that is globally recognized and accepted. The purpose and goal of this program is to develop, maintain, evaluate, promote, and administer a rigorous examination-based, professional certification program of the highest caliber. In 1999, PMI's certification program department became the first in the world to attain International Organization for Standardization (ISO) 9001 recognition. ISO is **a network of national standards institutes from 140 countries working in partnership with international organizations, governments, industry, business, and consumer representatives.** To achieve this certification, each candidate must satisfy all educational and experiential requirements established by PMI and must demonstrate, through rigorous examination, an acceptable and valid level of understanding and knowledge of project management. In addition, those who have earned this certification must demonstrate ongoing professional commitment to the field of project management by satisfying continuing education requirements. Employees with such a certification are often highly valued by customers and command higher billing rates.

General Training

In addition to formal project management certification, PS employees can increase their general knowledge and skills by attending general training classes. Such classes include but are not limited to courses on leadership, business case development, negotiation, and risk management. By allowing employees access to such courses, PS organizations will see the quality of their workforce climb and will stand a better chance of retaining employees.

PS Specific Training

Your organization, like every other PS organization, will have specific ways of conducting business and differentiating yourself from your competitors. Therefore, you may want to offer specific training classes and opportunities to your staff on your business strategies. By bringing all employees together for an intensive series of classes and workshops, you can focus on building communication, consulting, negotiating, and presentation skills. Actual business-case scenarios can be used to demonstrate appropriate ways to run a PS engagement. This is also an excellent opportunity for some team building and for employees to share their experiences and ideas.

▶ Staff Reports

These are the reports that support the staff.

Time Reporting

As we discussed in Chapter 6, it is critical to the success of your business to keep your delivery force utilized 65 percent to 85 percent of the time. In order to ensure this utilization rate, you need to have a mechanism for time tracking and approval. Although it is possible to track time manually (i.e., on a spreadsheet), it is not advisable. There are too many opportunities for errors and you may find your delivery staff spending more time on record-keeping than on customer engagements. This could sink your ship. Therefore, most PS organizations invest in some kind of time reporting system. Again, there are several on the market that range from basic recording systems to complex management systems. Whatever you decide is appropriate to your business, make sure that it is easily accessible to your entire delivery force, simple to use, and capable of providing basic time reporting information. While time reporting is a tool critical to the delivery force, it can also be used to track the time of sales, marketing, engineering, and support personnel. Many PS organizations mandate that all PS personnel record their time regardless of whether they are involved in billable engagements. This provides management with a better understanding of how people are allocating their time and helps capture costs beyond those of delivery personnel.

▶ Roles and Responsibilities

The Services Operations function is staffed by an operations director and a business analyst. See Table 9-1 for more on their roles and responsibilities.

▶ Key Interfaces for Operations

Again, the Services Operations function is not a frontline but a support function in the corporate organization (see Figure 9-4). It ensures that the infrastructure necessary to run the business exists and is functioning appropriately. The operations staff will ensure that the appropriate systems and processes are in place to better allow each group to understand and manage their businesses more effectively. All groups will be doing some amount of reporting and will look to the operations group to gather and help present their results to management.

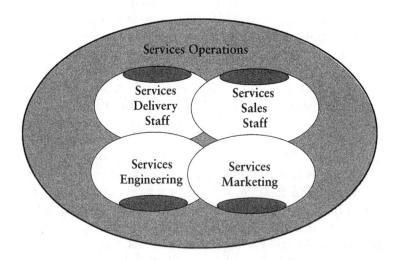

Figure 9–4   Key interfaces for the Services Operations function.

Table 9–1 Roles and Responsibilities of Services Operations Staff.

Role	Purpose	Responsibilities			Requirements		
		General	Managerial	Financial	Experience	Education and Training	Technical
Operations Director	Assist in closing business Establish policy and procedures that benefit the organization Manage system requirements	Assure the successful implementation of new processes and reports Monitor engagements to ensure high quality results	Manage operations staff	Manage operations expense budget Help business units achieve margin and profitability targets Assure that revenue and expenses flow through the sales and financial systems appropriately	10+ years management experience Prior experience managing budgets and staff 5+ years in consulting business	4-year degree, Master's preferred	Strong knowledge of tools and business processes

Table 9–1   Roles and Responsibilities of Services Operations Staff. (cont.'d)

| Role | Purpose | Responsibilities | | | Requirements | | |
		General	Managerial	Financial	Experience	Education and Training	Technical
Business Analyst	Assist in closing business	Collect information		Summarize key financial data for management	5+ years general business experience	4-year degree	Knowledge of tools and business processes
	Resolve system flow issues	Analyze and summarize results			2+ years in consulting business		
	Implement new business processes	Prepare and distribute reports					

Key inputs and outputs between these entities are shown in Table 9-2.

Table 9–2 Inputs and Outputs for Services Operations.

Services Operations	Services Sales	Services Delivery	Services Engineering	Senior Management	Services Marketing
Outputs To	Funnel and backlog reports	Utilization reports	Knowledge warehouse and IP capture processes	Financial reports Metrics reports	Customer reports
Inputs From	Probability ratio Hardware pull Revenue by quarter	Project completion data Time tracking Project data	Intellectual property	Strategic objectives	Pricing Competitive analysis
Comments					

▶ Compensation for Operations

The operations team is not directly responsible for generating or bringing in new revenue. However, by providing the infrastructure necessary to run the business, it plays an important role in assuring the organization meets its commitments to customers and the company. Therefore, the operations team needs to feel they are an integral part of the PS team and should be compensated to help ensure the organization's success. This variable compensation could be either in the form of a bonus when specific programs or tools are delivered or through participation in a compensation program similar to that in other parts of the organization. A sample compensation matrix for operations staff is shown in Table 9-3.

Table 9–3 Compensation for Services Operations Staff.

POSITION	PLAN TYPE	MONEY			MARGIN		MIX	MILE-STONES	MIN-UTES	TOTAL VARIABLE COMPEN-SATION
		Bookings	Revenue	Gross Margin	Target Project Margin	Actual Project Margin	Revenue Mix	Project Comple-tion Ratio	Billable Utiliza-tion Rate	
Director Operations	80/20							20%		30%
Business Analyst	80/20							20%		30%

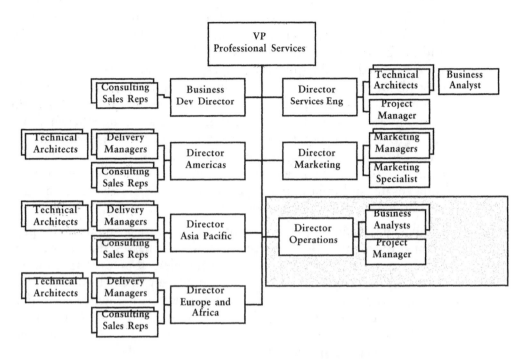

Figure 9–5 Organizational structure for Services Operations.

▶ Organizational Structure and Sizing

As was mentioned earlier in the chapter, it's important that the director of operations report directly to the VP of professional services to ensure that all the needs of the organization are met. As shown in Figure 9-5, reporting to the director should be at least one business analyst who processes and analyzes the key metrics outlined earlier in this chapter. Also reporting to the director should be a project manager who is responsible for ensuring that the systems and tools needed to run the business are in place and properly maintained.

To summarize, the operational infrastructure provides you the ability to manage and maneuver your business. The infrastructure is comprised of processes and reports that are developed and implemented to support three separate areas: the general business, the projects, and the staff. Processes and reports for the general business should be developed first, followed by processes and reports for the projects, and then those for the staff. This will ensure that the infrastructure is established and can grow with the business. Many different processes and reports were outlined in the previous pages, and choosing the best ones depends on the maturity of your business and the amount you can invest in your infrastructure. Any infrastructure that is created should be monitored constantly to ensure that it is functioning efficiently and adding value to the organization. It is very important that some investment be set aside for operations infrastructure or your vessel will not be able to stay afloat. Likewise, your business must be willing to hire, compensate, and treat operations personnel as if they were an integral part of your overall organization.

Establishing the appropriate level of infrastructure is an important part of any PS organization's success. Those businesses that invest too heavily in their infrastructure waste valuable resources that could be better utilized building the business. Conversely, those businesses that do not invest enough in their infrastructure risk inefficiencies that could severely hamper the ability of the business to grow. Once established, the appropriate level of infrastructure will make sailing your vessel much easier and your voyage more successful.

10

Putting It All Together

We B Solutions

In the last five chapters, we presented the core components of the PS organization. We reviewed the functions of Services Sales, Services Delivery, Services Engineering, Services Marketing, and Services Operations. Now it's time to put these pieces together, to see what this sample $100 million service organization looks like. It's time to christen this vessel.

▶ Organizational Parameters

To review, there are several key parameters (assumptions) that are in play for the creation of this PS business unit. All the critical parameters are shown in Table 10-1.

Table 10–1   Critical Parameters.

Description	Parameter	Reference Chapter
Target revenue	$100M	5: Selling
Revenue mix	60/40	6: Delivery

Table 10–1 Critical Parameters. (cont.'d)

Description	Parameter	Reference Chapter
Revenue from solutions	$ 40M	7: Productizing
Global regions	3	5: Selling
Focus	Geography	5: Selling
Quota per rep	$ 4M	6: Selling
Target billable utilization	65%	6: Delivery
Target billable rate	$220 hr	6: Delivery
Number of target solutions	3	7: Productizing

Changing any of these variables will alter the organization, sometimes slightly, sometimes significantly. To understand the impact of each variable individually, please return to the chapter in which the variable was introduced.

▶ Organizational Interfaces

There are a variety of organizational interfaces including those within the PS part of the organization, those between professional services and the larger organization, and those with the outside world.

Interfaces within Professional Services

First, let's look at the core of the service organization. Figure 10-1 identifies where the five service departments interact with each other. While all of these have been reviewed in previous chapters, let's highlight a few of the key internal interfaces here. The Services Sales staff must be educated by Services Marketing staff on what service offerings to sell. Then Services Sales staff must work tightly with Services Delivery staff to bid and win the business.

Services Delivery staff count on receiving technical training and insights from Services Engineering staff surrounding the target solutions the company is driving.

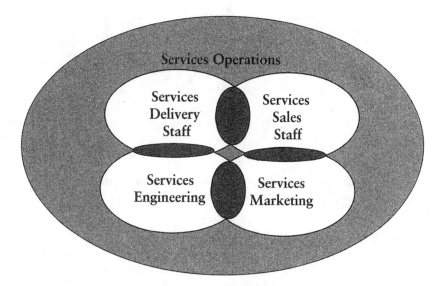

Figure 10–1 Interfaces within professional services.

Finally, Services Engineering staff and Services Marketing staff must work tightly to manage the overall solution portfolio.

Interfaces with the Larger Company

The next layer of data is to look at how the service organization touches the rest of the product organization (see Figure 10-2). Once again, all of these interfaces have previously been reviewed. Notice that the overlay Services Sales staff must interact with the Product Sales staff. The Services Delivery team must have a good working relationship with the pre-sales field engineers. The Services Engineering team should work hand-in-hand with the Product Engineering team as the technical specifications for new customer solutions are debated. And, the Services Marketing team must coordinate marketing efforts with the other marketing departments in the company.

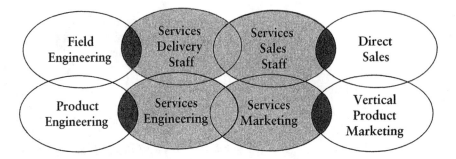

Figure 10–2 Interfaces within the larger company.

External Interfaces

Now, we can see where the PS staff interface with the outside world (Figure 10-3). Specifically, we see that Services Delivery staff and Services Sales staff provide the primary interfaces from professional services to the end customers. Meanwhile, the Services Engineering staff spend a great deal of time with partners who provide products and services that round out solution offerings. The Services Marketing staff works with channel partners to market and sell services.

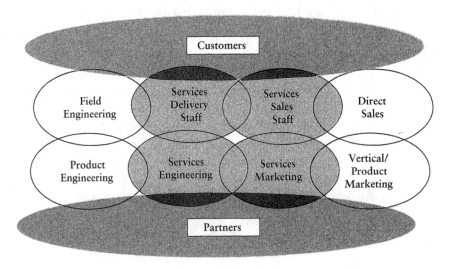

Figure 10–3 Interfaces to the outside world.

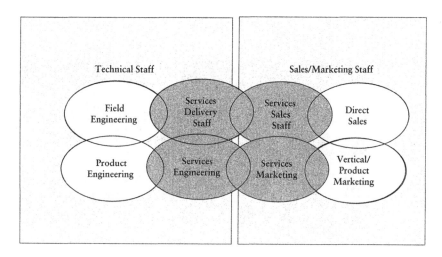

Figure 10–4 Interfaces by function.

Interfaces by Function

Since we have all of these nice bubbles drawn, we can use them to demonstrate some of the other ways you can view organizational interfaces.

▶ Technical Staff versus Sales and Marketing Staff

With the interface diagram shown in Figure 10-4, we can easily separate our technical staff from our sales and marketing staff. On the left-hand side of the diagram, the technical staff are focused on developing and delivering solutions. In other words, they focus on the supply side of the supply-and-demand equation. The functions on the right-hand side focus on the demand side of the equation by promoting and selling services.

▶ Field Staff versus Corporate Staff

Next, we can use the interface diagrams to demonstrate where the classic division between corporate (i.e., staff) and field (i.e., line) responsi-

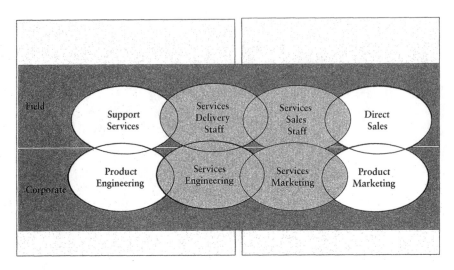

Figure 10–5 Corporate (Staff) vs. Field (Line).

bilities occurs (see Figure 10-5). Incidentally, the greater the tension and gap between the field box and the corporate box, the more ineffective the overall company is. Of course, you already knew that.

Finally, we can overlay the customer and partner interfaces across all the company departments (see Figure 10-6).

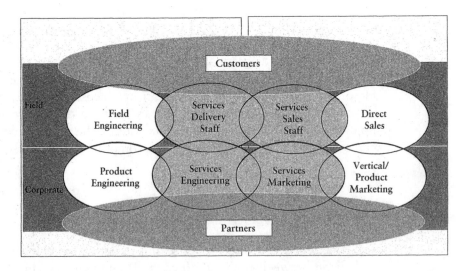

Figure 10–6 Interfaces to the outside world.

OK, I think we've viewed this topic from every angle possible. The key inputs and outputs of all these interfaces are documented in the previous chapters. Chapter 5 reviews the Services Sales function interfaces. Chapter 6 reviews the Services Delivery function interfaces. Chapter 7 reviews the Services Engineering function interfaces. And, Chapter 8 reviews the Services Marketing interfaces.

▶ Organizational Structure

In the previous chapters, we built each individual function from the ground up and populated the functions to support a PS organization with a $100 million revenue target. Putting all of the functions together, this new $100 million organization has a staff of 282 highly skilled professionals. The head count by function is shown in Table 10-2. As you can see, the Services Delivery function has the majority of the staff. This is good because everything outside the Services Delivery function is typically nonbillable labor that represents overhead. The next largest part of the organization is the Services Sales function. This also makes sense since these are your rainmakers—the individuals who drive the demand for your services. The remaining parts of the organization are thinly staffed with high-end talent. They must use the services of outside vendors to meet their departmental charters.

Table 10–2   Organizational Head Count.

Function	Head Count	Total
VP	1	
Admin	1	
Sales		
Management	4	
Staff	25	
TOTAL		29

Table 10–2 Organizational Head Count. (cont.'d)

Function	Head Count	Total
Delivery		
Management	12	
Staff	222	
TOTAL		234
Solutions Engineering		
Management	1	
Staff	5	
TOTAL		6
Solutions Marketing		
Management	1	
Staff	5	6
Operations		
Management	1	
Staff	4	5
TOTAL		282

Putting these 282 employees together, you might arrive at an organizational chart for professional services that looks like the one in Figure 10-7.

As you can see, there is a clear line between field-based activities (sales and delivery) and corporate-based activities (productizing and promoting). In general, the only time an activity or department should be centralized at the corporate office is when centralizing the activity creates

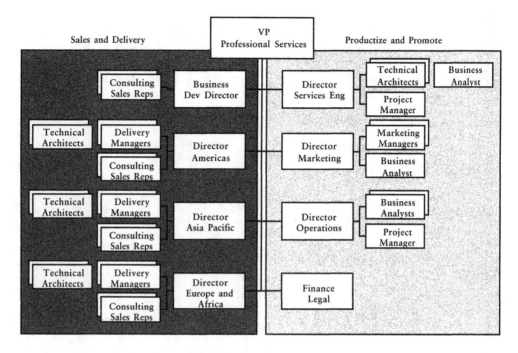

Figure 10–7 Organizational structure for professional services.

an economy of scale that benefits the overall PS organization. Solution development is a great example of an activity that can be performed more efficiently when centralized.

▶ Roles and Responsibilities

The key roles required to run the service organization are outlined in Table 10-3. The responsibilities of each role and the background required to perform each role is also provided.

▶ Processes and Metrics

Now, let's review the charters, processes, and metrics that apply to each of the PS functions (see Table 10-4).

Table 10–3 Professional Services Roles and Responsibilities.

| Role | Purpose | Responsibilities | | | Requirements | | |
		General	Managerial	Financial	Experience	Education and Training	Technical
Services Sales Rep	• Identify and qualify opportunities • Generate proposals • Close business • Forecast demand for his or her territory	• Manage accounts • Manage proposals • Provide weekly sales forecasts	Manage virtual teams assigned to proposals	• Meet bookings target • Meet expense objectives	• 4+ years general sales experience • 2+ years selling services	4-year degree	• Understand company's product line • Understand how customers are using technology in their business
Sales Director	• Assist in closing business • Forecast demand for his or her region • Upsell existing programs	• Provide weekly sales forecasts • Manage customer escalations • Prospect for new business	Manage sales reps	• Meet bookings and revenue targets for region • Meet expense objectives • Ensure collection of A/R	• 8+ years general sales experience • 4+ years selling services • 2+ years managerial experience	4-year degree	• Understand company's product line • Understand how customers are using technology in their business

Table 10–3 Professional Services Roles and Responsibilities. (cont.'d)

Role	Responsibilities				Experience	Degree	Knowledge
Business Development Manager	• Build relation-ships with prospects • Educate customers on company offerings	• Generate leads • Qualify prospects	• Educate sales force • Advise staff	Meet bookings and revenue targets for target-solution areas	• 4+ years general sales experience • 2+ years selling services	4-year degree	Understand customers use technology in their business
Delivery Manager	Manage delivery staff	• Schedule resources scheduling • Oversee staff develop-ment	• Manage delivery staff • Evaluate employees • Train employees	• Meet overall expense objectives • Meet project expense objectives	• 4+ years general manage-ment experience • 2+ years delivery manager	4-year degree	• Understand technical skills being requested by customers • Understand project life cycle
Project Manager	Manage customer projects	• Create project plans • Manage projects • Provide weekly project updates	• Manage virtual project teams • Manage subcon-tractors	Meet project expense objectives	• 8+ years general work experience • 2+ years project manage-ment experience	2-year degree	• Understand project life cycle • Understand how customers are using technology in their business

Table 10-3 Professional Services Roles and Responsibilities. (cont.'d)

Role	Purpose	Responsibilities			Requirements		
		General	Managerial	Financial	Experience	Education and Training	Technical
Senior Technical Consultant	• Create system architectures • Implement solutions	• Create system architectures • Provide effort estimations • Implement solutions • Assist in closing business	Manage and mentor technical consultants	Meet project expense objectives	• 10+ years general work experience • 4+ years technical consultant	4-year degree	Deep understanding of technologies being deployed
Technical Consultant	Implement solutions	• Provide effort estimations • Implement solutions	None		4+ years work experience	4-year degree	

Table 10–4 Charters, Processes, and Metrics for Professional
Services.

Function	Charter	Key Processes	Key Metrics
Services Sales	Identify Close Forecast	Engagement Life cycle • Identify • Qualify • Propose • Negotiate • Forecast	• Bookings • Target project margin • Hit ratio • Forecast accuracy
Services Delivery	Estimate Execute Educate	Project estimation Project-Delivery Life Cycle • Requirements Review • Project Planning • Design • Implementation • Sign-Off • Project Review • Project Follow-On Staff Training	• Revenue • Gross margin • Project completion ratio
Services Engineering	Capture Improve Leverage	Solution-Development Life Cycle • Project Review • Solution Review • IP Capture • Solution Development • Training • Sales Support	• IP Capture Rates • Project completion ratio
Services Marketing	Differentiate Validate Evangelize	Solution review Solution Rollout Process • Campaign Development • Demo Development • Benchmarking • Channel management • Sales Training • Lighthouse Accounts	• Bookings • Project completion ratio

▶ Compensation

In Chapter 3: Levers for Profitability, we reviewed the key levers that
encourage PS profitability. These levers include developing higher margin revenues, acquiring critical customer references, and identifying

solutions that can be repeated at better and better margins. To gauge progress in these areas, we identified the five Ms a PS organization must measure and manage: money (revenue), margin, mix, milestones (customer deliverables), and minutes (billable utilization). Each member of the PS organization should have his or her compensation linked directly to the success of the organization. This can be accomplished by linking, in some way, each employee's compensation to these five Ms. Table 10-5 provides an example of how different employees could be compensated with this strategy in mind.

▶ Business Model and Budget

When we first introduced our fictional services business unit in Chapter 3: Levers for Profitability, it had a pretty solid financial scorecard (shown here in Table 10-6). We B Solutions is working to achieve at least 30 percent gross margin. A revenue mix that consists of 60 percent direct revenues, 30 percent low-margin pass-through revenues, and 10 percent high-margin revenues from reusable IP produces this overall 30 percent gross margin target.

On this $100 million in revenue, We B Solutions is planning to bring home a 13 percent operating profit as shown in Table 10-7. In this table, COGS is equal to the cost to deliver the services, or the Services Delivery budget; the costs associated with sales are a direct reflection of the sales budget; the costs associated with R&D are from the engineering budget; and the costs associated with G&A, or general accounting, are from the VP and operations budget.

For this $100 million business, the vice president of professional services is managing an $87 million budget. The budget is allocated as shown in Figure 10-8.

Table 10–5 Compensation for Professional Services.

POSITION	PLAN TYPE	MONEY		MARGIN			MIX	MILE-STONES	MINUTES	TOTAL VARIABLE COMPEN-SATION
		Bookings	Revenue	Gross Margin	Target Project Margin	Actual Project Margin	Revenue Mix	Project Completion Ratio	Billable Utilization Rate	
Sales Director	70/30	10%			10%		10%			30%
Business Development Director	70/30	10%			10%		10%			30%
Sales Rep	60/40	20%			10%		10%			40%
Regional Director	70/30		20%	10%						30%
Delivery Manager	80/20					10%			10%	20%
Delivery Project Manager	80/20					5%		5%	10%	20%
Delivery Senior Technical Consultant	80/20								20%	20%
Delivery Technical Consultant	80/20								20	

Table 10–5 Compensation for Professional Services. (cont.'d)

POSITION	PLAN TYPE	MONEY	MARGIN	MIX	MILE-STONES	MINUTES	TOTAL VARIABLE COMPEN-SATION
Director Services Engineering	80/20	10%			10%		20%
Director Services Marketing	80/20	10%			10%		20%
Director Operations	80/20				20%		20%
Marketing Manager	80/20	10%			10%		20%

Chapter **10** | Putting It All Together

Table 10–6   We B Solutions Financial Scorecard.

Area to Measure and Manage	Specific Metric	We B Solutions
Financial	Annual Revenue (millions)	$100
	Direct Revenue	$ 60
	Pass-Through Revenue	$ 30
	Reusable IP Revenue	$ 10
	Average margin on Pass-Through Services	15%
	Average margin on Direct Services	35%
	Average margin on Reusable IP	50%
	Average Gross Margin Percentage	30.5

Table 10–7   We B Solutions Operating Profit.

Target Business Model		
Element Description	Target Percent	Target Dollars
Revenue	100%	$100,000,000
COGS	70%	<$ 70,000,000>
Gross Margin	30%	$ 30,000,000
Sales	5%	<$ 5,000,000>
R&D	2%	<$ 2,000,000>
Marketing	2%	<$ 2,000,000>
G&A	8%	<$ 8,000,000>
Operating Profit	13%	$13,000,000

Services Sales		
Number of Employees: 29		
Salaries and Benefits	$2,600,000	52%
Commissions and Bonuses	$1,000,000	20%
Occupancy	$ 145,000	3%
Travel	$1,055,000	21%
Outside Services	$ 55,000	1%
Depreciation	$ 145,000	3%
TOTAL	$5,000,000	

Services Delivery		
Number of Employees: 234		
Salaries and Benefits	$24,528,000	35%
Commissions and Bonuses	$ 6,132,000	9%
Occupancy	$ 1,170,000	2%
Travel	$ 2,910,000	4%
Outside Services	$ 90,000	1%
Depreciation	$ 1,170,000	2%
Third Party COGS	$34,000,000	49%
TOTAL	$70,000,000	

Figure 10–8 Budget for We B Solutions.

Services Engineering		
Number of Employees: 6		
Salaries and Benefits	$950,000	48%
Commissions and Bonuses	$120,000	6%
Occupancy	$ 30,000	2%
Travel	$200,000	10%
Outside Services	$300,000	15%
Depreciation	$400,000	20%
TOTAL	$2,000,000	

Services Marketing		
Number of Employees: 6		
Salaries and Benefits	$950,000	48%
Commissions and Bonuses	$120,000	6%
Occupancy	$ 30,000	2%
Travel	$200,000	10%
Outside Services	$670,000	34%
Depreciation	$ 30,000	2%
TOTAL	$2,000,000	

Figure 10–8 Budget for We B Solutions. (cont.'d)

VP & Operations		
Number of Employees: 8		
Salaries and Benefits	$1,600,000	20%
Commissions and Bonuses	$ 600,000	8%
Occupancy	$ 40,000	1%
Travel	$ 200,000	3%
Outside Services	$5,520,000	69%
Depreciation	$ 40,000	1%
TOTAL	$8,000,000	

Figure 10–8 Budget for We B Solutions. (cont.'d)

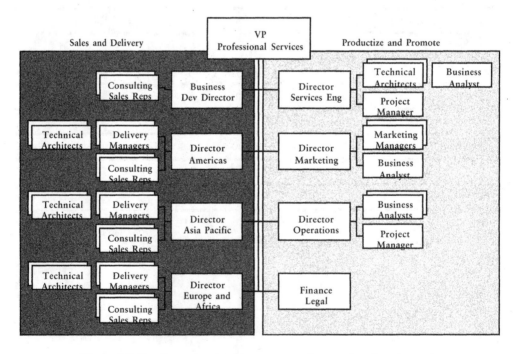

Figure 10–9 Organizational structure for professional services.

Summary

So, there you have it: a $100 million service business that produces $13 million in profits. It has 282 employees and an $87 million operating budget. Stop. Pause and reflect for a moment on what the real learning for you has been so far. The size and target business model for We B Solutions is really irrelevant. It's not important that you just reviewed a $100 million organization; we could have scoped a $50 or $250 million service organization. What's important is that in the previous 10 chapters, you've learned *how* to build and size a PS organization of almost any size. You should now comprehend the key variables needed to initially size the organization. In Chapter 12: Four Phases of Building PS, we will build on this knowledge and take the next step. In that chapter, we will look deeper into revenue mix and organizational maturity levels to guide you through the process of establishing and growing your PS business. But first, we want to take the current organization out for a test drive!

11

Customer Engagement Workflow

From request to review

Up to this point in the journey, the focus has been on the strategies and tactics required to build a PS organization. We have presented an almost overwhelming amount of information regarding the functional areas of the PS organization. If we were building a ship, our focus would have been on the detailed design specifications as we hammered the ship together in dry dock. We would have been concentrating on how large it must be, how much weight it must bear, and how best to craft its various components. Now, we finally have her together. Now, we want to take our newly christened vessel out to sea. We want to know how she actually handles.

We are now moving from the strategic and tactical levels to the operational level, as mentioned in Chapter 1. We have crafted this new business unit; now we want to review the day-to-day issues of bidding, winning, delivering successful customer engagements, and collecting revenue. We want to see our business in action! This chapter will revisit the engagement life cycle and the project-delivery life cycle to clearly demonstrate what occurs from the initial customer request through implementation, sign-off, and the final project review. The workflow being defined is not complex, but there is an order you must be able to envision if you want to be a competent service manager.

▶ Workflow Overview

To help you get a feel for how the PS team actually engages a customer, we will only focus on the first five phases of the engagement life cycle (identify, qualify, propose, negotiate, and deliver). We will also focus on the eight most important steps in these first five phases:

1. **Request:** A request is received from a customer to engage the PS team.
2. **Qualify:** The request is reviewed and qualified to determine if the PS team should bid the business.
3. **Bid:** The Services Sales team and the Services Delivery team actually create a proposal and submit it to the customer.
4. **Negotiate:** The sales team and the customer arm wrestle over the details in the proposal.
5. **Develop:** The delivery team works to develop the customer-specific solution named in the agreed-upon proposal.
6. **Implement:** The solution is actually installed at the customer site.
7. **Sign off:** The customer officially accepts the delivered solution.
8. **Review:** The delivery team performs a project review and captures important lessons and knowledge.

These eight steps are illustrated in Figure 11-1 as a workflow diagram. The following information is also included in the diagram:

- **Step:** This is the current step in the workflow. Each step is related back to the engagement life cycle that was outlined in Chapter 5: Selling.
- **Key Roles:** These are the staff members from your service organization that will be engaged in the process. On the chart, the role that has a checkerboard associated with it has primary ownership of that step. That is, he or she is responsible to complete the tasks required in this step. The role that has a picket fence associated with it holds the secondary responsibility for that task. That is, skills held by this individual may be required to complete the task, but the person holding those skills is not the point person.

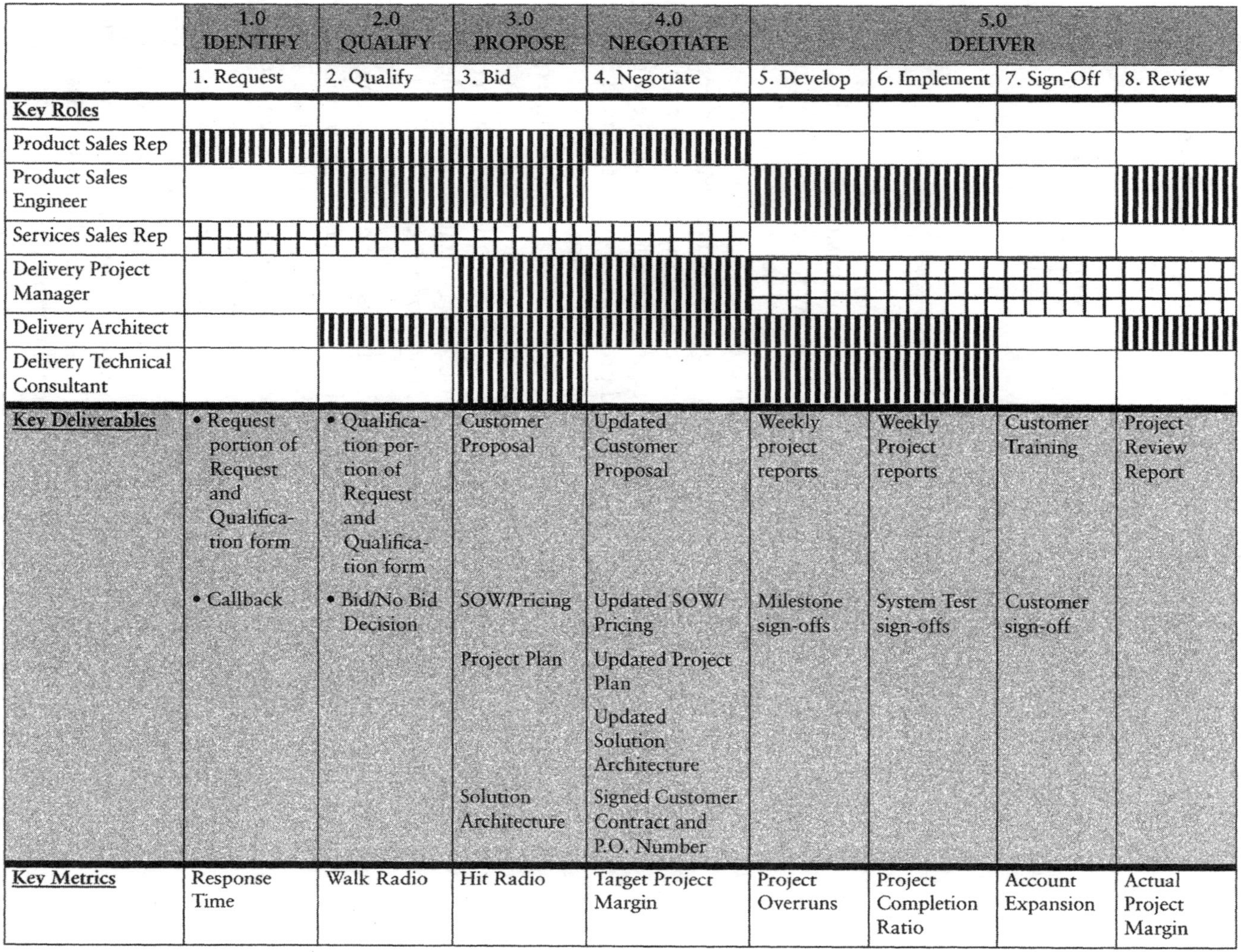

	1.0 IDENTIFY	2.0 QUALIFY	3.0 PROPOSE	4.0 NEGOTIATE	5.0 DELIVER			
	1. Request	2. Qualify	3. Bid	4. Negotiate	5. Develop	6. Implement	7. Sign-Off	8. Review
Key Roles								
Product Sales Rep								
Product Sales Engineer								
Services Sales Rep								
Delivery Project Manager								
Delivery Architect								
Delivery Technical Consultant								
Key Deliverables	• Request portion of Request and Qualification form • Callback	• Qualification portion of Request and Qualification form • Bid/No Bid Decision	Customer Proposal SOW/Pricing Project Plan Solution Architecture	Updated Customer Proposal Updated SOW/Pricing Updated Project Plan Updated Solution Architecture Signed Customer Contract and P.O. Number	Weekly project reports Milestone sign-offs	Weekly Project reports System Test sign-offs	Customer Training Customer sign-off	Project Review Report
Key Metrics	Response Time	Walk Radio	Hit Radio	Target Project Margin	Project Overruns	Project Completion Ratio	Account Expansion	Actual Project Margin

Figure 11–1 Customer engagement workflow.

- **Key Deliverables:** These are the actual deliverables generated during this step. Typically, these are tangible documents that can be analyzed at a later date if required.

- **Key Metrics:** These are the metrics that apply to this specific step.

So, here we go. Let's walk through the customer engagement from *request* to *review*.

▶ Step 1: Request

It all starts with a simple request. An existing customer that has purchased your company's product wants to know if your service organization can do this, that, or the other thing. The request might come through a variety of channels: the product account executive may be contacting you; your telesales team may have generated the lead; or perhaps a customer is following up from a recent trade show he or she attended. Regardless of how or why the initial request is made, the service organization needs to process it and respond promptly. One of the most common complaints surrounding a service organization that's part of a product company is its response time. Product Sales reps want, expect, and actually deserve a prompt response to requests for service. In fact, it doesn't even matter how poorly qualified or outlandish the request may be. What matters is that the service organization acknowledges the request and quickly begins the qualification process.

Now, let's review the actual workflow that is initiated by a new customer request as outlined in Figure 11-2. The primary responsibility to manage the request falls within the Services Sales organization. Typically, a request is assigned to the appropriate Services Sales representative based on territory or account ownership. In this step, the goal of the Services Sales rep is to document the request and quickly respond to the person that made the request. The key metric to watch here is response time. How long did it take for the requestor to receive a call back or an email acknowledging the request? Anything over two business days is too long. In Appendix F, there is a sample Request and Qualification form that outlines the key information the Services Sales rep needs to collect in this step.

	1.0 IDENTIFY
	1. Request
Key Roles	
Product Sales Rep	||||||||||||||||||||||||
Product Sales Engineer	
Services Sales Rep	┼┼┼┼┼┼┼
Delivery Project Manager	
Delivery Architect	
Delivery Technical Consultant	
Key Deliverables	• Request portion of Request and Qualification form • Callback
Key Metrics	Response Time

Figure 11–2   Customer request.

▶ Step 2: Qualify

Once the request has been submitted and documented, it needs to be qualified (see Figure 11-3). In the qualification process, the Services Sales representative works with the product account team to assess how real the opportunity is. Key qualification criteria include whether the customer has the budget to pay for the requested services and whether your service organization can even deliver what is being requested. In the sample Request and Qualification form in Appendix F, more detail is provided about areas that can be used to qualify an opportunity.

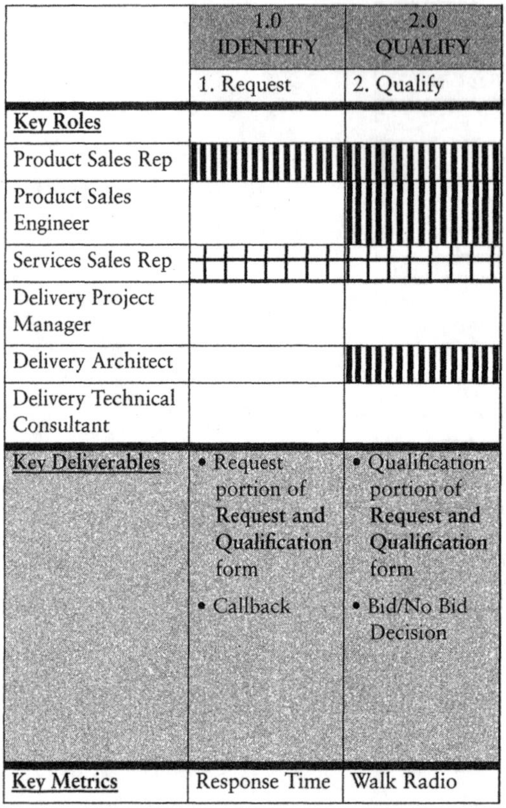

	1.0 IDENTIFY	2.0 QUALIFY
	1. Request	2. Qualify
Key Roles		
Product Sales Rep	▓▓▓▓▓▓	▓▓▓▓▓▓
Product Sales Engineer		▓▓▓▓▓▓
Services Sales Rep	▦▦▦	▦▦▦
Delivery Project Manager		
Delivery Architect		▓▓▓▓▓▓
Delivery Technical Consultant		
Key Deliverables	• Request portion of Request and Qualification form • Callback	• Qualification portion of Request and Qualification form • Bid/No Bid Decision
Key Metrics	Response Time	Walk Radio

Figure 11–3 Request qualification.

Once all of the qualification information has been collected by the Services Sales representative, a decision needs to be made. Will the services organization bid this opportunity or not? Who ultimately makes that call depends on several factors:

Qualification Rating For opportunities with high ratings, the Services Sales rep may be authorized to start the bid process. For opportunities with very low qualification ratings, the Services Sales rep may be authorized to walk away from the business without further discussion. For opportunities with ratings in the middle, discussion will most likely be required with services management staff and a local Product Sales team.

Deal Size For opportunities with a high dollar value, the regional services director may be required for approval to bid or walk.

Account Importance For opportunities with strategic value to the company, there may be different criteria applied when making bid/no bid decisions.

After reviewing all relevant factors, the final decision to bid or not to bid is made by the service organization and communicated to the local product account team.

▶ Step 3: Bid

Let's assume the services organization decides to bid on the opportunity (see Figure 11-4). At this point, the Services Sales representative is still in charge and responsible for managing the process. However, there are some other key service personnel that need to be engaged. A project manager must be assigned to assist in the creation of a proposal. The project manager is responsible for validating any project schedules that are being proposed. And a project manager must be involved now so the sales staff doesn't create a proposal that meets the customer's time frames but cannot realistically be executed. No project schedules should be submitted to the customer without being reviewed by the project manager.

A solution architect must also be engaged in this step. The solution architect is responsible for the technical feasibility of the proposal. Without the guidance of a solution architect, the sales staff could make unrealistic technical commitments to satisfy the customer. The solution architect researches, validates, and stands behind any technical commitments made.

Based on the complexity of the proposal, several other resources may be engaged. The local Product Sales engineer may need to provide information about a customer's technical environment. Also, other technical consultants with specialized expertise may need to assist with solution specifications.

Once the core proposal team is assembled, it will work to create a proposal that includes an architecture for the solution, a statement of work (SOW) to deliver the solution, and a project plan for the delivery schedule. This body of work is submitted to the customer for review.

	1.0 IDENTIFY	2.0 QUALIFY	3.0 PROPOSE
	1. Request	2. Qualify	3. Bid
Key Roles			
Product Sales Rep	▓▓▓	▓▓▓	▓▓▓
Product Sales Engineer		▓▓▓	▓▓▓
Services Sales Rep	░░░	░░░	░░░
Delivery Project Manager			▓▓▓
Delivery Architect		▓▓▓	▓▓▓
Delivery Technical Consultant			▓▓▓
Key Deliverables	• Request portion of Request and Qualification form • Callback	• Qualification portion of Request and Qualification form • Bid/No Bid Decision	Customer Proposal SOW/Pricing Project Plan Solution Architecture
Key Metrics	Response Time	Walk Radio	Hit Radio

Figure 11–4 Bid process.

In the proposal step, the key metric is the hit ratio, that is, how many proposals are accepted by customers and move forward to the step of final negotiations. Incidentally, a hit ratio of 50 percent is considered very respectable in the consulting world. A hit ratio lower than 50 percent may indicate the service organization is spending precious resources bidding business that is poorly qualified, the organization's services are not unique or well positioned, or the services are priced higher than competitors' services. An exceedingly high hit ratio could indicate pricing is too low compared to competitors'.

▶ Step 4: Negotiate

Once a proposal makes it past that initial acceptance, the real fun begins. The customer will want to discuss and negotiate almost all the key parameters of the proposal: pricing, timing, key deliverables, everything. In this step, the Services Sales representative and Product Sales representative need to work very closely (see Figure 11-5). Remember from Chapter 3: Levers for Profitability that the objective is to win the business without giving away the farm. If customer demands lead to an unacceptable target project margin or include unrealistic deliverables, it is always better to walk away than to sign; there can be such a thing as bad revenue. To keep the sales team in check, require any proposal changes to be reviewed and approved by the assigned project manager and solution architect. They should assure that any changes have not compromised the schedule or technical feasibility of the project. Also, the regional services director may need to review and approve any final discounts.

Assuming negotiations go well, a final version of the proposal will be generated in this step. This includes a version of the statement of work (SOW) that becomes the Bible for the delivery team implementing the solution. The most important outcome of this step is for the customer to sign a contract. This signed contract should generate a purchase order from the customer. The signed contract and valid purchase order number are critical documentation. Without these two items in place, it is unwise for the service organization to assign or deploy any resources for the project. Incidentally, premature deployment can be one of the most embarrassing and costly behaviors for a service organization.

Finally, the key measurement of your success during this step is target project margin. If the target project margin is at or higher than your standard objective, negotiations went well. If the target margin for the project is now lower than your standard, there should be some benefit to the service organization to compensate for the lost margin. One acceptable benefit might be that this specific customer is willing to serve as a key reference for other customers.

	1.0 IDENTIFY	2.0 QUALIFY	3.0 PROPOSE	4.0 NEGOTIATE
	1. Request	2. Qualify	3. Bid	4. Negotiate
Key Roles				
Product Sales Rep	▓	▓	▓	▓
Product Sales Engineer		▓	▓	
Services Sales Rep	▓	▓	▓	▓
Delivery Project Manager			▓	▓
Delivery Architect		▓	▓	▓
Delivery Technical Consultant			▓	
Key Deliverables	• Request portion of Request and Qualification form • Callback	• Qualification portion of Request and Qualification form • Bid/No Bid Decision	Customer Proposal SOW/Pricing Project Plan Solution Architecture	Updated Customer Proposal Updated SOW/Pricing Updated Project Plan Updated Solution Architecture Signed Customer Contract and P.O. Number
Key Metrics	Response Time	Walk Radio	Hit Radio	Target Project Margin

Figure 11–5 Negotiate.

▶ Step 5: Develop

Having identified and closed the business, the Services Sales rep now hands over the primary responsibility to the project manager. With signed contract in hand and final SOW in folder, the project manager can accept that responsibility and officially start the project of developing a solution (Figure 11-6).

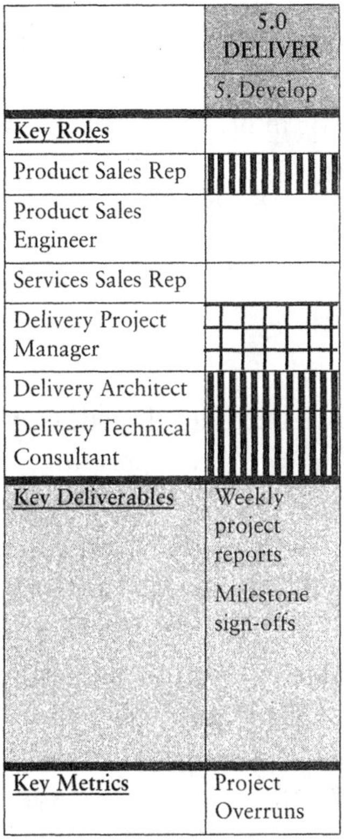

	5.0 DELIVER
	5. Develop
Key Roles	
Product Sales Rep	▓▓▓▓▓▓▓▓
Product Sales Engineer	
Services Sales Rep	
Delivery Project Manager	▦▦▦▦
Delivery Architect	▓▓▓▓▓▓
Delivery Technical Consultant	▓▓▓▓▓▓
Key Deliverables	Weekly project reports Milestone sign-offs
Key Metrics	Project Overruns

Figure 11–6 Developing a solution.

As the development process begins, additional technical resources are assigned and third-party partners are engaged. There will be few if any projects where a previous solution can be used as is. Therefore, for most projects, some level of planning and development will need to occur. Thanks to the wonder of technology, this development can often occur away from the customer site. During this development step, the project manager should provide regular project updates to the customer. Also, if any documented milestones are achieved (e.g., demonstrated new data entry screen to customer), the project manager should acquire official customer sign-off.

During development, a key metric to watch is project overruns. These could be overruns in staff hours or other expenses. If overruns are exceptionally high during development, the entire project should be immediately reviewed. Perhaps the customer has changed requirements. Perhaps there are technology issues we were not aware of. Whatever the cause, it needs to be identified and dealt with. Otherwise, the project team is digging a hole of unprofitability it most likely will not climb out of during the next step.

▶ Step 6: Implement

Once the pieces of the solution have been developed, they need to be assembled at the customer site and put into operation. Welcome to implementation (Figure 11-7). In this step, the project manager maintains primary responsibility for success. The project manager is aggressively coordinating the activities of service staff, partners, and the customer's staff to install and test the new solution. In reality, a project can bounce from development to implementation and back again. The delivery team starts implementing the solution, the customer finds a flaw, and more development must be done before implementation can continue. This is all standard system-development life-cycle stuff. Eventually, however, the delivery team and customer team will enter into the hard-core implementation step where all eyes are focused on cutover (i.e., when the new solution is actually being used by the customer).

During that final implementation phase, weekly project status reports are more important than ever. All individuals involved must clearly understand where the critical bottlenecks may exist. Also at this time, the project manager should be collecting customer sign-off for specific system elements that have been tested and have performed well. It is important these small milestones are not overlooked. If they go undocumented, the project manager may have a difficult time demonstrating progress to senior management.

In this home stretch, the measure of success is project completion. You'll be watching to be sure the project is on time and nearing completion.

	5.0 DELIVER	
	5. Develop	6. Implement
Key Roles		
Product Sales Rep		
Product Sales Engineer	▓▓▓▓▓	▓▓▓▓▓
Services Sales Rep		
Delivery Project Manager	▦▦▦	▦▦▦
Delivery Architect	▓▓▓▓▓	▓▓▓▓▓
Delivery Technical Consultant	▓▓▓▓▓	▓▓▓▓▓
Key Deliverables	Weekly project reports	Weekly Project reports
	Milestone sign-offs	System Test sign-offs
Key Metrics	Project Overruns	Project Completion Ratio

Figure 11–7   Implementation process.

▶ Step 7: Sign-Off

Ah, that most glorious of glorious steps: sign-off (Figure 11-8). This is the step where the customer acknowledges you did what you said you would do.

The project manager has primary responsibility to acquire the customer's sign-off on the project. Incidentally, this is a heavy and difficult responsibility. On one hand, the service organization is dependent on a quick sign-off to receive critical revenue. On the other hand, the customer wants time to validate the work. And in between these opposing objectives sits the poor project manager. If your service organization

	5.0 DELIVER		
	5. Develop	6. Implement	7. Sign-Off
Key Roles			
Product Sales Rep			
Product Sales Engineer	▊	▊	
Services Sales Rep			
Delivery Project Manager	▦	▦	▦
Delivery Architect	▊	▊	
Delivery Technical Consultant	▊	▊	
Key Deliverables	Weekly project reports Milestone sign-offs	Weekly Project reports System Test sign-offs	Customer Training Customer sign-off
Key Metrics	Project Overruns	Project Completion Ratio	Account Expansion

Figure 11–8   Sign-off.

receives the revenue on time and the customer is willing to serve as a reference, you know you have a terrific project manager on your hands. Don't forget to include a bonus for him or her!

The interesting metric to review in this step is account expansion (also called project follow-on). This is the measurement of how much additional service revenue was generated during the project or is now actively being proposed. If no additional business was generated with this customer, the management team should ask why. Was the customer happy with the people we provided? Did our competitors beat us to the punch? Did we price ourselves out of the account? Understanding lack of account expansion is the key to account expansion.

▶ Step 8: Review

And finally, we reach the end of the customer engagement workflow. The project has been delivered, the customer has signed off, and revenue has been collected. However, your work is not entirely complete. The final step of the customer engagement workflow is review (Figure 11-9). You must take the time to review the business experience you just had. This moment of reflection will pay massive dividends in the future.

The project manager remains at the helm by collecting all relevant project data to complete a formal project review. A sample project review has been provided in Appendix D. This review should be conducted as soon after the project is complete as possible (i.e., when the project data is still available and memories of the project team are still fresh). The review will focus on the following elements:

| | 5.0 DELIVER | | | |
	5. Develop	6. Implement	7. Sign-Off	8. Review
Key Roles				
Product Sales Rep				
Product Sales Engineer	‖‖‖‖	‖‖‖‖		‖‖‖‖
Services Sales Rep				
Delivery Project Manager	⊞⊞⊞	⊞⊞⊞	⊞⊞⊞	⊞⊞⊞
Delivery Architect	‖‖‖‖	‖‖‖‖		‖‖‖‖
Delivery Technical Consultant	‖‖‖‖	‖‖‖‖		
Key Deliverables	Weekly project reports Milestone sign-offs	Weekly Project reports System Test sign-offs	Customer Training Customer sign-off	Project Review Report
Key Metrics	Project Overruns	Project Completion Ratio	Account Expansion	Actual Project Margin

Figure 11–9 Review.

- Who was involved in the project?
- What was done for the customer?
- How close was the actual effort to the estimated effort?
- How close were actual expenses to estimated expenses?
- Was there anything developed for this customer or learned during this engagement that can be reused with other customers?

From the final review, the management team can determine the actual project margin. This metric is often the final word regarding the success of any completed project. Did you actually make money or not? If the project did not make money, what were the reasons? Were there other benefits, besides profit, that were gained? This type of analysis and insight translates to improvement for the next engagement. If no review is conducted, the delivery team runs the risk of repeating the same costly mistakes again and again.

▶ Summary

So, there you have it, from request to review. It's important for the entire PS organization to understand and internalize this eight-step workflow. Whenever service employees are reviewing various opportunities or projects, they should be able to articulate where they are in the workflow. Missing any step can be a costly mistake. For example: it's not uncommon for the sales staff to want to jump from the request step to the bid step, skipping over the qualify step. What if this particular opportunity doesn't meet your business criteria or the customer is not in a position to pay for your services? Or, sometimes delivery teams will want to jump into the development step before the negotiation step is complete. This too is risky. What if you and the customer never arrive at agreeable terms? And finally, regional directors are famous for flashing revenue from an engagement before the sign-off step has occurred. From a fiscal reporting perspective, this is a huge no-no. You see, whether you like it or not, these eight steps should be followed in a very linear, sequential, and disciplined manner. Otherwise, your service ship won't handle at all as you expected—she'll buckle under the additional and unnecessary strain you place her under when the crew engages in guesswork. But, if you follow proper procedures and keep her design parameters in mind, she should carry you wherever you need to go.

12

Four Phases of Building PS

Turning the wheel

You have come a long, long way. In this journey, you have been introduced to frameworks that will help you understand your PS business. You have been educated on metrics to help run your business. You have seen a sample PS business built from the ground up. You have even taken a virtual ride on a customer-engagement workflow, felt the wind in your hair, and saw how the organization handles in action. But in many ways, the real challenges are still ahead.

In the *Odyssey*, Odysseus thought his trials and tribulations were over when Troy fell. Little did he know that his ten-year odyssey home was just beginning. While the journey of building a successful and profitable PS business should not take ten years to complete, it will take some time. If you assembled a new crew to sail a boat, you would not expect them to perform exceptionally the first day at sea. Even if they were expert sailors (which most people are not), the crew would need time to familiarize themselves with the new boat and each other. The same learning curve applies when launching your new service business. In fact, when launching and managing a services business, there are very distinct phases of learning and maturity your organization will reach. The journe through these phases is the subject of this chapter.

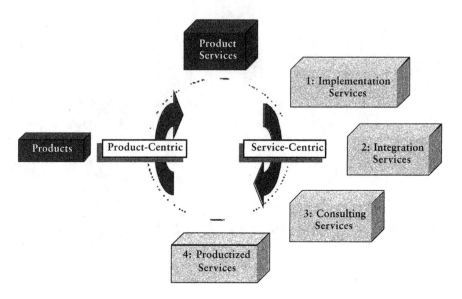

Figure 12–1 Four phases of building PS.

▶ Overview of Phases

When a product company makes the decision to move from basic product-support services to more solution-oriented consulting services, the company will experience several distinct phases during the journey (see Figure 12-1). Each phase has unique challenges and priorities. The key is to understand which phase your PS organization is experiencing.

The first phase happens when a product company begins offering *implementation services*. This often occurs because the company is pulled by its customers into offering services beyond basic support services. To close a deal or guarantee customer satisfaction, the product company may promise to provide customer-requested implementation assistance. In this phase, the product company is willing to take on more responsibility for the overall success of a customer project, including the implementation of products from other companies. If, and we do stress if, a product company survives this phase successfully, the company migrates to a phase where it provides *integration services*. In this phase, the product company typically realizes there are critical components required to glue together (i.e., to integrate) a customer solution that doesn't already exist in the marketplace. The product company invests in specific technical skills required to create the glue. If the product company masters this new level of complexity, the company becomes a critical business partner to the customer. Basking in this newfound glow, the product company may move to the next phase by offering *consulting services*. These are services designed to solve high-level business problems, where discussions regarding technology and products are secondary. This is good business if your company has the credibility and expertise to deliver it. Finally, there is one last phase. This is a phase most product-centric PS organizations will not reach, although it is the most profitable phase a product-centric PS organization can operate in. In this phase, the *productized-services* phase, the PS team has mastered the skill of identifying the most profitable intellectual property, capturing that knowledge, and effectively using that knowledge for the benefit of the entire organization, across the entire organization. As detailed in Chapter 7, managing intellectual property requires great discipline. This is why few service organizations reach the shores of this phase.

In this chapter, we will review each one of these phases in detail. Specifically, we will analyze the following elements and how they differ during each phase:

Value Proposition: This is how the solution is positioned to your customer, that is, the proposed value of the solution to your customer. This review will outline the value proposition for each phase.

Focus: These, as you will remember from the profitability triangle in Chapter 3 (revenue, references, and repeatability), are the three aspects of profitability. This review will outline the most critical aspect(s) of profitability to each phase.

Critical Skills: These are the skills relating to the four key service functions (i.e., sales, delivery, productizing, and promoting). This review will outline which functions are critical during each phase.

Required Operational Infrastructure: These are the infrastructure elements important to each phase. This review will help you prioritize your infrastructure elements.

Target Mix: This is the revenue mix that you hope to achieve. This review will outline the different revenue mixes you might reasonably expect for each phase.

Revenue Growth Rate: This is how fast can you expect your gross revenue to increase. This review will outline the different growth rates you might expect in each phase based on mix and business maturity.

Target Margins: These are overall gross and operational margins. This review helps frame what margins your senior management should be expecting in each phase.

So, let us begin the review and analysis of each of these distinctive phases.

▶ Phase I—Implementation Services

A product-based company typically starts its service business with basic product-support services. Granted, many support services can be very sophisticated, but they are always, always, always focused on supporting the core products of the company. Implementation services are the first step beyond this comfort zone. As previously mentioned, product companies are often pulled into this phase by their customers who need help implementing complex products. Customers don't want to manage multiple vendors to implement one solution. Customers want someone on the hook, a single company and even a particular individual within that company.

Value Proposition

The value proposition the product company makes when offering implementation services is relatively straightforward: product expertise and risk reduction. Your pitch to the customer should include reminders that there is no one who knows your company's products better than your company's consultants. Your company, therefore, is the obvious best choice to implement your product. And, your company is happy to juggle, for a price, all the customer's various product relationships that must certainly be exhausting.

Profitability Triangle Focus

In this initial phase, revenue is king of the triad. Without revenue, it becomes very difficult for the fledgling service organization to justify itself and acquire much-needed resources. Bookings and revenue forecasts are watched with great anticipation. If the trends are not up and to the right, then why would the product company be compelled to continue the service experiment?

Critical Skills

There are two key skills required to successfully navigate this phase. First and foremost, your service organization will require staff with highly developed project-management skills. These project managers are critical to customer success and satisfaction and will be managing the multiple subcontractors you have now agreed to juggle for the customer. If your project managers are weak, your projects are doomed.

Second, to drive up top-line revenue growth, you need competent Services Sales reps. Only sales reps that can manage a solution sales cycle will be acceptable. Don't settle for product reps who think they might sell some services in their spare time, only for full-time Services Sales reps who increase bookings for your new business.

Required Operational Infrastructure

As outlined in Chapter 9: Operational Infrastructure, there are three levels your operational infrastructure must address: staff level, project level, the business level. During this first phase, there are some basic business-level infrastructure elements that are required.

Required Operational Reporting: Without basic business-level financial reports, it will be impossible to manage the business.

Required Operational Processes: It is critical to establish frameworks for dealing with partners and customers, including partner-agreement frameworks and customer-contract templates.

Target Mix

Almost by definition, implementation services involve assisting in the integration of your product with other surrounding products to create a business solution. This reality necessarily means your revenue mix will be heavily weighted toward pass-through revenue. Most of your direct revenue will come from the billable hours of your project managers. Therefore, you should expect a revenue mix of 30/70, with 30 percent of your revenue attributable to billable hours and 70 percent to product and service pass-through.

Revenue Growth Rate

During this phase, gross revenue can be grown at a phenomenal rate. Why? Because of the target mix previously discussed. You are adding revenue by reselling the products and services of others. You are not constrained by your own limited delivery capabilities. Based on this reality, it is not unreasonable to target revenue growth rates of 100 percent to 200 percent.

Target Gross Margin

With every upside comes a downside. The upside of a 30/70 revenue mix is that you can grow revenue aggressively. The downside is the impact on your gross margin. Due to the poor revenue mix, you should expect gross margins only around 4 percent. This may seem impossible, but it is true. The math is simple. Look at the simple calculations in Table 12-1.

Table 12–1   Implementation Services Gross Margin.

Revenue/Margin Type	Amount/Percentage
Annual revenue (millions)	$20
Direct revenue	$ 6
Pass-through revenue	$14

Table 12–1 Implementation Services Gross Margin. (cont.'d)

Revenue/Margin Type	Amount/Percentage
Average margin on pass-through services	15%
Average margin on direct services	25%
Average gross margin percentage	18%

Target Operating Profit

This is the part that stings. When product companies first engage in offering implementation services, they can be lured into a false sense of success. As customers sign large-dollar deals, the product company is enchanted by the swell to the top line. But to collect service revenue, you must deliver the services. In this phase, which almost always requires large payments to your subcontractors, you're also spending money to ramp up your sales and delivery staff. Also, you need to invest in some basic infrastructure. Putting this all together can result in operating profits ranging from –20 percent to –10 percent. Details on how we calculated this operating profit are offered later in this chapter.

So, there you have it, Phase 1, Implementation Services, in all its glory. As you can see, most product companies will be highly motivated to move through this phase and into a more profitable one.

▶ Phase II—Integration Services

By offering implementation services, you stepped up to the plate and offered to manage multiple vendors to make your customer successful. Your customer is thankful, but there is a fly the ointment. Even with the capabilities of your product and the products from other companies, the customer's problem is not being totally addressed. There are critical pieces of glue missing, that is, there are pieces of code missing. Whose problem is it? Once again, to close the deal and guarantee customer satisfaction, the product company is motivated to fix this issue.

The key is to make money in the process. Welcome to the integration-services phase.

Value Proposition

The value proposition the product company makes when offering integration services is slightly modified from the value proposed when offering implementation services. Beyond product expertise and risk reduction, the product company is now willing to provide specialized technical expertise required to integrate disparate products. The more rare the technical expertise, the greater the value to the customer.

Profitability Triangle Focus

In this second phase, as in all four phases, revenue remains a focal point. But as the PS organization matures into this phase, customer references become critical. Customers need to hear others validate your capabilities. Specifically, industry references are key. That is, customers need to hear from like customers. In his marketing how-to book, *Inside the Tornado*, Geoffrey Moore describes the strategy high-tech firms need to deploy to develop emerging customer markets. He uses the analogy of a set of bowling pins to describe how a company must leverage customer references to cause the adoption of a new solution:

> The purpose of the bowling pin model is to approach niche market expansion in as leveraged a way as possible, to bowl toward [a market] tornado...[Customers] find it much easier to buy in if vendors can supply references from an "adjacent niche," one within which it already has established word-of-mouth relationships.
>
> If you go after niches at random, driven solely by sales opportunity, there is no such leverage at all.[1]

In essence, when you make one customer successful, you are knocking that pin over. As that customer falls, it bumps into another target customer (at the same industry shows, at the same industry professional societies, etc.). The second customer can be from the same market

---

1. Geoffrey Moore, *Inside the Tornado*, New York: HarperBusiness, 1995.

niche or one closely related. The important point is you are acquiring references that are relevant to future target customers.

Critical Skills

Integration services still require highly skilled project managers. These project managers remain the key to profitable projects and satisfied customers. Assuming you have already invested effectively in Services Sales reps, you should now be investing in technical expertise. These technical consultants are the individuals who create the glue (i.e., write the code) required to complete your solutions.

Required Operational Infrastructure

In this phase, the project-level infrastructure becomes more important.

Required Operational Reporting: You'll need to implement some type of project-reporting system in order to determine whether your projects are being delivered on time and on budget.

Required Operational Processes: You need consistent project life cycle processes across all your geographical territories. By implementing such processes, you create a common language for your delivery teams. This investment will return great dividends when you focus on leveraging knowledge across all territories (i.e., when you develop a repeatable solution).

Target Mix

By adding technical expertise to your value proposition and by hiring more technical consultants to deliver that expertise, you increase your capability to collect direct revenue. Thus, your revenue mix improves. A target revenue mix of 40/60, or 40 percent from billable hours and 60 percent from product and service pass-through, is very reasonable in this phase.

Revenue Growth Rate

Your revenue mix is still heavily oriented toward pass-through revenue. This means you still have the ability to rapidly grow your top-line revenue. Revenue growth rates between 50 percent and 100 percent are achievable.

Target Gross Margin

Though your top-line revenue can grow aggressively, your gross margins improve at a slower rate. Gross margins of 11 percent or better should be very acceptable in this phase.

Target Operating Profit

The sting still remains. While this phase, the integration-services phase, maintains better margins, you are still building your business. You are still hiring new consultants and ramping up their billable utilization rates. There are also infrastructure investments that need to be made. Your executive management team should expect operating profits ranging from –12 percent to –8 percent.

Keep in mind, we are predicting a four-year growth plan for a PS organization that wishes to make it all the way to Phase IV—Productized Services. There are many product-centric service organizations that choose to settle into the integration-services business. If this is the strategy, executive management should expect the revenue mix to continue improving, with more and more business being delivered by the company's technical consultants. As this occurs, gross margins and operating profits will improve. World-class gross margins for this business would be in the order of 35 percent to 50 percent. The key is to acquire and maintain superior technical talent and keep those folks busy.

For those wondering what the next stage of maturity would look like, read on.

▶ Phase III—Consulting Services

Implementation and integration services are mostly about technical solutions, while consulting services are about business solutions. The first question to address is why your product company would ever want to stray beyond services closely related to your products? The answer is hidden in the purse strings, or who exactly holds the purse strings. The customer's technical staff greatly influences which products are purchased and who implements them. But the checkbook is often held, not by the technical staff, but by someone else who cares more about business solutions than technical ones. If your product company can converse in this business-solution arena, you will have greater control over your fate in the account. Hence, the birth of consulting services.

Value Proposition

By this phase, the product company has already established its value proposition: product expertise, risk reduction, and specialized technical expertise. By offering more general consulting services, the product company must demonstrate business-solution expertise to the customer. The more targeted this expertise is, the more credible the argument.

To illustrate this point, let's take the example of customer relationship management (CRM) systems. Your company makes a CRM software product. When offering integration services, your company provided the project management and technical skills required to successfully implement your product and integrate it into the customers' other software systems. Your proposals all dealt with implementing your product. Now, you hope to consult with the customers to help them make the best business decision. You want to offer to your current customers all your experiences with CRM packages and how companies can best choose, implement, and use them to their advantage. You want to talk strategy before tactics.

Profitability Triangle Focus

As you may suspect, revenue never drops from the radar screen. In this phase, references also remain critical. And now, for the first time, repeatability will gain some attention. To be credible on a consulting level, you must be able to demonstrate success patterns to your customers. You must be able to show what has worked or not worked for like customers. This requires a new level of knowledge management. Previously, best practices and knowledge sharing between delivery teams was nice to have. Now, it is mandatory.

Critical Skills

To break into this phase, you need a new skill set in your delivery teams. You need to hire business consultants who are comfortable with the technology but are focused on the business strategies of your customers.

At this point, marketing managers also become critical. You need people who can spin your story. In previous phases, customers could be convinced with references and data sheets. Now, you are selling higher; you are pitching vice presidents and CEOs. You need someone that can help soften the obstacles you may face in the selling process. You need some air cover.

Required Operational Infrastructure

In this phase, both your reporting and process needs will be focused on your individual delivery employees. Their numbers and skills have grown and, therefore, the expenses related to them have also grown. You need to optimize these resources to guarantee profitability.

Required Operational Reporting. Individual time reporting is an infrastructure element many consulting firms implement at conception. Not a bad idea. But, for the product-centric company employees, time reporting is an alien concept. Only after reaching a certain level of business maturity does it really make sense to push this concept. Now is the time.

Required Operational Processes. To maximize your expensive human resources, you need a professional-development program. For your technical staff to be effective and your projects profitable, your staff requires technical training. And for your new business consultants to be credible, they require training in best practices. Relying on grass-roots, trial-by-fire training is not the best strategy. It can be costly and your customers will not be appreciative.

Target Mix

By the time you reach the consulting-services phase, you should have developed a robust delivery organization. Your staff with billable time should be responsible for 50 percent of your revenue streams. This means you are looking at a 50/50 revenue mix.

Revenue Growth Rate

Top-line revenue growth is now more challenging. With a 50/50 revenue mix, you are more dependent on scaling your delivery teams to capture more revenue. Scaling your delivery capabilities requires you to identify new delivery staff, hire them, and train them. This slows down the revenue growth rate you should expect. Rates of 50 percent to 80 percent are very acceptable.

Target Gross Margin

Once again, your improving revenue mix will translate to improving gross margins. Gross margins of 18 percent to 22 percent are achievable in this phase.

Target Operating Profit

Welcome to the promised land of profitability! A healthier revenue mix means a better gross margin. A better gross margin produces dramatically improved operating profit. In this phase, you should expect to see some positive cash flow. Operating profits ranging from break even to +4 percent are within reach.

Finally, things are looking up! Your PS organization is actually making and not losing money. But there is a better place to be. A place where margins grow fatter and profits grow taller. The place of productized services.

▶ Phase IV—Productized Services

Please don't let the name scare you away. The concept of productized services is really quite simple. It is all about leverage. To enter this phase, a PS organization must be committed to using its valuable intellectual property to gain better margins and higher profits. The components of this valuable knowledge are outlined in detail in Chapter 7: Productizing. This section reviews how leveraging IP positively impacts your business.

Value Proposition

The product company with consulting services has several things to offer the customer: product expertise, technical expertise, business problem expertise, and risk-management knowledge.

If the product company has been disciplined enough to capture and quantify experiences from previous customer engagements, it can position risk management as one of its new areas of expertise. That is, by demonstrating proven delivery methodologies, the product company can greatly reduce the fears and risks of a customer. Also, the product company should have no trouble establishing its credibility with target solutions where you can show previous customer satisfaction.

Profitability Triangle Focus

As always, revenue remains a focus. and references remain important. However, repeatability is the hallmark endeavor of the productized-services phase.

Critical Skills

The most important skill required to develop repeatable, productized services are talented technical skills, especially those possessed by the more senior technical staff. This group of individuals is the brain trust that confirms your technical architectures and delivery strategies. The stronger they are, the more easily your services can be differentiated from other services.

Marketing managers who understand how to position and market business solutions are also critical to this phase. Remember from our discussion in Chapter 8 that product managers and solution-marketing managers are not the same. They hold different skills and different mind-sets. Product managers typically focus marketing efforts on differentiating product capabilities. In the world of computer hardware, this is called marketing based on "speeds and feeds" (how fast a computer can process and move data). Solutions are much mushier entities. They are often differentiated based on intangible concepts, such as lower risk or improved employee productivity. Therefore, solution-marketing managers must position solutions opposite specific business problems, while product marketing managers may design very successful marketing campaigns that never address a general business problem.

Required Operational Infrastructure

In this phase, we return to a project-level focus.

Required Operational Reporting Detailed, uniform, project reporting, across the organization, is critical for developing an understanding about which projects are most profitable and why. The most profitable projects in the overall organization then become candidates for productized services.

Required Operational Processes The process of IP capture must be added to the project management life-cycle. Each geographical area must now have delivery teams that are educated on how to capture and submit project IP, which can be reviewed by the Services Engineering team.

Target Mix

Valuable IP should be well managed and well implemented by staff, as opposed to by third-party providers. Therefore, a target revenue mix of at least 60/40, with 60 percent from direct revenue, should be the objective by this phase.

Revenue Growth Rate

Top-line revenue growth is much more challenging at this phase because the hiring and training of delivery staff is a longer and more complex endeavor. Revenue growth rates of 20 percent to 30 percent are manageable. Higher growth rates can impact the quality of your service delivery.

Target Gross Margin

And now for the real benefit. By aggressively managing a target-solution portfolio, you can realistically expect to enjoy a target gross margin of 30 percent or greater. This is true for three reasons. First, customers are willing to pay a premium for your well-referenced and valuable solution expertise. Second, your delivery teams have become extremely efficient at delivering your target solutions. And last, this is the phase where you start to see revenues from reusable components such as software. Remember the comparison we made way back in Chapter 3: Levers for Profitability between Solutions R Us and We B Solutions? One of the advantages We B Solutions had was the high-margin revenue (50 percent gross margin) from reusable IP components. Using Table 12-2, look again at these numbers and see how much that component can help lift overall gross margins for the business.

Target Operating Profit

Now for the best part. By offering productized services that are highly differentiated from your competitor's, you have improved your gross margin. This leads you to a very respectable operating profit of 13 percent.

Table 12–2 Comparing Revenue Mixes.

Area to Measure and Manage	Specific Metric	Solutions R Us	We B Solutions
Financial	Annual Revenue (millions)	$100	$100
	Direct Revenue	$ 30	$ 60
	Pass-Through Revenue	$ 70	$ 30
	Reusable IP Revenue	$ —	$ 10
	Average margin on Pass-Through Services	15%	15%
	Average margin on Direct Services	25%	35%
	Average margin on Reusable IP	60%	50%
	Average Gross Margin Percentage	18%	30.5%
Customer	Number of Product References	20	20
	Number of Capabilities	10	15
	Number of Industry References	4	8
	Number of Solution References	0	6
	Number of Repeatable Solutions	0	3
	Average margin on Direct Services	25%	35%
Learning & Growth	Average margin on Reusable IP	60%	50%

So, there you have it, the four phases a PS organization, based in a product company, can migrate through. Table 12-3 summarizes the data presented in this overview.

▶ Maturity Time Line

Now, you may ask the question you are dying to ask: How long? How long will it take to move through these phases? How long until my organization is profitable?

And, here is the answer you know is coming but don't want to hear: It depends. It depends on your overall business objectives. It depends on how heavily your company is willing to invest on the front end. It depends on what phase you would like your service business to reach (e.g., you may want to stop at integration services). And ultimately, it depends on the ability of your management team to execute its plan.

Having avoided a direct answer, we can provide some guidance. Assuming your company would like to establish a mature PS organization that offers high-margin, productized services, you could reasonably target a four-year horizon. This time line is documented in Figure 12-2. As you can see, We B Solutions starts its first year as an implementation-services organization. In its second year, it offers integration services, improving its gross margin and profitability in the process. It continues the evolution by providing consulting services in year three. By the fourth year, We B Solutions has successfully disciplined itself to provide higher margin, productized services. Could this time line be accelerated? Absolutely. Could this time line take longer than four years? Very likely. Once again, your specific business objectives and your team's ability to execute their jobs will greatly impact how quickly or slowly you navigate through these phases.

In earlier chapters, we discussed the *how* of building a PS organization. In this chapter, by describing phases of maturity and providing a time line, we have addressed the *when* (i.e., when you should expect various events to occur). The additional benefit of the time line provided in this chapter is that you should also understand the *where*, specifically, where is your organization in the journey. If you can accurately assess this, you can set realistic expectations for senior management regarding revenue growth and profitability. For every senior PS manager, the

Table 12–3 The Four Phases of Building PS.

Name	Value Proposition	Focus	Critical Skills	Required Operational Infrastructure	Target Mix	Target Margins
Implementation Services	• Single point of contact to manage implementation of product environment • Product-specific skills	• Revenue	• Services Sales reps • Project managers	• Financial reporting • Partner management (legal)	30/70 30%: Company services (25% gross margin [GM]) 70%: Third-party services (15% GM)	Gross Margin: 4% Operating Profit: –16%
Integration Services	• Single point of contact to manage implementation of product environment • Product-specific skills • Targeted technical skills	• Revenue • References	• Project managers • Technical consul-tants	• Project reporting	40/60 40%: Company services (30% GM) 60%: Third-party services (15% GM)	Gross Margin: 11% Operating Profit: –10%

Table 12–3   The Four Phases of Building PS. (cont.'d)

Name	Value Proposition	Focus	Critical Skills	Required Operational Infrastructure	Target Mix	Target Margins
Consulting Services	• Single point of contact to manage implementation of product environment • Product-specific skills • Targeted technical skills • Business problem expertise	• Revenue • References • Repeatability	• Business consul-tants • Marketing manager	• Time reporting • Staff training	50/50 50%: Company services (35% GM) 50%: Third-party services (15% GM)	Gross Margin: 20% Operating Profit: 2%
Productized Services	• Single point of contact to manage implementation of product environment • Product-specific skills • Targeted technical skills • Business problem expertise • Engagement methodologies	• Revenue • References • Repeat-ability	• Senior technical architects	• IP capture	60/40 60%: Company services (40% GM) 40%: Third-party services (15% GM)	Gross Margin: 30% Operating Profit: 13%

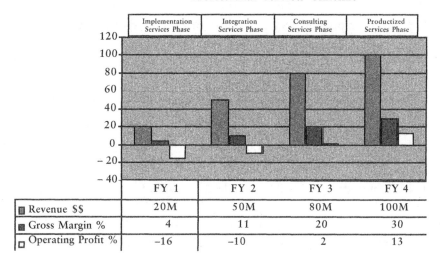

Professional Services Timeline

	Implementation Services Phase	Integration Services Phase	Consulting Services Phase	Productized Services Phase
	FY 1	FY 2	FY 3	FY 4
▣ Revenue $$	20M	50M	80M	100M
▣ Gross Margin %	4	11	20	30
▢ Operating Profit %	−16	−10	2	13

Figure 12–2 Financial performance during the four phases.

pain of missing financial objectives and not being able to articulate why is a very real and common experience. Hopefully, this framework removes much of the mystery.

▶ Services Phases Graph

There is an interesting graph you can draw when you combine the concept building PS in four phases with the actual service revenues, service margins, and service revenue growth rates that you would expect from the service business unit of a product company. But first, let's acknowledge that the financial models we outlined for each phase are purified for the purpose of example. In the real world, most product companies have a complex service business that cannot be mapped completely and cleanly into one of the four phases. Also, some product companies still lump revenues from support services, education services, managed services, and professional services into one big pot—making it extremely difficult to assess exactly which stage the PS business is operating in. And, by extension, this lumping of revenues masks the successes and failures of the PS business. Our intent is to develop a service business where we can necessarily identify successes and failures, and therefore, we hope to see some basic correlations between our financial data and these four phases. Based on our review, we should expect to see the specific patterns emerge as shown in Table 12-4.

Table 12–4   Phase Parameters.

Phase of Service Business	Service Revenue as a Percent of Total Company Revenue	Annual Growth Rate of Service Revenue	Gross Margin Achieved on Services
Phase 0: Support Services Only	Small: 15% or less	Locked to product revenues	High (just support services): 30% or more
Phase 1: Implementation Services	Growing: 15%–20%	30% or more	10%–20%
Phase 2: Integration Services	Growing: 20%–25%	30% or more	10%–20%
Phase 3: Consulting Services	30%	20% or more	20%–30%
Phase 4: Productized Services	30% or more	20% or more	30% or more

Using the parameters in Table 12-4, you can create a 2×2 graph mapping service revenue as a percent of total company revenue against gross margin achieved on services sold. Each of our four service maturity phases would fit into a quadrant of that graph (see Figure 12-3):

- When service revenues represent a low percentage of total company revenues, but they maintain high margins, the company is probably still very focused on support services.

- When service revenues are a low percentage of total company revenues, but their margins have dropped, the company is probably moving into the implementation-services phase.

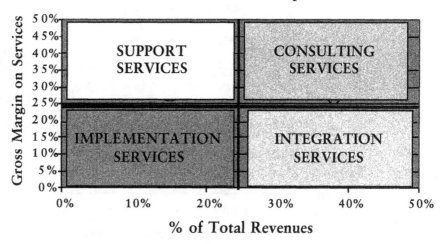

Services Landscape

Figure 12–3   Financial performance during the four phases.

- When service revenues are an increasing percentage of total company revenues, but their margins remain low, the company has probably moved into integration services.
- Finally, when service revenues are an increasing percentage of total company revenues, and their gross margins are improving, the company is probably successfully moving into consulting and productized services.

Therefore, mapping the time line with the financial results that a company would report for all their service revenues, we would expect a company working through the four phases to experience the curve shown in Figure 12-4.

Based on this visual presentation, you might start to wonder why a product company would ever embark on such a painful journey. It also makes you wonder why business analysts are so keen to see product companies move aggressively into services. But referring back to the Introduction, Why Product Companies Jump In, we offer several good customer-related reasons to provide more than just basic support services. And, don't forget, there is a powerful economic reason to take this painful journey: long-term revenues and margins. What if you are

Working Through the Phases

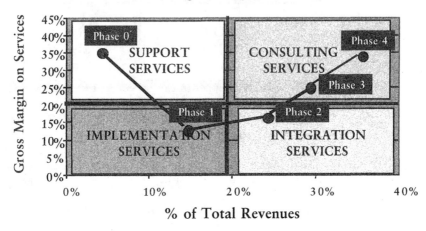

Figure 12–4 Financial performance during the four phases.

a product company sitting in Phase 0 with high-margin products, high-margin support services, but a low percentage of overall revenue from services. You are fat and happy. However, what if your product margins start to erode, and with them go your support-service revenues and margins? Now what? How are you going to maintain a product and service portfolio that continues to bring high margins and high growth to your investors? Suddenly, the curve in Figure 12-4 looks like a painful but viable option. And thus, the Sirens begin their singing.

▶ Skipping a Phase

Now, ask the other question you are dying to ask. Can we skip a step? Must we follow these defined phases? Why can't we start out with integration services and jump to productized services?

All of these questions are valid. And in fact, your company may have the skills and expertise to skip phases. However, be acutely aware that each subsequent phase requires higher level skills, greater infrastructure, and greater business discipline. However, there are no natural laws in play here. In nature, most babies crawl before they walk and walk before they run. There are facts of physiology that force that progression. In the development of a PS organization, there are no irrevocable laws restricting you from skipping a phase of development. As you contemplate leap-frogging phases, bear in mind your company size and your market focus. Smaller product companies with specialized market niches typically can traverse the product-service life cycle more easily. These smaller, more specialized companies often work to understand their customers' business environments from the top down and, therefore, may already have the skills for business-level consulting in house. Larger product companies may have a greater challenge skipping phases simply because they offer more generalized expertise to a more diverse base of customers from a wider spectrum of industries. This jack-of-all-trades reality will make it difficult for a larger company to begin positioning itself on the business-consulting level.

You may look to independent consulting companies as your guide. After all, many independent consulting companies are born into the consulting-services phase. But be cautious with your comparisons. Independent consulting organizations do not have the same product-oriented burdens you do. They have a clean slate. You do not. You are operating in an environment heavily tainted by product business-model thinking. Before you make any final decisions about skipping a phase, please read Chapter 13: Unique Issues.

▶ Stalling in a Phase

Stalling in a phase. Can it be done? Should it be done?

In the *Odyssey*, Odysseus is hell-bent on returning home to Ithaca after the fall of Troy. On his journey, he stumbles onto an island inhabited by a witch named Circe. Circe meets all of Odysseus's wants and needs. With the intention of staying only five days, Odysseus is enchanted by

Circe into staying five years. But Odysseus misses his wife and child. He misses his homeland. He is not content to spend his remaining days in listless luxury. He is driven to return home and manage his kingdom. Eventually, he breaks Circe's spell and leaves her island.

The same question ultimately faces the product company. What are you trying to accomplish? What is important to you? Many product companies may be very content simply offering implementation services. The low margins on these services may be more than offset by the high-margin products that are part of each installation. The effort required to offer more complex services may be too great a price to pay for some product companies. There is no shame in this. Each product company that offers professional services must find its comfortable niche. Once again, it is important for the product company to understand what types of services it's attempting to offer and, realistically, what margins it should expect from those services.

▶ Services Market Landscape

We cannot leave this chapter without stepping back and discussing the overall services marketplace. How do the four phases discussed in this chapter apply to the product-centric PS companies we all know by name? Does the above framework provide any insight into the services marketplace? Actually, if you map these four phases to the service strategies of various product companies, you may better understand their strategies and struggles.

To demonstrate how the four phases of service maturity can be applied to actual companies, we will focus on the computer hardware industry. In that industry, let's look at the following four companies:

- Hewlett Packard
- Compaq
- Sun Microsystems
- EMC

IBM is noticeably absent from this list. That's because the service strategy of IBM has been analyzed to death. Also, IBM has already worked itself completely through the four phases described in this chapter. The four companies we have chosen are not so fortunate and provide insight when examined.

Hewlett Packard: More Than Just an Integrator?

Let's start our analysis with Hewlett Packard, a large company that has received a great deal of press around its endeavors in the service arena. At least nine years ago, HP made a conscious and public decision to move beyond basic support services. Ever since then, HP has been struggling to move into the consulting-services phase with varied success. In an article titled "HP Keeps Mum on Future Plans,"[2] an International Data Corporation (IDC) analyst makes the following comment, "For HP, this is about becoming the prime contractor with end-to-end capacity. All too often, it is seen as an infrastructure vendor, and these days the consultancy is the high profit area." Interpretation: HP is caught in the implementation-services phase, perhaps more by perception than reality. But, based on the comments of this analyst, customers do not believe HP has mastered integration services (providing end-to-end capacity by managing subcontractors and hiring critical skill sets), nor are customers willing to embrace HP as a business-level consultant. HP has attempted to buy its way to the consulting-services phase by purchasing Price Waterhouse consulting. Unfortunately, that strategy did not come to fruition; to date, HP continues the struggle, and the merger with Compaq will not greatly improve the situation.[3] In March of 2001, HP announced the creation of a new services business unit reporting directly to the chairman.[4] In a press release, HP reiterated its commitment to service capabilities that help customers transform their businesses. HP is a large company with over $7 billion in service revenues.[5] If anyone can continue the journey and make it successfully to the phase of consulting services, HP can. But its 2001 Q2 results tell you it's not there yet. In a press release reviewing those results, HP provided the following insight on its IT services business unit:

> The IT services segment includes consulting, outsourcing, support, and customer financing services. Revenues overall for the segment grew 9% (16% in local currency) with improving profitability. HP's consulting business achieved

2. Sarah Arnott, "HP Keeps Mum on Future Plans," *Computing*, November 24, 2000.
3. See "The Services Alignment Risk Factor: The Real Challenge for HP," available at *www.thomaslah.com*.
4. HP Elevates Role of IT Services Business, Company Press Release, March 22, 2001.
5. *HP 2000 Annual Report*.

33% revenue growth, driven by increased size and scope of engagements. Outsourcing revenues were up 23% worldwide, while support services grew at 7%. "Our IT services business turned in a solid quarter. Our increased focus is resulting in good successes and we believe this business is a significant growth engine for us," said [CEO Carly] Fiorina. Operating margin was 6.0%, compared to 6.6% for the same period last year and 5.3% for the last quarter.[6]

Unfortunately, HP provides no insight into its revenue mix. There are clues to how much service revenue is coming from basic support services as opposed to professional services. However, based on the revenue growth rate quoted for professional services and blended operating profit of 6 percent, it is probably safe to say HP is somewhere between the implementation-services phase and the consulting-services phase. Solidifying its consulting services and moving into more productized services should help drive the overall operating profit higher.

Compaq: Buying Its Way Around the Wheel

Compaq is another interesting case study. Like HP, Compaq has been determined to move quickly through the four service phases. And, like HP, Compaq felt buying its way through was a viable strategy. The difference with Compaq is that it actually purchased service capability when it acquired Digital Equipment Corporation (DEC) in 1998. DEC came to the table with the perception of having implementation, integration, and possibly consulting services. Compaq previously possessed only basic support services and a spattering of implementation services. The potential for synergy seemed high. But alas, sometimes you need to create your service capabilities the old-fashioned way; you need to earn your credibility and not buy it. Since the merger, Compaq has suffered several missteps in its services strategy. In a 1999 news.com article, Kim Girard reported that "Compaq's services push hasn't been dynamic, even though the company picked up an army of services employees (30,000) when it acquired Digital Equipment last year."[7] In the article, one analyst is quoted as saying that Compaq

---

6. HP Reports Second Quarter Results, Company Press Release, May 16, 2001.
7. Kim Girard, "Compaq Services May Get New Sheen," April 19, 1999, *www.news.com*.

"says they're a full-line vendor but they're having a tough time fitting into that pair of blue jeans."

In May of 2001, Gartner Inc. issued an alert regarding Compaq's intention to purchase an e-business consulting firm named Proxicom. In the article, Gartner provides good insight into the state of Compaq's service business:[8]

> Compaq Global Services is divided into two groups. Compaq's customer services unit accounted for $4.3 billion in revenue in 2000, and Compaq professional services accounted for $2.7 billion in revenue in 2000.

> Outsourcing revenue was approximately $1 billion in 2000. Consulting and systems integration revenue was approximately $1.7 billion.

What this tells you is that true implementation, integration, and consulting services make up less than 25 percent of Compaq's $7 billion in services revenues. This is after the purchase of DEC! A press release regarding its 2001 Q2 results provides an update on the services business:

> Compaq Global Services revenue grew 7 percent year-over-year, or 13 percent in constant currency. Global Services now represents 23 percent of the company's revenue, up from 21 percent in the first quarter of 2001, showing steady progress towards the company's goal to grow services to more than 30 percent of overall revenue. In certain countries—including Japan, the United Kingdom and Switzerland—services already represent in excess of 30 percent of total revenue.[9]

Looking at the financial numbers from Q2, you can see why Compaq wants desperately to grow the service revenues. Gross margins on the product side of the house barely exceeded 19 percent. Gross margins on the service side exceeded 28 percent. The bottom line: the services business is now providing buoyancy to Compaq's overall gross margins—despite the erosion in product margins.

But to get to where Compaq wants to go, it still has some very heavy lifting to do in the services arena. To date, Compaq continues to struggle with its external positioning. To quote the Gartner article again:

---

8. *Compaq Expands Professional Services by Making a Bid to Acquire Proxicom, Dataquest Alert,* Gartner, Inc., May 7, 2001.

9. Compaq Reports 2001 Second Quarter Results, Company Press Release, July 25, 2001.

Largely viewed as a provider of application integration and infrastructure services, particularly in Microsoft technologies, Compaq's consulting and system integration organization has made numerous attempts over the past several years to bolster its vertical industry and business solution capabilities. The acquisition of Proxicom enhances Compaq's ability to provide vertically focused business solutions and could help Compaq engage earlier in the sales cycle and establish relationships with business managers.

Conclusion: Compaq is stuck somewhere between Phase I—Implementation Services and Phase II—Integration Services. Compaq continues to attempt to buy its way upstream. Whether this will work is yet to be seen.

Sun: Not Sure They Want In

Unlike HP and Compaq, Sun Microsystems is less enthusiastic about jumping onto this spinning product-services wheel. The company has appeared to make a conscious effort to restrain itself from blindly following the Sirens' song of services and prefers to create partnerships in this arena. Interestingly, Sun does provide lip service to the financial analysts by stating its commitment to broadening service capabilities. However, it's the intuition of these authors that Sun seriously questions the value of embarking on the services journey only to be shipwrecked in a low-margin phase.

If you look at Sun's quarterly financial statements, it does not even break out service revenues—everything is lumped together. This is not a sign the company has much to say regarding services. The *2000 Annual Report for Sun* included this sentence describing its services:

> Our 10,000-person service organization supports more than 1.2 million systems worldwide and is a leading provider of training for JAVA and the Unix platform.

This is a great description of support services and training services. In fact, it almost appears as if Sun hasn't even entered the first phase of offering implementation services, although its 2000 annual report states that it is experiencing more revenues from education and professional services. What is interesting is that all services (support services and professional services) represent less than 15 percent of Sun's revenues.

Sun wants to achieve service gross margins of the mid to high 30 percent range. The gross margin on the product side was over 50 percent in 2000. Now you can see why: Sun is less than enthusiastic about jumping into the service waters. Sun is in the exact opposite position from where Compaq finds itself. Compaq is desperate to grow the services portfolio to offset lagging product margins. For Sun, growing service revenues too aggressively would diminish the gross margin of its overall portfolio. The real test for Sun will occur when product margins are not so fat. What will Sun do if Linux takes off and suddenly Sun cannot command margins of 50 percent or greater on the product side? Consulting services here we come? It appears Sun does intend to move into services, but on its terms—focusing on hosted ASP-type services where customers pay as they go for infrastructure. This is very different than jumping into the services game as it is currently defined. Clearly, it will be interesting to see how Sun maneuvers through the service waters. What we know for sure is that capitalism abhors fat margins. If a company is making as much money as Sun is on hardware, someone else will figure out how to get a piece of that pie. When that occurs, Sun must look to other revenue streams like advanced services if it intends to sustain the same gross margins.

EMC: Knows the Way to Go

If you visit the home page for EMC Global Services (*www.emc.com/ global_services*), you immediately get the sense that EMC is very serious about services. The home page crisply presents pointers for support services, education services, and professional services. The page has all the right buzzwords like "best practices," "implementation services," and "integration services." But beyond the hype, it appears EMC is very focused on providing more complex services to complement its product portfolio. Its 2000 annual report states that services represented about 10 percent of EMC's overall revenues. These services had overall gross margins of about 33 percent. These numbers look reasonable for a product-centric company providing mostly support services.

On July 18, 2001, EMC released its financial results for Q2 2001. Service revenues had grown to represent 14 percent of EMC's overall revenues. Also, gross margins on service revenues had increased to almost 37 percent (a four-point improvement in less than six months). The press release stated:[10]

> Revenue from information storage services grew 73% compared with a year-ago quarter to $232 million, reflecting the expansion of EMC Professional Services as a major factor in helping customers design, deploy, and manage their networked information infrastructures.

Based on the market positioning and financial results, it is clear EMC is committed to successfully navigating the transition from being a strictly product-oriented company to a product- and services-oriented company.

Now, let's take these four companies, add IBM in as a benchmark, and map them to the phases graph we created earlier in the chapter. The financial numbers for the five companies from their 2000 annual reports appear in Table 12-5.

We have used these numbers to show the companies' positions on a new graph of the services landscape (see Figure 12-5).

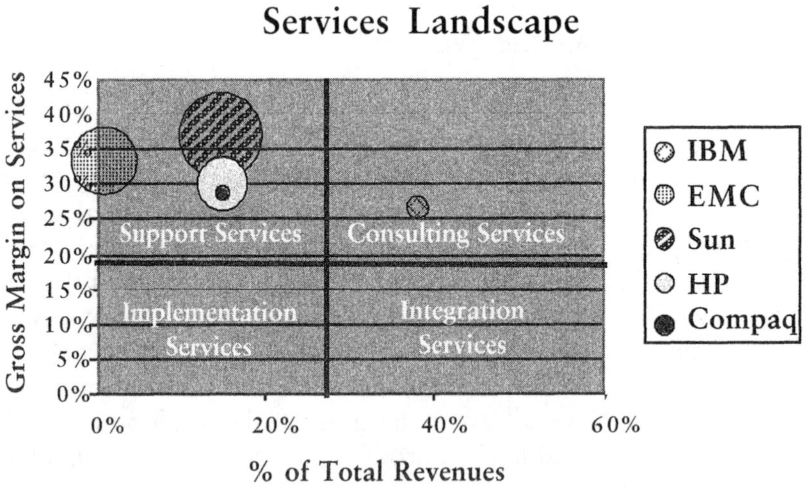

Services Landscape

Figure 12–5   Services landscape.

10. EMC Reports Second Quarter Results, Company Press Release, July 18, 2001.

Table 12–5   Financial Performance of Product Technology Companies.

	2000			1999			Growth of Services Revenues	Growth of Product Revenues	2000 Gross Margin on Services	% of Total Revenues
	Service Revenues	Total Revenues	Service Costs	Services Revenues	Total Revenues	Service Costs				
IBM	$33,152	$88,396	$24,309	$32,172	$87,548	$23,304	3.0%	1.0%	27%	38%
HP	$ 7,336	$48,782	$ 5,137	$ 6,335	$42,370	$ 4,415	15.8%	15.1%	30%	15%
EMC	$ 0.906	$ 8,872	$ 0.604	$ 0.733	$ 6,715	$ 0.507	23.6%	32.1%	33%	0.01%
Compaq	$ 6,716	$42,383	$ 4,793	$ 6,623	$38,525	$ 4,535	1.4%	10.0%	29%	16%
Sun	$ 2,300	$15,721	$ 1,453	$ 1,635	$11,806	$ 974	40.7%	33.2%	37%	15%

What does this graph tell us? First of all, it appears IBM is the only company in this small sample that has transitioned into a consulting-services company. That's the good news for them. The bad news is that the growth rate for IBM services has slowed significantly (see the itty-bitty bubble). Sun is exactly where you would expect it to be: service revenues are a low percentage of total company revenues, but margins are high. The high growth rate for Sun's support-oriented services is in direct relationship to the high growth rate Sun experienced on the product side in 2000.

Now, Compaq's recent issues become more apparent. Even after the purchase of DEC, Compaq's services are still a relatively low percentage of overall revenues. Also, the growth rate is weak. Most likely, Compaq's service-revenues mix is still largely dominated by support services and implementation services.

HP services don't fare much better than Compaq's. Better growth rate, but still a small percentage of overall revenues. HP, too, seems stuck in the profile of a support-service and implementation-service company.

Finally, look at EMC. Services are just now getting on the radar screen. But, margins and growth rates remain high. EMC will face a massive challenge as it moves right—challenges not to dip down into the implementation-services or integration-services quadrants where the percentage of total revenues represented by services increases but service margins suffer. It will be interesting to see if EMC pulls off the migration and maintains service margins.

▶ Management Positioning

> Overall, professional services have not reached the level of margins that had been hoped for or expected. While traditional services gross margins tend to be at about 40 percent, professional services gross margins have been running at 15 to 20 percent. At the bottom line, that translates into barely breaking even.
>
> Shera Mikelson, Hahn Consulting

In this chapter, we have explained why the above quote is so true. By outlining the four distinct phases of building a PS organization in a product company, we have explained why the margins for professional services have, in fact, been so dismal. We have also reviewed how some companies currently align with those phases.

The real world of services is not exactly as cut and dry as presented here. However, understanding the four distinct phases and their specific business models can be extremely helpful to the stressed services management team. This team is often in a position of wondering why it can't get the nice fat margins that a support services team always seems to achieve. The VP of professional services is also often in the hot seat to explain poor margins and zero profitability. Hopefully, the information in this chapter can provide insight and frameworks for more constructive conversations with the executive management team of a product company.

Unique Issues

Undertows and riptides at a product company

Throughout this book, we have been emphasizing the critical differences between a consulting organization and a product company. Unfortunately, when the services organization is within the product company, these differences create friction and overhead as opposed to leverage and economy. This is opposite of what most business executives and analysts believe. In fact, the press is awash in articles emphasizing the benefits awaiting product companies, if only they would offer more services. A May 2000 *Industry Standard* article highlights this point: "Goaded by restive investors, most of the firms that made their names in the PC era of the '80s and '90s—not only Compaq and HP, but also Dell and Intel, which last month announced the addition of 1000 consultants—are trying to reposition themselves as service companies."[1]

In other articles, the analysts incessantly beat the services drum. "Strategically it makes sense for HP to acquire a services company in order to be able to compete with the likes of IBM."[2] "What Eckard failed to do at Compaq is play anything that didn't touch on hardware—including services. If you look at IBM, those were things they did very well."[3]

1. Todd Waserman, "Compaq and HP Rush to Fill Roleson Web," *The Industry Standard,* May 3, 2000.
2. Sarah Arnott, "HP Keeps Mum on Future Plans," *Computing,* November 24, 2000.
3. Kim Girard, "Compaq Services May Get New Sheen," April 19, 1999, CNET *news.com.*

But, as we have been emphasizing, service is not a panacea. In the previous chapter, we explicitly demonstrated the painful maturity curve that product companies must work through. We also highlighted specific struggles of some product companies. In fact, if you lightly scratch beneath the headlines and opening paragraphs, you gain a more balanced insight from the business press. "Sun has been hiring chiefly in the services area, although services such as technical support and choosing the right Sun equipment come with lower profit margins than Sun's traditional products business."[4] "Compaq is struggling with bringing Digital into the mix and building a coherent plan for services."[5] "Though HP service revenues were up to $1.9B for the quarter, profits were down."[6]

In this chapter, we will review the most critical issues that a product company faces as it dives into the services waters. These are the undertows and riptides that a PS business encounters when sailing off the shore of a product company. These are the often hidden forces preventing the HPs and Compaqs of the world from optimizing the economic engine of their service unit. Our recommendation is to prepare for these strong currents, or expect to be dragged out to sea against your will.

▶ Alignment

The first strong headwind that can impede your progress is the issue of alignment. In the *Odyssey*, Odysseus reclaims his crown by proving he is indeed the long lost ruler of Ithaca. How does he do this? By performing a feat that no other man has been successful in completing. Odysseus strings his mighty hunting bow and shoots an arrow through the opening of twelve axe handles set in a line. Such a feat required strength and concentration. But it also required perfect alignment of the axe handles. Without that alignment, even the best placed shot in the world would have ricocheted to failure.

Alignment is not a new or unique concept to product companies. The better-aligned the resources of any company are to corporate objectives,

---

4. Stephen Shankland, "Sun Reports Record Profits," July 22, 1999, *CNET news.com*.
5. Kim Girard, "Compaq Services May Get New Sheen," April 19, 1999, *CNET news.com*.
6. Daniel F. Delong, "HP Says It Has Nowhere to go but Up," *NewsFactor Network*, May 17, 2001.

the more successful the company tends to be. Explicitly or implicitly, executive leaders of all companies spend an inordinate amount of time aligning resources. In fact, the topic is gaining much-needed analysis. George Labovitz and Victor Rosansky of Organizational Dynamics, Inc., in a book titled *The Power of Alignment*[7] draw upon their dealings with large multinational companies, such as Federal Express, to create a straightforward framework that captures the issue of company alignment. In their framework, they define two types of alignment a company must strive for: vertical alignment and horizontal alignment. Vertical alignment refers to aligning from the top down (i.e., from high-level corporate strategy, crafted by the executive staff, all the way down to the frontline employee). "When vertical alignment is reached, employees understand organization-wide goals and their role in achieving them." Horizontal alignment refers to aligning your company processes and infrastructure to meet the real needs of your customers. "The best companies align their processes with customer requirements and then work constantly at improving them. Most of the organizations that have stalled in their progress toward superior performance have mastered local or departmental processes, but not the cross-functional processes that lead to customer satisfaction and retention. In other words, they had mastered easier, smaller processes, but not the big ones that matter most." Figure 13-1 provides a picture of these two types of alignment and how they relate to each other.

Now, Labovitz and Rosansky maintain that both types of alignment are required to ultimately be successful:

> Neither a great strategy nor the full commitment of managers and employees will have the right results if a company's processes for creating and delivering value have targeted the wrong customers—or worse, if they have targeted the right customers with the wrong product...Nor will the company that is fully aligned on the horizontal dimension succeed if its strategy or implementation is flawed.

When creating a new service business, the issues of vertical and horizontal alignment remain paramount. In fact, alignment takes on a heightened sense of urgency. Why? Remember, the success of a service business is dependent upon having the right skills to sell to the customer. If your service unit develops skills and capabilities that are not aligned with your company or customer needs, you create an expensive inventory of human resources. You could also inadvertently create

7. George Labovitz and Victor Rosansky, *The Power of Alignment*, New York: John Wiley & Sons, 1997.

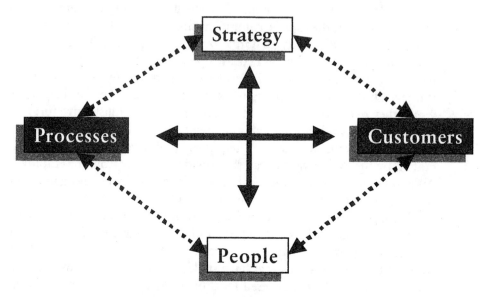

Figure 13–1 Vertical and horizontal alignment.

redundant business functions and processes in your service unit. This will not help the cause of profitability. So, to reduce the risk of misalignment, let us review the issue in more detail.

Vertical Alignment: Aligning Service Solutions and Capabilities

As you may recall from Chapter 8 on promoting professional services, there are two key ways a PS organization can differentiate itself: through capabilities or through solutions. Capabilities refer to the unique skills your consultants possess that can be applied to solve various technical and business issues. Solution differentiation refers to the technology and methodology you apply to solve a specific business problem. To align solutions and capabilities, you must insist on vertical alignment.

To align your service organization vertically, you need to start with the company strategy. A company must have a business strategy it can articulate to its employees, customers, and shareholders. That business strategy should define what core competencies the company possesses or intends to develop. These are the competencies that differentiate the company and drive up profitability. In *Living on the Fault Line*, Geoffrey Moore defines a core competency as "any behavior that can raise your stock price." Every other activity is context that can and should be outsourced. The concept of core competencies is very hot right now. Companies are constantly being asked to take a hard look and determine what their core competencies truly are. Understanding the core competencies of your company is a key step in aligning your service organization.

Defining your business strategy and core competencies is a complex topic that warrants its own book. For our purposes, we will assume your company has already completed this work and has a clear understanding of the core competencies it intends to nurture.

Once your company has defined its core competencies, it can formulate go-to-market plans (i.e., plans articulating how the company intends to deploy its core competencies to specific industry markets). These market strategies will involve specific solution strategies. What business problems can your core competencies help solve? What solutions do you bring to the table using these competencies? These solutions should make up the core solution portfolio of your service organization. These are the solutions that the Services Engineering team should be productizing and the Services Marketing team should be promoting. Finally, now that you understand what solutions you intend to take to market, you can itemize the specific skills you need to add into your Services Delivery team.

In summary, business strategy determines core competencies, core competencies define market strategies, market strategies consist of target solutions, and target solutions determine skills sets. Figure 13-2 demonstrates the linkages from overall business strategy to specific solution offerings and capabilities.

As demonstrated previously, the capabilities and solutions of your service organization should be aligned with your company's business strategy. It makes no sense for your company to hang its hat on one set of competencies while your service organization builds another set of competencies. Also, misaligned solution portfolios generate no benefit. In fact, vertical alignment (i.e., the alignment of PS capabilities and solutions to the strategic objectives of the company) is one of the tethers that holds your professional services to the company portfolio. Let's quickly revisit the SAR factor introduced in Chapter 2. Figure 13-3

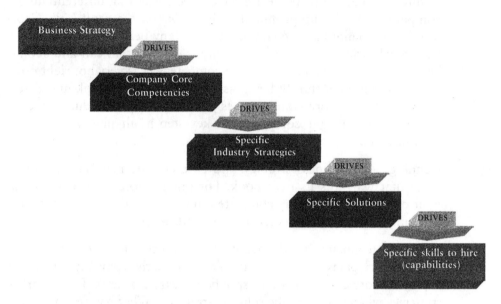

Figure 13–2   Linking business strategy to PS offerings.

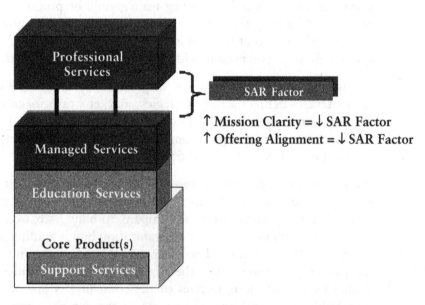

Figure 13–3   SAR and aligned solutions and capabilities.

shows that both a clear mission and aligned PS capabilities help to anchor the PS portfolio to the rest of the company portfolio.

Why would your service organization ever develop solutions that do not support the specific market strategies of the company? What senior management team would not choose to align products and services in order to gain leverage and economies of scale? The answers may seem obvious. However, there is a reason alignment is such an elusive state for companies to reach.

Let's work through an example to demonstrate how easy it is to get twisted and misaligned. What if you are an Enterprise Resource Planning (ERP) software vendor that offers integration services to your customers. Your consultants are focused on installing your product successfully. One day, a key customer is having problems administering its computer servers. The customer desperately needs some operating-system expertise. Now, your company doesn't focus at the operating-system level; it's not a core competency. However, the customer is desperate. Your project's success depends on this skill being available for the project. The customer is willing to pay you for the skill. Your local PS manager is anxious to get the revenue. If you hire the skill directly, you can get a great margin. OK, just this once, for this one customer. A month later that same key customer needs a second operating-system expert. Since you did such a great job finding the first expert, won't you find another? Once again, the local PS manager is happy to take the revenue and margin. But can you see the pending end game? If each local manager agrees to offer skills or solutions to satisfy local customers' needs, your core competencies and solutions quickly become diluted. Soon, your PS organization is offering a plethora of localized capabilities and solutions that may or may not be aligned to the core competencies of the company. This new collection of skills may not even be required to deliver the target solutions your company is trying to promote.

But what about the benefit? Didn't you satisfy a customer's need? Didn't you gain revenue at an acceptable margin? Yes and yes. But, at what cost? Offering operating-systems skills to customers is not core to your business. This is not a capability on which you can differentiate yourself. Numerous other competitors offer the same skill at the same or better prices. So, here you are, using precious time and energy to manage resources that will not sustain their margin. Again, Moore, in *Living on the Fault Line*, provides wonderful insight into the dangers of pursuing revenue not associated with your core competencies. He reminds us, the lesson is simple: constantly review your capabilities and solutions; make sure they remain aligned with your company's business strategy.

Horizontal Alignment: Aligning Service Departments

So, the first miss can occur when your service organization does not diligently align its capabilities and solutions with your business strategy. The second miss can occur when business units and departments do not align their tactical go-to-market efforts. This gap causes inefficiencies and inconsistencies. Figure 13-4 maps all the various business departments that are involved in creating a business solution and successfully delivering it to the customer. The process must be coordinated across departments for it to be truly successful. As Product Engineering and Product Marketing craft new products, they need to coordinate with Services Marketing and Services Delivery. The PS organization needs to be educated about product features and enhancements. PS also needs to understand competitive positioning and future product road maps. In this way, selling services can be the most effective channel possible for taking products to market. Scott McNealy is famous for encouraging internal alignment. Even when commenting on competitors, he uses alignment as the measuring stick:

> Apple will succeed if it can get from this to that and if the company can articulate its message of differentiation and innovation better than ever before. Marketing has got to be crisp, clear, and direct. The marketing dollars have to be spent in areas Apple can succeed in and not in areas where it's traditionally failed. The whole company has to look in the same direction.[8]

As Scott McNealy has always said, it's got to get all their wood behind one arrow.

The centerline in Figure 13-4 represents a specific solution the company would like to take to market (the arrow being shot into the marketplace). The closer each business department sits to the centerline, the greater the horizontal alignment is. The more interdepartmental

8. Macuser, *Between the Lines*, July 1997.

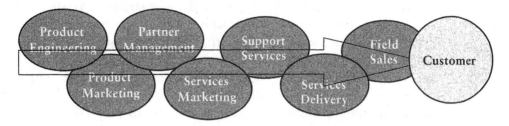

Figure 13-4 Horizontal alignment.

alignment, the more energy behind the arrow, and the greater the potential for success.

Once again, let's use an example of how quickly unaligned efforts can sabotage a solution strategy. Let's say your company sees an incredible market for digital collaborative work environments. These are technology centers where disparately located engineers can meet virtually to discuss and modify product designs in real time. Your company makes a key component of the solution, let's say the software that enables large documents to be edited simultaneously. However, there are several other critical components to the solution. There is the computer hardware that runs the software and the specialized high-bandwidth networking equipment required. The Product Engineering and Product Marketing teams create and validate an architecture that will do the job. Then, the global Partner Management team negotiates a favorable relationship with preferred hardware and network providers. This relationship provides discounted pricing from selected vendors. So far, so good. But then, the solution is rolled out to the field. When the solution hits the local Services Delivery team, there is a glitch. The local team has been butting heads with the newly anointed preferred hardware vendor for over a year now. In fact, there is bad blood over several deals that the hardware vendor threw to a competing software vendor. There is no way the local delivery team will ever implement anything on *that* hardware platform. Unfortunately, the corporate Partner Management team never consulted anyone in the field to assess the various hardware vendors. Now what happens? In one very likely scenario, the local Services Delivery team does take the solution to market, but never delivers it on the preferred hardware platform. This creates problems in the strategic relationship and leads to your company losing the preferred pricing. What to do?

To help build horizontal alignment, there are three key mechanisms that can be implemented. First, you need a mechanism to verify there is an on-going, two-way communication between various departments. In the above example, the global Partner Management team could have instituted quarterly status meetings where potential partner candidates were reviewed with the help of senior field management. There must be venues for open and honest dialogue regarding business decisions that impact multiple departments. Everyone needs to play fairly and the rules of engagement need to be agreed upon and well documented.

Second, roles and responsibilities need to be clearly defined. If the global Partner Management team is chartered to make the final decision on your strategic partners, then its final call stands. If those partner decisions can be trumped by any ole field manager that doesn't like the call, then what's the point? Get rid of the global team and save some money. Why pay people to negotiate contracts they can't enforce? And, if the global team has no real authority, how can they be held accountable for their decisions?

Last and most important, make sure everyone understands what the company's overarching objectives are. Labovitz and Rosansky refer to this as defining the "main thing." If your employees and departments have a clear understanding of what the main thing is, they can use that information to anchor their decisions. If that vision of the main thing is missing, the anchor is lost and various departments start to drift apart. Also, when there is a void, employees fill it. Soon, departments will each be developing their own version of the main thing. Often, these versions directly conflict with each other! Guidelines for defining the main thing are provided in *The Power of Alignment.* [9]

- The main thing for the organization as a whole must be a common and unifying concept to which every unit can contribute.

- Each department and team must be able to see a direct relationship between what it does and this overarching goal.

- The main thing must be clear, easy to understand, consistent with the strategy of the organization, and actionable by every group and individual.

9. George Labovitz and Victor Rosansky, *The Power of Alignment,* New York: John Wiley & Sons, 1997.

To summarize: Clearly define what the main thing is. Make sure the departments are talking. Determine who owns final decisions and live by them. Otherwise, watch the arrow of horizontal alignment continually miss the bull's-eye.

Aligning Skills

Like the existing product organization, the new service organization must acquire both technical and sales/marketing skills. Figure 13-5 was first introduced in Chapter 1: Mapping the Voyage, but can be used here to demonstrate where skill linkages need to be made.

First, the Services Sales staff needs to effectively link to the Product Sales staff. There are several types of connections that need to be made at the skills level. Training Product Sales staff and Services Sales staff on a common sales cycle methodology is a great place to start. The two sales forces should be trained in the same steps and processes regarding opportunity management and terminology. Another linkage involves account planning; strategic account plans should be developed jointly allowing the two sales forces to coordinate opportunity management.

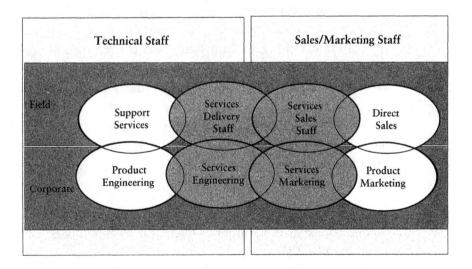

Figure 13–5 Aligning skills.

Services Marketing also needs to link its skills. It should closely coordinate its efforts with the company's other marketing efforts, such as those for product marketing, vertical marketing, field marketing, and corporate marketing. As go-to-market plans are created, the Services Marketing team should clearly understand its roles and responsibilities in conjunction with larger company efforts. If Services Marketing staff members operate in an isolated fashion, they can create two problems: They may create marketing messages that are inconsistent with company messages, and they may create go-to-market plans that are inconsistent or ineffective with how the overall company delivers messages to customers.

The skills of Services Delivery staff and product field engineers must also closely be aligned. If these two pools of technical resources do not sing from the same songbook, customers will be frustrated and confused. The depth of technical knowledge in these groups must be consistent. Their training should be coordinated.

Finally, the Services Engineering and Product Engineering teams should spend quality time together. There is a two-way data path that needs to form to prove very beneficial to the company. On one path, the Product Engineering team needs to provide real-time training to the Services Engineering team regarding product capabilities. This allows Services Engineering to incorporate these capabilities into differentiated solution offerings. On the return path, Services Engineering needs to provide information about real customer requirements back to the Product Engineering team to influence future product developments. If this two-way communication is not successfully established, the Service Engineering team will end up creating customer solutions that could have been solved with new standard product capabilities. And the Product Engineering team will end up creating product features that don't meet customer needs.

In conclusion, alignment of the service organization with the other organizations in the company is critical to the success of the service business. Misaligned capabilities, solutions, positioning, and skills will negatively impact the potential for profitability for the service organization.

▶ Overlap

Let's assume your organization operates with optimal levels of communication between departments. This guarantees that departments are addressing all of the potential alignment issues highlighted in the previous section. But even if this optimal state were achievable, there would still exist some areas where departmental charters and activities overlapped. Areas for potential overlap are highlighted in Figure 13-6. These areas of overlap can be approached as "issues" or as "opportunities." We consider them untapped opportunities for most product-centric service organizations.

Let's analyze the overlap that occurs in sales. In Chapter 5: Selling, we were adamant that an overlay Services Sales function is required to jump-start your PS organization. Overlay is a nice way of saying overlap. You are intentionally creating overlap and, in essence, are paying twice for the same capability. In Chapter 3, we discussed why this additional overhead is justified. Here, we want to emphasize the importance of minimizing that overlap. Do not create two stovepipe sales organizations that do not benefit from each other's infrastructure. Also, the potential for the sales-cycle mismanagement is high. If the Product Sales and Services Sales forces do not clearly define their boundaries, customer opportunities can be lost in the gaps or disputed in the overlaps. The opportunity comes by positioning the Services Sales reps as content experts who can be effectively leveraged by the product account managers who ultimately own the account.

The next area of overlap opportunity occurs between the technical delivery consultants and field sales engineers. Managed incorrectly, this overlap becomes painful and expensive. Sales engineers may design solutions that PS staff don't understand or can't actually implement. The company ends up paying for two expensive, technical, resource pools that don't benefit from each other. However, if these two entities are treated as interchangeable, a whole new world of efficiency is born. Sales engineers, working closely with service staff, can be used to design customer solutions. Well-spoken technical delivery staff can be used early in the sales cycle to establish credibility. Ultimately, there is the potential to merge field engineers and Services Delivery staff into one organization. However, this is not an action we recommend you attempt early in the existence of your service business; the resistance will be too great. Instead, focus on optimizing the resources of these two technical groups to help sell and deliver business.

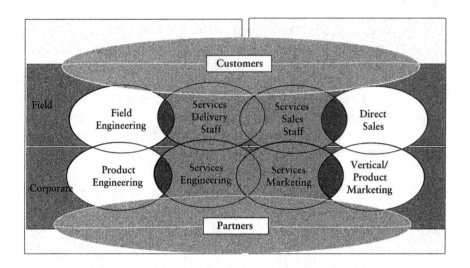

Figure 13–6 Skill overlaps.

And, what about the work of the Services Engineering team? What happens when it develops technologies that could be directly incorporated into the product line? Is that team now engineering products? Yes. And, handled incorrectly, this reality can be a great source of angst, threat, or resentment for the Product Engineering team. These feelings can cause the product engineers to ignore the work of the service engineers. This is a huge lost opportunity. If the product and services engineers coordinate their efforts, Product Engineering can greatly benefit from the development work of the service engineers. In fact, Services Engineering efforts should be classified as R&D spending on the company balance sheet and as an actual extension of core Product Engineering spending. The company should be greatly motivated to see technical developments started on the Services Engineering side migrated to the Product Engineering side. That is the win that offsets any overlap.

Finally, there can be overlap between the Services Marketing department and the other marketing departments in the company. If Services Marketing management is not careful, its staff will perform tasks that are currently being performed by other functions. Examples could include the creation of product data sheets, success stories, and customer presentations. To drive operating expenses down, the Services

Marketing team must benefit from the marketing infrastructure already in place.

Once again, overlaps that exist can be viewed as issues or opportunities. When managed as opportunities, your service organization can gain advantages that directly improve the bottom line.

▶ Partner Conflict

We have already touched on this issue in the section on horizontal alignment, but this is one of the greatest issues a product company can face once it decides to create a PS organization. To give you a sense of perspective, compare it to the greatest challenge that Odysseus faced in the *Odyssey*. To return to his homeland, he was required to navigate a narrow strait past two terrible monsters. One was Scylla, a multi-headed fiend that plucked men from ships as they sailed by. The second was Charybdis, a massive creature that swallowed ships whole. The experience cost Odysseus his six best crewmen. Partner management for the service organization is no less terrifying.

Before the birth of the service organization, the product company chose partners that could help build and maintain product sales. If you were a hardware product company, these could be software companies that used your platform. You could sign up system integrators that you trained to implement your product. But, now you have a PS organization that could be creating specialized software to meet customer needs, a PS organization that wants to prime all implementation engagements. Now what? The real showdown occurs when a product marketing manager devises a go-to-market strategy centered on an outside system integrator. The Product Marketing manager probably has good business reasons for engaging the outside firm (better skill sets, better geographical coverage, etc.). But this new partner is now in direct competition with the internal-service organization for the customer's business. This can get very ugly very quick.

The issue of partner conflict is really an issue of poor horizontal alignment. When discussing horizontal alignment, we used the example of a corporate Partner Management team choosing platform partners that caused Services Delivery staff great angst. The two keys to addressing potential partner conflicts are clearly defined processes and clearly defined overall company objectives (i.e., the main thing). Once a product company establishes a PS organization, it needs to acknowledge that past mechanisms for establishing partners may not suffice any longer. Before, the main thing was to push product. That still is the case, but having services adds new complexity to how that objective is achieved. Is the new objective to sell product or to maximize company revenues and margins (even if that means products must take a back seat at times)? Senior management must acknowledge the rules have changed and they need to support a well-documented process for identifying, qualifying, negotiating, and signing new strategic partners. If an agreed-upon and above-the-board process is not established, partner conflict will compromise your market strategies as ruthlessly as Scylla plucked away capable men. One by one, your product managers will become frustrated and ineffective. When no clear process exists, each one will operate by his or her own business rules, sometimes establishing partnerships that undermine overall company profitability. When confronted with this issue, your product managers will be confused. Their plans and partnerships support product sales. Is that not what they are paid to do? Who changed the rules? On the service side, senior managers will be infuriated as Product Marketing managers create relationships that steal revenue and profits from the service coffers. By establishing a formal Partner Management process that incorporates the updated objectives of your company, the service managers can get their day in court. They can articulate the impact a potential partnership may have on their service business.

Be aware that partner conflict will always exist for the product company once it establishes a PS organization. You cannot totally remove this conflict; your objective should be to minimize it. If not, you are sailing directly into the gaping jaws of Charybdis-like business decisions.

▶ Product Infrastructure versus Service Infrastructure

The list of unique challenges continues: alignment, overlap, partner conflict. Isn't that enough bad news for one book? Unfortunately, the list of issues is not quite complete, and it grows subtler as we progress.

If a product company hires an executive from a consulting company to manage the new service organization, an interesting phenomenon occurs, especially if the new executive spent his or her career working exclusively in independent consulting companies. When the executive arrives, he or she does not realize his or her new environment is not necessarily hospitable to a service business. The executive is accustomed to being surrounded by basic infrastructure required to run a service business profitably. For example, employee time-reporting systems are a basic staple in a service-centric company. Every consulting organization has a time-reporting system. Been there forever. Not only does the product company not have a time reporting-system, it has no intentions of implementing one. Why? If the service organization is just starting, and the revenue streams are so small, why would the product company spend precious IT dollars on a time-reporting system? This resistance to something so basic to consulting is a foreign experience to the newly hired leader. And, it's just the beginning.

Besides time reporting, there is a host of infrastructure needs unique to service companies and foreign to product companies. In Chapter 9: Operational Infrastructure, we reviewed all the infrastructure needs for professional services. Here, we want to specifically call out the ones that a product company may find difficult to embrace, fund, and support:

- **Time Reporting** (as mentioned): A system that allows PS employees to easily and accurately capture their billable hours.

- **Project Account Reporting:** A system that captures project efforts (staff hours) and expenses, then generates reports for critical metrics, such as actual project margin and project completion ratio.

- **Milestone Billing:** A system to invoice the customer when project milestones are achieved, and then to recognize that revenue.

- **Work-in-Process (WIP) Revenue Recognition:** A system to move revenue from booked revenue to recognized revenue before an entire project is completed and signed-off.

Internal Education and Promotion

This issue is an extension of the previous partner-conflict and infrastructure issues. Partner conflict and infrastructure are two specific areas in which the service organization must work to influence, educate, and change the way the product company does business. This is actually part of a much broader internal education campaign that must be waged by Service Management.

When a product company marries itself to a service organization, it must accept the service organization whether rich or poor, in sickness and in health, until death, bankruptcy, or a spin-off parts them. As with most newlyweds, the product company is blinded by initial infatuation. Those service revenues are like big, baby-blue eyes that product executives get lost in. However, eventually the honeymoon ends. Service revenue growth slows. Profitability comes too slowly. Expenses seem high. The list can go on.

If executives that are product oriented see only surface-level metrics, such as revenue and operating profit, they may come to incorrect and harsh conclusions regarding their service business unit. If they do not have some understanding about the unique challenges involved in growing the service business, they will not appreciate or support the efforts. If they have zero sense of the four phases of maturity the service team must manage, these product executives will have unrealistic expectations regarding profitability. This potential disconnect must be averted. The senior managers of a service organization must constantly educate their product companions about the world of services. Specifically, the following areas need to be discussed and promoted internally.

Service Business Model.   News Flash: The business model for a service organization is different than the business model for a product organization. A reasonable businessperson should expect different gross margins, R&D spending levels, and operating profits. For some reason, many product executives have a difficult time internalizing this fact. Sure, they look at you and nod their head and say "Yeah, yeah, yeah, clearly service is a different business." But deep down, they have not really processed what that means financially. So, you must educate them. Again, and again, and again. Because if they don't get it, you, the service manager, will. To assist in this education process, we have provided a discussion on business models in Appendix B: Key Financial Models, including comparisons between the business models of various service and product companies.

Also, for some unknown reason, many product executives maintain the belief that services draw a very high margin, as high as 50 percent+ gross margin. In Chapter 12: Four Phases of Building PS, we demonstrated the slow evolutionary improvement of service margins in a product company. The Service Management staff needs to constantly educate other managers regarding this reality.

Service Metrics. Beyond revenue bookings and operating profit, there are many metrics that help assess the health of a service business. These metrics will be foreign to most product executives. Key metrics discussed earlier include project-completion ratios, proposal-hit ratios, and IP capture ratio.

Positioning Services. Finally, the Service Management team must kick and scratch and gouge its way into the overall psyche of the Marketing staff. Sure, corporate communications will be happy to add an encouraging, easily understood line like the one in an IntelliNet press release, December 14, 2000:

> IntelliNet's product line includes a multiprotocol, openly-flexible SS7 to IP Gateway, the IntelliSS7 Application Development Environment (ADE) and a strong Professional Services.

It's the word *strong* that really sells the service organization, right? Wrong. If the product company is serious about services, it must lead with solutions and follow with product information, not lead with product specs and follow with an honorable mention for services.

▶ Global Differences

Finally, the issue of global differences should be discussed. When the product company first went global, it learned how to effectively distribute products through different channels, in different countries, with different cultures. With the advent of new services, the learning curve begins all over again. Let us state that again. The learning curve begins all over again. Countries have developed their own cultures around services. For example, naming conventions are not universal. In the United States, the terms *professional services* and *consulting services* can be used interchangeably. In Europe, this is not true. These cultural differences must be considered when crafting promotional literature and customer presentations.

Deployment of services is also impacted by global differences. Local labor laws can dramatically impact how and where you employ your delivery resources. A one-size-fits-all delivery model may not be realistic for your business.

Finally, your service-processes and service-infrastructure needs may vary based on national labor laws. Areas like time reporting may need to be altered from region to region.

▶ Closing Comments

Hopefully this chapter has successfully delivered the message that managing a professional services firm within a product company is very different than managing an independent consulting firm. As discussed, alignment takes on a new level of complexity for an internal PS business. Successfully managing this effort requires an astute and patient management team. Partner conflict, lack of infrastructure to run a services business, and global differences in the services business simply make the task even more challenging.

Hopefully, by calling out these issues and by writing this book, we have provided a framework to assist any person who intends to tackle the challenge of developing professional services within a product company. Once again, we do not believe there are multiple case studies of success in this area. This is a very new and immature management discipline. However, successfully building professional services has become a critical success factor for so many product companies. We do not see that reality changing in the near future. So as product companies take this voyage, we encourage them to be cautious, open, and disciplined. And most importantly, we hope our warnings on the many Sirens' songs they will hear help them complete this journey successfully.

Summary of Key Concepts

Framework cheat sheet

We realize that many folks in business struggle with reading a business book. They don't have the time or perhaps the patience. For this reason, we wanted to summarize the key concepts we introduced. By reviewing this summary, you can decide which topics warrant more study, then refer back to the text for more detailed information.

▶ The SAR Factor

The SAR factor was introduced in the Introduction: Why Product Companies Jump In.

When product companies create a new PS organization, they run a high risk of creating a new business unit that is not synergistic to the overall objectives of the product company. We call this the **service alignment risk factor,** or the **SAR factor** (see Figure 14-1). The higher this risk factor becomes, the greater the potential to create an unprofitable service organization becomes. There are three areas that must be addressed to greatly reduce this risk factor.

287

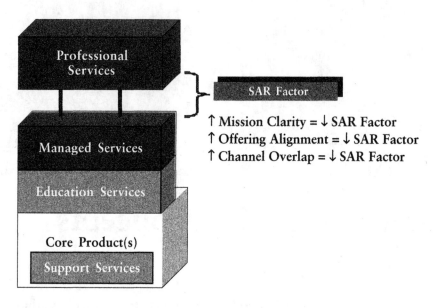

Figure 14–1 SAR factor.

Clarity of Mission: The mission of the new PS business unit must be well defined. Senior executive management must agree on what the mission of the new PS unit is. If there is ambiguity regarding what the company expects from the professional services organization, the SAR factor is greatly increased.

Alignment of Capabilities and Solutions: The PS unit should develop skills and solutions that develop and support the rest of the company portfolio. If professional services develops skills and solutions that maximize PS revenues but do not support other company offerings, the SAR factor is increased.

Channel Overlap: The new services being offered by the PS unit should be targeted at the existing customer base. Also, the existing sales channels should be effective at selling the new services. If professional services creates offerings that cannot be sold through the current company channels or are not designed for current customers, the SAR factor is greatly increased.

Chapter **14** I Summary of Key Concepts

▶ Four Qualifying Questions

These four qualifying questions were introduced in Chapter 2: Setting the Parameters.

Before you jump head-first into the service waters, your executive team should consider the following four questions to better qualify the professional service opportunities of the company:

1. **Can your management team articulate what would differentiate your professional services from everybody else's?** Typically, product companies possess some type of unique technical expertise. If you cannot identify any unique skills or solutions that will set you apart in the service world, perhaps partnering with another service provider is the better play.

2. **Do you intend to make fee-based, professional expertise a core competency of your company?** The story goes that way back when, IBM made the fundamental decision it was actually a service company, not a product company. Today, offering everything from technology-planning consulting services to full-scale outsourcing is core to IBM. Will your new services be core to who you are? Or, are they just expensive window dressing you really can't afford?

3. **Is there a market for your services?** You may be able to articulate a unique set of new services that you feel is core to someone's future success, but is there a viable market? Before diving in head first, make sure the water is deep enough. In other words, is the customer base actually there?

4. **Can you sell these new services to your existing customers through your existing channels?**[1] You have identified the service, you are committed to it, and it looks like there is a healthy market. All good. But there are two potential issues you must consider. What if the buyer of your new services is not your current customer?

---

1. The insight on this issue is based on a conversation one of the authors had with Tom Pencek of Pencek and Associates. Tom highlighted how so many product companies struggle as they attempt to shove new services down a channel optimized to sell products.

Ten Parameters for Running a Business

These ten parameters were introduced in Chapter 2: Setting the Parameters.

To successfully run a business unit in the long term, the management team must understand the following ten parameters:

1. The **mission** of your business unit
2. Your **strategic objectives** for the business (long-term objectives)
3. The **guiding principles** (or policies) that apply to your business
4. Your overall financial **business model**
5. The key **levers** you can use to increase profitability in your business
6. Your **organizational structure** (including roles and responsibilities)
7. The **metrics** you will use to manage the health of your business
8. Your **compensation strategy** (including incentives you will use to encourage the right behaviors)
9. Your **current key objectives** (short-term objectives)
10. **Unique issues** you face in running this particular business

The remainder of this chapter is a summary of all ten parameters as they are specifically applied to a PS organization in a product company.

Key Levers of a Professional Services Business

These key levers were introduced in Chapter 3: Levers for Profitability. Every business has levers that can be turned to improve profitability. In the professional services business, you need to focus on the levers summarized in Table 14-1 to drive profitability.

Organization Structure, Metrics, and Compensation

These components were introduced in Chapters 4 through 9. Each one of these chapters defines a functional component of the professional

Table 14–1 Key Levers of the PS Business.

Primary Lever	Secondary Lever	Where Introduced
Revenue	Revenue Type *Pass-Through Revenue:* Revenue that comes from reselling other people's services. Typically receive 10%–20% gross margin on this revenue. *Direct Revenue:* Revenue that comes from selling your own services. Can receive 20%–60% gross margin based on value of service. *Solution Revenue:* Revenue from reusable solution components **TOTAL REVENUE = (DIRECT REVENUE + PASS-THROUGH REVENUE + SOLUTION REVENUE)**	Chapter 3
	Revenue Mix: Amount of revenue that comes from direct revenue vs. pass-through revenue. ↑DIRECT REVENUE = ↑PROFITABILITY	Chapter 3
	Revenue Growth Rate: How fast you are growing your revenues. ↑GROWTH RATE = ↓PROFITABILITY	Chapter 3
References	**Solution References:** References you have regarding your success in implementing a specific solution (Example: ERP system implementation). ↑SOLUTION REFERENCES = ↑PROFITABILITY	Chapter 3
	Industry References: References you have regarding your ability to make a type of customer successful (Example: oil and gas customers). ↑INDUSTRY REFERENCES = ↑PROFITABILITY	Chapter 3
	Capabilities References: References you have regarding the specific specialized skills of your delivery staff (Example: network security skills). ↑CAPABILITY REFERENCES = ↑PROFITABILITY	Chapter 3

Table 14–1 Key Levers of the PS Business. (cont.'d)

Primary Lever	Secondary Lever	Where Introduced
References (cont.'d)	**Product References:** References you have attesting to the quality of company products you are implementing. ↑PRODUCT REFERENCES = ↑PROFITABILITY	
Repeatability	Your ability to capture lessons learned from one project and apply it to new projects of similar nature. ↑REPEATABILITY= ↑PROFITABILITY	Chapter 3

services organization, along with its charter and how it is structured, measured, and compensated. Table 14-2 summarizes this information.

Business Model and Objectives

These phases were introduced in Chapter 12: Four Phases of Building PS.

A PS organization matures through four distinct phases (see Figure 14-2). Each phase has unique challenges that require specific objectives. Also, each phase has a different financial business model. The challenges and business parameters for each phase are summarized in Table 14-3.

Maturity Time Line

The maturity time line was introduced in Chapter 12: Four Phases of Building PS.

It takes time and energy for a service business to work through the four distinct phases described previously. A four-year time line of financial performance for the professional services business could look similar to the one shown in Figure 14-3.

Table 14–2 PS Function Summary.

Organizational Department	Charter	Key Processes	Key Roles	Metrics	Compensation	Where Introduced
Services Sales	Identify, Close, Forecast	Sales-cycle process: • Identify • Qualify • Propose • Negotiate Forecasting	• Sales director • Sales representative • Business development director	• Bookings • Target project margin • Hit ratio Forecast accuracy	Variable 60/40, 70/30 Bookings Target project margin	Chapter 5
Services Delivery	Estimate, Execute, Educate	Project estimation Project life cycle process: • Requirements review • Project planning • Design • Implementation sign-off • Project follow-on • Project review Staff training	• Delivery manager • Project manager • Solution architect • Technical consultant	• Revenue • Actual project gross margin • Utilization • Project completion ratio	• Variable 80/20 • Utilization • Actual project margins • Project completion ratio	Chapter 6
Services Engineering	Capture, Improve, Leverage	Solution review IP capture Solution development Delivery Training Sales support	Services engineering director	• Target project gross margin • IP capture ratio • Project completion ratio	• Variable 80/20 • IP capture ratio • Project completion ratio	Chapter 7
Services Marketing	Differentiate, Validate, Evangelize	Solution rollout: • Campaign development • Demo development • Benchmarking • Channel strategy • Sales training • Lighthouse accounts	• Services marketing director • Services marketing manager			Chapter 6
Operations						

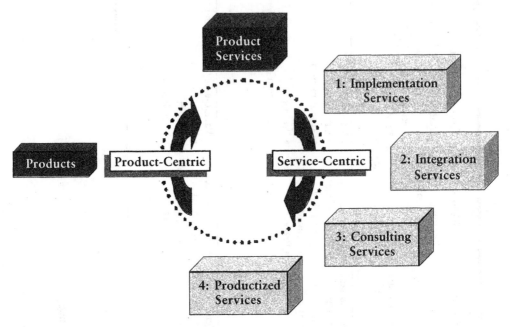

Figure 14–2 Four phases of building PS.

Table 14–3 Challenges and Business Parameters.

Phase Name	Value Proposition	Key Business Objective	Target Business Model
Implementation Services	Single point of contact to manage implementation of product environment Product-specific skills	• Grow top-line revenue • Hire sales reps that can sell services • Hire delivery staff to grow direct revenue • Implement infrastructure to support basic financial reporting • Implement infrastructure to engage partners and subcontractors	• **Target Mix: 30/70** 30%: Company services (25% GM) 70%: Third-party services (15% GM) • **Gross Margin: 4%** • **Operating Profit: –16%**

Table 14–3 Challenges and Business Parameters. (cont.'d)

Phase Name	Value Proposition	Key Business Objective	Target Business Model
Integration Services	• Single point of contact to manage implementation of product environment • Product-specific skills • Targeted technical skills	• Continue to grow top-line revenue • Develop key industry references • Hire project managers and technical delivery staff • Implement project reporting system	• **Target Mix: 40/60** 40%: Company services (30% GM) 60%: Third-party services (15% GM) • **Gross Margin: 11%** • **Operating Profit: –10%**
Consulting Services	• Single point of contact to manage implementation of product environment • Product-specific skills • Targeted technical skills • Business problem expertise	• Develop solution references • Start to manage IP to reap the benefits of repeatability • Hire more specialized technical delivery staff • Hire Services Marketing staff to promote solutions and capabilities • Implement time reporting • Create staff-training and staff-development processes	• **Target Mix: 50/50** 50%: Company services (35% GM) 50%: Third-party services (15% GM) • **Gross Margin: 20%** • **Operating Profit: 2%**
Productized Services	• Single point of contact to manage implementation of product environment • Product-specific skills • Targeted technical skills • Business problem expertise • Engagement methodologies that reduce implementation risks	• Increase solution revenues, solution references, and solution repeatability • Hire Services Engineering staff • Implement IP capture processes and infrastructure	• **Target Mix 60/40** 60%: Company services (40% GM) 40%: Third-party services (15% GM) • **Gross Margin: 30%** • **Operating Profit: 13%**

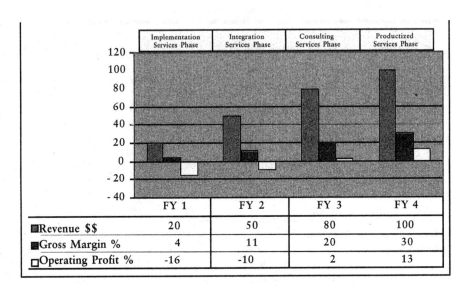

	Implementation Services Phase	Integration Services Phase	Consulting Services Phase	Productized Services Phase
	FY 1	FY 2	FY 3	FY 4
■Revenue $$	20	50	80	100
■Gross Margin %	4	11	20	30
☐Operating Profit %	-16	-10	2	13

Figure 14–3   Financial timeline.

If you combine the professional services business with the other existing service units in a product-oriented company (e.g., support services, education services), you could expect overall financial performance for the professional services to map as shown in Figure 14-4.

Working Through the Phases

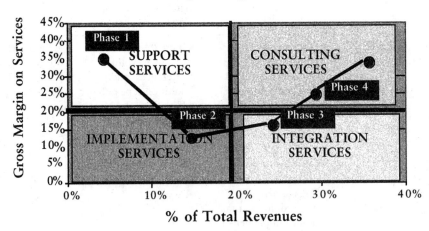

Figure 14–4   Four-year financial performance of PS.

▶ Unique Issues

Building and managing a PS organization within a product company is a very different experience than managing a stand-alone consulting business (see Table 14-4). In Chapter 13: Unique Issues, we highlight the unique issues the service management team will face as they incubate their business within the walls of a product-oriented company.

Table 14–4 Summary of Unique Issues.

Primary Issue	Secondary Issue	Resolution Strategies
Alignment	Vertical Alignment: Aligning core competencies and target solutions	• Tight linkage between services and company strategy • Rigorous bid/no bid criteria to avoid nonstrategic business
	Horizontal Alignment: Aligning departments	• Two-way communication channels between Services and other key departments • Clearly defined roles and responsibilities across departments • Clear definition and communication of the overarching objectives of the company to all departments
	Skills Alignment	• Joint training with Services Sales staff and Product Sales staff • Joint account planning • Joint go-to-market planning between Services Marketing and Product Marketing • Joint solution development between Services Engineering and Product Engineering

Table 14–4 Summary of Unique Issues. (cont.'d)

Primary Issue	Secondary Issue	Resolution Strategies
Overlap	• Services Sales reps and Product account reps • Field sales engineers and delivery staff • Services Engineering and Product Engineering	Joint sales training Common business processes across business departments
Partner Conflict	Channel partners that offer same services Third-party revenues	Well-defined partner qualification process
Product Infrastructure vs. Services Infrastructure	Time reporting Project account reporting Milestone billing Revenue recognition	Review of gaps between current IT infrastructure and IT infrastructure required by Services Time line and investment schedule to address gaps
Internal Education and Promotion	• Service business model vs. product business model • Service metrics vs. product metrics • Positioning services vs. positioning products	• Presentation of service business models and metrics to senior executives • Review sessions with product marketing managers, educating them on integrating Services message into product literature
Global Differences	Positioning of services from region to region Local labor laws	• Review of regional differences • Adjustment to business processes as required

▶ Sirens' Song

Finally, throughout this book, we highlight something we call Sirens' Songs. These are misconceptions or false truths that often surround the business of professional services when it is being developed within a product company. Table 14-5 lists all of these Sirens' Songs.

Table 14–5 Summary of Sirens' Songs.

Sirens' Song (Perception)	Boulder Ahead (Reality)	Where Discussed
Professional services are not dramatically different than support services or education services.	Professional services are dramatically different from other services typically offered by product companies. They are different in size, scope, and risk. They operate under a different financial model. And they are the first services a product company offers that do not have to be directly linked to the product portfolio of the company.	Introduction
Professional services should be a high-margin component of a product company's portfolio.	Many product companies operate professional services as a break-even or slightly unprofitable business.	Introduction
Services are services. Managing professional services within a product company are not very different from managing professional services outside a product company.	There are fundamental differences in managing a professional services organization within a product company. If those differences are not understood, it will be very difficult for the product company to build and sustain a profitable services organization.	Chapter 1
Offering high-margin professional services is a sound business move for most product companies.	Like any business decision, the decision to offer professional services should be reviewed before being agreed to. Not all product companies are well positioned to offer professional services.	Chapter 2
The existing product sales force will effectively sell the new professional services.	Less than 10 percent of your product sales force will learn to effectively sell solutions.	Chapter 5
The more service business you bid, the more profitable you will be.	Bidding service contracts that you have a low probability of winning can be the most expensive mistake your service organization can make.	Chapter 5

Table 14–5   Summary of Sirens' Songs. (cont.'d)

Sirens' Song (Perception)	Boulder Ahead (Reality)	Where Discussed
When bidding service opportunities, effort estimations are relatively accurate.	The first time your service organization estimates the effort to deliver a solution, they typically underestimate by a factor of two. Fifty percent of consulting engagements are delivered late and over budget.	Chapter 6
Once a proposal is signed by a customer, the service team can begin delivery.	At least 30 percent of customer requirements change after the initial proposal is signed.	Chapter 6
The more delivery staff you have, the more money you'll make.	Poorly aligned hiring leads to low utilization and poor profitability.	Chapter 6
Managing intellectual property from past engagements is cost prohibitive and unnecessary.	It will be difficult to maintain gross margins greater than 25 percent without some level of IP management.	Chapter 7
Your existing product-marketing managers can also market services.	Product marketing managers will market their products. If you don't invest in marketing your services, no one will be marketing your services.	Chapter 8
Why start your service business with low-margin implementation services? Why not start by offering high-margin business consulting services.	Customers may not accept your credibility as an inexpensive, business-level consulting firm. Your organization may not possess the level of expertise required to deliver those high-margin services.	Chapter 12

Evaluating Your Service Vendors

In the introduction, we defined three target audiences for this book: the existing management team of the product company thinking about building a service business, the actual service management team, and the actual customer of the professional services organization. We have dedicated Appendix A to those of you in the last category.

As a customer of professional services, you may find yourself sifting through proposals and assessing the true capabilities of service firms. The ability to accurately predict how service firms perform on projects can be career enhancing or career debilitating. Selecting a competent contractor is a wonderful thing. Incorrectly placing your trust in a struggling or mismatched service organization can be painful and costly. To help you assess service organizations, we have compiled the following three-tiered checklist. We will focus on a solution scenario, which is when your company has a specific business problem it is trying to address. For example, your company needs to implement a new CRM system or the marketing department wants to create a new database to mine customer trend information. As you start to engage service organizations that could help solve your problem, consider the following three levels of evaluation:

Tier I—Solutions and capabilities

Tier II—Ability to execute

Tier III—Strategic fit

▶ Tier I—Solutions and Capabilities

We keep emphasizing that a service organization needs to identify and manage core skills and target solutions to drive up profitability. As a customer, this is the place to start when assessing if a service organization has what you are looking for. Therefore, if this is a solution scenario, you need to determine if the service organization can actually help you implement the solution. There are three basic questions you need to ask the service firm you are evaluating:

1. Have you implemented this solution before?
2. If yes, do you have references?
3. If no, do you at least have the skills or partners required to implement the solution now?

Based on the answers, you can quickly determine if engaging this firm is a high-risk, low-risk, or medium-risk proposition (see Figure A-1).

Now you can see why references become so key to the service organization. After working through the above questions, you hopefully can

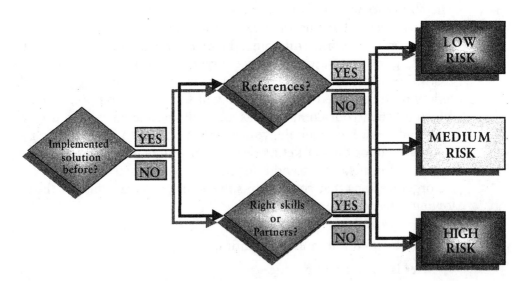

Figure A–1   Tier I Evaluation of a PS Firm.

focus on service organizations that are medium to low risk. High-risk firms should be engaged only if you are asking for a solution that nobody has ever delivered before.

▶ Tier II—Ability to Execute

After assessing how well the service firm's solutions and capabilities can address your current business problem, you need to assess the firm's actual ability to execute your contract. Here, you want to focus on the structural and human intellectual property the firm will bring to the project. In this step, you want to ask the following three questions:

1. Are you, as a matter of course, capturing and leveraging solution IP?

2. Are you developing your staff?

3. Do you follow some type of standard methodology when delivering projects?

As highlighted in Chapter 7: Productizing, Thomas A. Stewart has identified three types of intellectual property a company has and can manage: structural, human, and customer. You will need to assess how well the service firm courting you manages its solution IP. It's great that the firm has implemented the solution before and has several references. But what if those customers are halfway around the world and the lessons learned from those engagements remain with that team rather than being shared with those who will work on your account? Beyond that, does the firm have some type of engagement framework? Does it have access to previous project data? Does the firm know what problems other customers have hit? If the answer is *no* to any of these queries, you can assess that the service organization is not serious about managing IP. This makes all those great customer references almost meaningless. Once you get a *no* on IP management, you should determine if the service firm at least has some type of standard project life cycle methodology it follows. If not, you should be really concerned at this point. The firm has now become high risk in terms of its ability to deliver on time and on budget since it will be making it up as it goes.

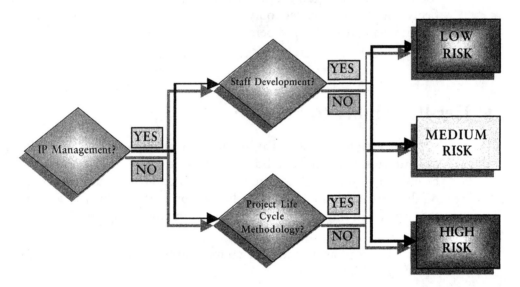

Figure A–2   Tier II Evaluation of a PS Firm.

If the firm does manage IP, you should be armed with a follow-up question concerning how the service firm manages its human capital. You are satisfied that the firm is capturing lessons learned, but if the firm cannot articulate how those lessons learned are disseminated to other staff, you should be concerned. How are technical staff trained and developed? If the answer is fuzzy, then how do you know the team assigned to your account will be well prepared? This is an issue of quality control.

Figure A-2 summarizes the process for assessing the service firm's ability to execute its job. At this point, you can focus on firms that present low to medium risk (i.e., they have a higher probability of actually delivering what they say they will deliver than not delivering).

▶ Tier III—Strategic Fit

Now we arrive at the final and most subtle level of assessment. In fact, for many small to medium projects, this level of assessment may not make sense. If a service firm successfully survives Tier I and Tier II assessment with a low-risk rating, you may be able to stop right there. But, if this is a very large project—something you are betting your career on or the future of the company on—you probably want to ask these final questions:

1. Is the solution I am requesting a target solution for your service organization?
2. Describe your current revenue streams to me.

With the first question you are trying to determine if this solution is strategic or simply opportunistic revenue for the service firm. If it is committed to taking this solution to market (i.e., offering the solution beyond your situation), it will be committed to making you successful and using you as a reference. You can probe this commitment by asking what promotion activities are planned for this solution area. The more cryptic the future plans, the more doubtful the commitment. The service firm may be reluctant to share its strategy here, but keep prying. You want its future success to depend on yours. If there is no discernable strategic intent with the solution, be concerned.

The second question is designed to help you assess what phase of maturity the service firm has reached. This is important when you consider what services you are asking its staff to perform. For example, if the service firm is squarely in the middle of providing implementation services (e.g., lots of pass-through revenue, not a great deal of internal capability), it may be unrealistic to ask for a complex integration or business-consulting project. The service firm will most likely resist questions that assess its overall business model, as it may have done with questions concerning strategic intent. However, never forget that you possess the ultimate trump card: the checkbook. If you are not comfortable with the answers around strategy and business, close the checkbook. It's better to stop now—before your futures are married—than to attempt a painful divorce later in the relationship.

Figure A-3 summarizes the flow of Tier III questioning. If a service vendor is deemed low risk after all three levels of assessment, you potentially have a solid partner with whom to conduct business. Of course, its staff will need to pass all the other technical, financial, and business requirements you will throw their way during the request for proposal (RFP) process, but at least you know you have lowered the risk of finding the wrong contractor.

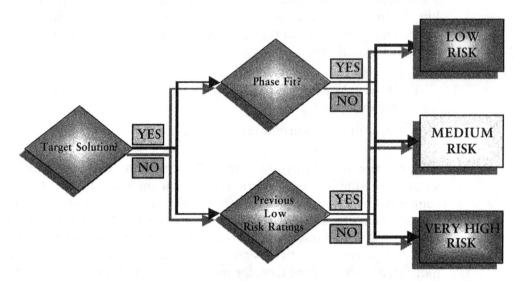

Figure A–3 Tier III Evaluation of a PS Firm.

Based on the answers, you can quickly determine if engaging this firm is a high-risk, low-risk, or medium-risk proposition (see Figure A-1).

Now you can see why references become so key to the service organization. After working through the above questions, you hopefully can focus on service organizations that are medium to low risk. High-risk firms should be engaged only if you are asking for a solution that nobody has ever delivered before.

Key Financial Models

Managing your business

When establishing the strategic direction of your organization it is important to build your overall business model around the appropriate financial model for your business environment. Not all professional service organizations (PSO) are the same and therefore cannot be expected to produce the same results. Table B-1 provides the financial model of a typical computer hardware manufacturing company as well as the financial models of three different types of professional service organizations including the model for a PSO within a product company.

Model for a Product Company—As you start to determine the appropriate financial model for your PSO, it is helpful to look also at your company's overall financial model. If your organization is part of a company that already has high gross margins, you will have to educate your senior managers about what is realistic for your PSO to deliver. Conversely, if your company is looking to have the PSO raise the company's margins, then you will want to set realistic expectations about that as well.

Model for PSO within a Product Company—PSOs that are part of a product company typically have lower margins and profitability compared to other PS firms. This is usually the result of the company's decision to take on less-profitable engagements in order to maintain

Table B–1 Financial Models.

	Financial Models				
		Product Companies w/ PS			
	Product Company	Industry Average	Industry Target	Management Consulting Firm	System Integration Firm
Revenue	100.0%	100.0%	100.0%	100.0%	100.0%
Gross Margin	42.5%	25.0%	30.0%	40.0%	45.0%
Operating Expenses					
R & D	10.0%	1.8%	2.0%	10.0%	10.0%
Sales	11.0%	8.9%	5.0%	5.0%	8.0%
Marketing	7.0%	1.4%	2.0%	5.0%	6.0%
General & Administration	7.0%	15.7%	8.0%	5.0%	13.5%
Total Operating Expenses	35.0%	27.8%	17.0%	25.0%	37.5%
Operating Profits	7.5%	-2.8%	13.0%	15.0%	7.5%

customer loyalty or to potentially increase its product sales. Table B-1 shows both the industry targets as well as the industry averages for a series of product companies that have PSO. As you can see, there is a rather large disparity between the target and the averages that companies are actually achieving. This is the result of the increased sales effort needed to sell PS and the high cost of getting a PSO started. It is also very useful to compare your own PSO results with the industry averages and targets to see where to focus your resources.

Model for Management Consulting Firm—Management consulting firms are those companies that specialize in pure consulting services with special emphasis on large-scale implementations like ERP systems. They generally take on higher margin engagements and are neutral regarding hardware choices, allowing them to provide a wide spectrum of services.

Model for System Integration Firm—System integration firms are those companies that specialize in providing the labor to perform certain engagements much like a job shop. They are labor intensive and often are less profitable as a result of a more erratic business cycle.

PS Business Review

Typically, most business units conduct some type of formal review process monthly, quarterly, or annually. This is what an outline might look like for the professional services business review.

▶ Timing

- Quarterly

▶ Attendees

- VP of Professional Services
- Services Financial Manager
- Regional Service Directors
- Director of Services Operations
- Director of Services Marketing
- Director of Services Engineering

▶ Agenda

Figure C-1 shows one possible agenda, including the topic, presenter, and timing.

Topic	Presenter	Time
DAY 1		
Welcome and Agenda Review	VP of Professional Services	30 Minutes
Financial Review	Finance Manager	60 Minutes
Region 1 Business Review	Region 1 Service Director	120 Minutes
Region 2 Business Review	Region 2 Service Director	120 Minutes
Region 3 Business Review	Region 3 Service Director	120 Minutes
DAY 2		
Services Marketing Review	Services Marketing Director	90 Minutes
Services Engineering Review	Services Engineering Director	90 Minutes
Operational Infrastructure Review	Director of Operations	90 Minutes
Guest Speaker: Product Marketing Update	Director of Product Marketing	60 Minutes
Critical Action Plan Review	VP of Professional Services	60–180 Minutes

Figure C–1   Agenda for PS business review.

▶ Sample Review Packages

A week before the quarterly review, each presenter should submit his or her quarterly review package to the group for review. This package should contain all the critical information and updates for that business area. In the actual meeting, each participant will present to the group a subset of information from his or her package. The assumption for the presentations should be that the audience is already familiar with the base information. The objective during the presentations should be to elaborate on key areas that warrant discussion, input, debate, and decisions. Tables C-1, C-2, C-3, and C-4 offer examples of review packages by a financial manager, a regional director, a marketing director, and an engineering director, respectively.

Quarterly Financial Review prepared by: Services Financial Manager

Table C–1 Quarterly Financial Review Package.

Section	Subsection	Description	What to Watch For
Revenue Trend	Total	Trend over the past X quarters of planned revenue for professional services vs. actual revenues recognized. Total services revenues = Direct revenues + Pass-through revenues + Solution revenues.	Revenue growth rate = target revenue growth rate.
	By Region	Revenue trend broken out by geographic areas.	
Bookings Trend	Total	Trend over the past X quarters of planned bookings for professional services vs. actual bookings recognized.	Bookings should be 1.5 times greater than revenue targets to meet next quarter revenue targets.
	By Region	Bookings trend broken out by geographic areas.	
Backlog Trend	Total	Backlog over the past X quarters for professional services.	
	By Region	Backlog trend broken out by geography.	Backlog entering a quarter should be 75% of that quarter's revenue target. Backlog trend should be increasing or holding steady.
Gross Margin Trend	Total	Gross margin for professional services business over the past X quarters.	Gross margin trend should be improving or holding steady.
	By Region	Gross margin trend broken out per geography.	

continued

Table C–1 Quarterly Financial Review Package. (cont.'d)

Section	Subsection	Description	What to Watch For
Average Deal-Size Trend	Total	Average revenue experiences per engagement broken out per quarter over the past X quarters.	Average deal size should be increasing or holding steady.
	By Region	Average revenue per deal broken out by geography.	
Product Pull-Through Trend	Total	Dollar value of company products that were sold as part of a professional services engagement.	Product pull-through revenue should be increasing or holding steady.
	By Region	Product pull-through broken out per geography.	

Quarterly Regional Review prepared by: Regional Services Director

Table C–2 Quarterly Regional Review Package.

Section	Subsection	Description	What to Watch For
BUSINESS METRICS			
Revenues, Gross Margin, SG&A (Sales and General Administration expenses)	Current quarter actuals	P&L statement for the region over the past quarter.	• Gross margins should be increasing or holding steady. • Operating profit at the regional level should be improving or holding steady.
	Next quarter projected	Project P&L for upcoming quarter.	
Head Count	Current quarter actuals	Broken down by functional area (sales, delivery, marketing, G&A).	Large increases in sales or delivery staff should correlate with increases in revenue commitments.
	Next quarter projected		
Revenue per Employee	Per quarter	Total service revenues from region divided by Total PS head count in region over the past X quarters.	Number should be increasing or holding steady.
SALES METRICS			
Bookings	Current quarter actual	Compare actual to target.	
	Next quarter projected	Compare projected to target for next quarter.	
Hit Ratio	Current quarter actual	Number of proposals made during the quarter and the number accepted.	Ratio should be increasing or holding steady.

continued

Table C–2 Quarterly Regional Review Package. (cont.'d)

Section	Subsection	Description	What to Watch For
Target Project Margins	Current quarter actual	Average project margins for projects actually completed over the past X quarters.	Actual project margins should be improving or holding steady.
	Next quarter projected	Average project margins for projects projected to be completed in the upcoming quarter.	Projected project margins should be improving or holding steady compared to past results.
Mix	Current quarter actual	Actual revenue mix over the past X quarters.	Improving mix (i.e., more direct and solution revenues).
	Next quarter projected	Projected revenue mix for the upcoming quarter.	

DELIVERY METRICS

Section	Subsection	Description	What to Watch For
Backlog	Current quarter actual	Backlog over the past X quarters for the region.	Backlog should be healthy. However, a dramatic increase in the backlog could be a warning sign that the delivery team is struggling to execute and collect revenues.
	Next quarter projected	Backlog going into the upcoming quarter.	Backlog should be 75% of the revenue target for the upcoming quarter.
Utilization	Current quarter actual	Actual billable utilization rates for the region over the past X quarters.	Region is achieving target utilization rates set in the business model. Rates are improving or holding steady.
	Next quarter projected	Projected billable utilization rate for the upcoming quarter.	

Table C–2 Quarterly Regional Review Package. (cont.'d)

Section	Subsection	Description	What to Watch For
Actual Project Margins	Current quarter actual	Actual average project margins experienced over the past X quarters.	
	Next quarter projected	Project margins for the projects that will be completed next quarter.	
ACCOUNT METRICS	Top five for revenue generating accounts	List of top five revenue-generating customers including revenue generated from each account over the past quarter.	
	Top five for profitability	List of top five accounts that generated the best project margins.	
	Recent wins	List of recent and significant wins.	
	New references	List of customers in the region willing to serve as references.	
Solutions and Capabilities	Revenues by solution	List of solutions sold last quarter and the revenues generated from those sales. Force ranked by revenues.	
	Revenues by capabilities	List of specific capabilities sold last quarter. Force ranked by revenues generated.	
Initiatives and Issues	Current quarter	List any business initiatives the regional team was working last quarter and how they were resolved.	Tangible progress on business objectives.
	Next quarter	List any business initiatives the regional team intends to work moving forward. Identify any issues impacting business.	Correct priorities and focus.

Quarterly Services Marketing Review prepared by:
Director of Services Marketing

Table C–3 Quarterly Services Marketing Review Package.

Section	Subsection	Description	What to Watch For
BUSINESS METRICS			
Budget Review	Quarterly actuals	Actual quarterly spending of the marketing department over the past X quarters.	Marketing spending should stay within business model (e.g., no more than 2% of total service revenues).
	Next quarter projected	Projected spending for upcoming quarter.	
SOLUTION METRICS			
Solution Bookings	Current quarter actual	Compare actual solution bookings to target solution bookings.	
	Next quarter projected	Compare projected bookings for next quarter to target for next quarter.	
Portfolio Revenue/ Maturity Revenue	Per solution	Summary of revenue mix for professional services over the past X quarters.	Improving mix. More revenue coming from target solutions being managed by Services Marketing.
Accounts	References and success stories	List of most important wins and references.	
Sales Training	Current quarter actual	List of sales training events conducted by Services Marketing.	
	Next quarter projected	List of planned events for the upcoming quarter.	

Table C–3 Quarterly Services Marketing Review Package. (cont.'d)

Section	Subsection	Description	What to Watch For
Initiatives and Issues	Current quarter	List any business initiatives the Services Marketing team was working last quarter and how they were resolved.	Tangible progress on business objectives.
	Next quarter	List any business initiatives the Services Marketing team intends to work moving forward. Identify any issues impacting business.	Correct priorities and focus.

Quarterly Services Engineering Review prepared by:
Director of Services Engineering

Table C–4   Quarterly Services Engineering Review Package.

Section	Subsection	Description	What to Watch For
BUSINESS METRICS			
Budget Review	Quarterly actuals	Actual quarterly spending of the engineering department over the past X quarters.	Engineering spending should stay within business model (e.g., no more than 2% of total service revenues).
	Next quarter projected		
SOLUTION METRICS			
Solution Maturity Ratings	Current quarter actual vs. targeted vs. next quarter	Graph showing how mature the IP for the current solution portfolio is.	
IP Capture	Actual vs. target	List of projects that were targeted to be reviewed and IP that was to be captured by Services Engineering.	
Delivery Training	Current quarter actual	List of delivery training events conducted by Services Marketing.	
	Next quarter projected	List of planned events for the upcoming quarter.	
Initiatives and Issues	Current quarter	List any business initiatives the Services Engineering team was working last quarter and how they were resolved.	Tangible progress on business objectives.
	Next quarter	List any business initiatives the Services Engineering team intends to work moving forward. Identify any issues impacting business.	Correct priorities and focus.

Sample Project Review

Project Review Executive Summary

▶ 1.0 Project Overview

We B Solutions primed the design and implementation of Our-Partner 3.2 for Key-Customer. This was We B Solutions' first full-scale implementation of Our-Partner and Our-Partner's second implementation of Our-Partner 3.2 software anywhere in the world.

The original customer requirements were captured during a three-week interview engagement in July 2000, which was conducted by We B Solutions corporate PS division. At that time, We B Solutions advised Key-Customer to start implementation as soon as possible, specifically no later than September 2000 in order to complete the transition and have ample time for tuning prior to the holiday rush (i.e., increased order sizes and volume). Key-Customer delayed but finally made its decision and the second PS portion of the engagement (system design) started in October 2000. System implementation started 15 October 2000, which placed We B Solutions in a challenging position to complete the system transition from the current application environment to the Our-Partner environment prior to 15 December 2000, the beginning of Key-Customer's internal system brownout period and start of the holiday rush.

▶ 2.0 Project Team

Every project review should include a roster of staff and their roles in the project (see Table D-1).

Table D–1 Project Team.

Role	Person	Company/Department
Global Account Manager	Tim Smith	We B Solutions, Field Sales
Services Sales Rep	Brad Kite	We B Solutions, Professional Services, Americas
Solution Architect	Johnny Knogh	We B Solutions, Professional Services, Services Engineering
Project Manager	Jill Jenkins	We B Solutions, Professional Services, Americas
Technical Consultant	Sue Simpkins	We B Solutions, Professional Services, Americas
Account Manager	Kim Keops	Our-Partner, Field Sales, Americas
Technical Consultant	Matt Monough	Our-Partner, Professional Services, Americas

▶ 3.0 Project Statistics

Project statistics for the design and implementation phases should be presented separately to facilitate interpretation. The statistics for the design phase are shown in Table D-2. The graph in Figure D-1 more clearly illustrates the differences between planned and actual deliverables mentioned in Table D-2.

▶ 3.1 Phase I: Detailed Design

Table D–2   Phase I: Detailed Design Statistics.

Planned Deliverables	• Design of Our-Partner System (technical architecture diagram and overview)
	• Analysis Reports
	  Service Level Analysis
	  User Profile Analysis
	  Risk Analysis
	  Capacity Analysis
	• Detailed Functional Requirements
	• Site Survey
	• Project Plan for Implementation
	• Project Reporting
		Actual Deliverables	• Design of Our-Partner System (technical architecture diagram and overview)
			• Analysis Reports
			  Service Level Analysis
			  User Profile Analysis
			• Detailed Functional Requirements
			• Site Survey
			• Project Plan for Implementation
			• Project Reporting
			  (Detailed project Web site)

Estimated Schedule	12 August–4 September 2000	Actual Schedule	12 October–11 November 2000 (system design review delayed one week due to customer availability)
Estimated Effort	320	Actual Effort	516
Estimated Expenses	$25,000	Actual Expenses	$27,000
Estimated Revenue	$80,000	Actual Revenue	$78,000

Key Customer Phase I

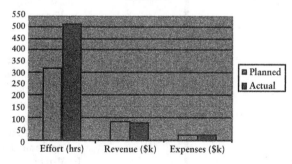

Figure D–1   Planned versus actual in the design stage.

The statistics for the implementation phase are shown in Table D-3. The graph in Figure D-2 more clearly illustrates the differences between planned and actual deliverables mentioned in Table D-3.

▶ 3.2 Phase II: Interpretation

Table D–3   Phase II: Implementation Statistics.

Planned Deliverables	Actual Deliverables
• Gantt Chart • Project Plan Document • Provisioning Interface Code • System Reports • Implement Hardware • Our-Partner 3.2 Installation • Interface Implementation • System Administration Implementation Modified Reporting Scripts Modified System Monitoring Scripts • System Testing • Operational Readiness Review • Migration of Existing Post Office Accounts • System Turnover	• Gantt Chart *(Detailed project Web site: Architecture, Project Plan, Meeting Minutes, Action List, Issues List, Decisions List, Presentations, Project Documentation, Change Control Process, Management Summary Schedule)* • Project Plan Document • Provisioning Interface Code • Additional Functionality: Store/Forward List Mgmt Automated Tape Change Log Rolling Journal Duplication • Documentation: Risk Analysis (from Phase I) Capacity Analysis (from Phase I) Provisioning Specification Rewrite Operational Recovery Procedures • System Reports Volume Reports Log Summary • Implement Hardware • Our-Partner 3.2 Installation

Table D–3 Phase II: Implementation Statistics. (cont.'d)

Planned Deliverables		Actual Deliverables	• Interface Implementation • System Administration Implementation Modified Reporting Scripts Modified System Monitoring Scripts • System Testing • Operational Readiness Review • Migration of Existing Accounts • System Turnover
Estimated Schedule	14 September–8 December 98	Actual Schedule	21 November–18 December 98
Estimated Effort	742	Actual Effort	1550
Estimated Expense	$85,000	Actual Expenses	$42,082
Estimated Revenue	$220,000	Actual Revenue	$262,917

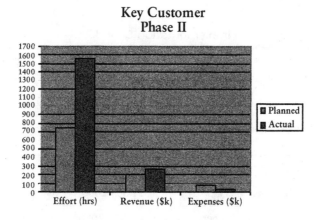

**Key Customer
Phase II**

Figure D–2 Planned versus actual in the implementation stage.

3.2 Phase II: Interpretation

325

▶ 3.3 Project Statistics Interpretation

This was a challenging project for the PS team, both from a technical and managerial perspective. For the Americas sales region, it was a make-or-break project in regard to future business with Key-Customer. The original schedule was aggressive, and the available slack was quickly depleted due to customer documentation delays, hardware delays, customer requirement changes, migration errors, and Our-Partner 3.2 bugs. This was also the first engagement by Corporate Professional Services using the newly created delivery methodology. Deficient areas of the methodology also accounted for an increase in the overall project hours.

Phase I, System Design, began with a revalidation of the functional requirements documented way back in March 2000. It was agreed that We B Solutions would identify and implement Key-Customer's business-continuance requirements only, due to the project's delayed start. Phase II, Implementation, satisfied the business-continuance requirements, provided additional documentation, and provided customer's additional functional requirements not originally documented in the Detailed Functional Requirements Report from Phase I. Phase II started at risk for failure on 21 September 2000; Key-Customer signed the Project Plan (i.e., the proposal) on 13 October 2000. The required project end date remained 8 December 2000.

Table D-4 identifies the major schedule impacts that occurred during Phase II, Implementation.

Table D-4   Impacts on Implementation Schedule.

Reference	Requested	Provided / Occurred
Provisioning specification (from Key-Customer)	21 Sep 2000	16 Oct 2000
Rewrite of the provisioning specification (We B Solutions)		28 Oct 2000
Reporting scripts (from Key-Customer)	21 Sep 2000	14 Oct 2000
Monitoring scripts (from Key-Customer)	21 Sep 2000	15 Oct 2000
Hardware decision/purchase (Key-Customer)	27 Aug 2000	3 Sep 2000
Second server purchase	27 Aug 2000	22 Oct 2000

Table D–4 Impacts on Implementation Schedule. (cont.'d)

Reference	Requested	Provided / Occurred
Change request PII002, shuffle disk capacity (hardware reconfiguration and root file system rebuild)	2 Nov 2000	9 Nov 2000
Key-Customer's backup strategy (increase in We B Solutions staff hours)	16 Sep 2000	9 Nov 2000
Installation of the tape drive		16 Nov 2000
Hardware relocation followed by hardware failure	15 Nov 2000	17 Nov 2000 [mig: 20 Nov 2000]
Hardware relocation (prior to customer account migration); hardware failure occurred after the move	23 Nov 2000	25 Nov 2000 [mig: 27 Nov 2000]
Change request PII004, list management	4 Dec 2000	6 Dec 2000
Key-Customer's continuing configuration changes	------	------
Post migration issue resolution (increase in We B Solutions man hours)	------	29 Nov – 17 Dec 2000

The hardware relocations on 15 and 20 November 2000, respectively, substantially increased the risk of project completion. We B Solutions documented this risk to the customer, and the customer chose to accept the risk. Had the hardware failures after each relocation not been resolved quickly, the implementation phase could have abruptly ended, with We B Solutions scrambling to ensure Key-Customer's current environment could survive and support the holiday rush (i.e., it would have been in We B Solutions' best interest to save the customer relationship). In hindsight, the current environment system could *not* have handled the approximate 21GB per day during the mid-December period.

Our-Partners' bid included two on-site engineers; however, only one engineer was on site during the entire project. Although the customer account migration occurred as originally scheduled (27 November 2000) and the system was operational, migration errors and Our-Partner 3.2 bugs slipped the project end date from 8 December 2000 to 18 December 2000. On 2 December 2000, We B Solutions started a prolonged round of requests for a second Our-Partners' on-site engineer; the engineer arrived 11 December 2000. Our-Partners agreed to provide on-site operational transitional training to Key-Customer's operational staff during the period 14–18 December 2000, which established 18 December 2000 as the date for final project acceptance.

Additional tasks completed by We B Solutions were Our-Partners' responsibility:

- Migration planning
- Migration verification
- Accounts
- Domains
- Aliases
- Migration repair
- Missing aliases (1200)
- Missing accounts (240+)
- Accounts with incorrect settings
- Wildcard forwards configured as aliases named
- Store-and-forward customers configured as wildcard
- Wildcard customers configured as store-and-forward

This was the first large engagement by the PS unit in the Americas, and it was critical to achieve success and receive a positive referral to ensure future business in that market. The priorities were on success, schedule, scope, and cost, in that order. Based on the success of this project, Americas Professional Services is discussing Phase III requirements with Key-Customer.

The project's main focus was to provide the features and capabilities that were critical for Key-Customer to continue offering services on a scalable architecture and ensure Key-Customer could support its customer base during the upcoming holiday rush. That goal was achieved. Key-Customer praised We B Solutions PS unit and was very pleased with the services provided. In the words of Mr. Kay, Key-Customer, "This project has been the most successful IT project I have been involved in at Key-Customer. If we can succeed at a complex project like this, then the smaller ones should be easy." Key-Customer did feel, however, that Our-Partners misrepresented their product to make the sale, which has caused operational impacts requiring adjustments to Key-Customer's IT operations group.

▶ 4.0 Repeatable Components

The repeatable components that can be offered as products in the future are as follows:

- High-availability failsafe integration with Our-Partner 3.2
- Operational-recovery procedures

Also, the delivery methodology will be updated based on the experiences of this project. The failsafe and operational-recovery procedures information is being managed by Bobby Smith, and the methodology update is being managed by Scott Wilkens, both in Services Engineering.

▶ 5.0 Conclusions

The main goal of this project was to transition Key-Customer from its current environment to Our-Partner 3.2 to meet its critical business requirements prior to 15 December 2000. We met and exceeded that goal and now have a very pleased customer whose excellent referrals will help increase We B Solutions' credibility in the marketplace. It will be important in future projects to make sure all of the project stakeholders are in agreement about the services to be provided, all prices for the services are sufficient to increase project profitability, and all penalties are written into subcontractor contracts. See Figures D-3 and D-4 for specific elements of the project and to note where and by how much actual effort varied from estimated effort. This was a very successful project based on the desired outcome of ensuring the customer's success, ensuring future business between Americas PS and Key-Customer, and further developing We B Solutions' reputation in the Our-Partner solution market.

Key-Customer Phase I

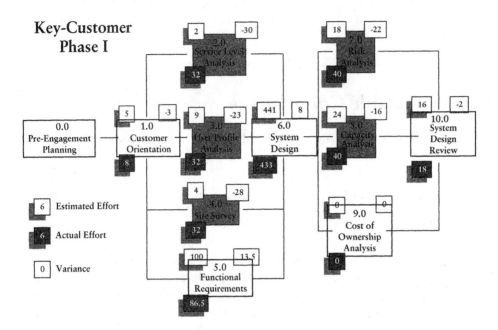

Figure D–3   Key-Customer phase I effort variance.

Key-Customer Phase II

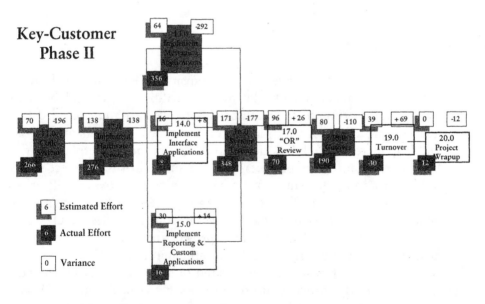

Figure D–4   Key-Customer phase II effort variance.

Solution Portfolio Management

This is when the MBA in each of us comes out. There is no way two business school graduates and a lawyer can collaborate on a book without creating at least one stellar McKinsey-like two-by-two chart. Appendix E contains the evidence of this indulgence.

▶ Solution Portfolio Graph

Throughout the text, we have emphasized the importance of revenue, references, and repeatability to the long-term success of the PS business unit. We have also contended that a set of core, target solutions should be the focal point for identifying high-margin revenue, collecting critical customer references, and creating repeatable, consistent execution. In this appendix, we will review how the service unit can assess and manage this target solution portfolio.

For each solution a PS team decides to target, there are three critical variables that must be managed.

Solution Revenue

For each solution, the company must list current and projected revenue streams it will enjoy from the solution (see Table E-1). This analysis should be inclusive of all revenue streams the company receives from implementing a solution (i.e., product revenue, support services revenue, and professional services revenue).

Table E–1   Solution Revenue Table.

FY 1 Solution Revenues	Solution ABC	Solution XYZ	Solution 123	TOTAL Component Revenue
Professional Services Revenue	$20,000,000	$12,000,000	$8,000,000	$40,000,000
Support Services Revenue	$3,000,000	$9,000,000	$2,400,000	$14,400,000
Product Revenue	$10,000,000	$30,000,000	$8,000,000	$48,000,000
TOTAL Company Revenue	$33,000,000	$51,000,000	$18,400,000	$102,400,000

Solution Maturity

Maturity sounds like a very subjective term, but it can be assessed in a very objective manner. In Chapter 7: Productizing, we itemized 23 go-to-market components of a solution. A simplistic yet effective technique to assess solution maturity is to checkmark these 23 components for each target solution as demonstrated in Figure E-1. Does the component exist or not? If *yes*, place the number 1 next to it. If *no*, place a 0 there. For each solution, you can review the percentage of the 23 components that exists for that solution. If you want to get sophisticated, you can begin to weight the components. For now, let's keep it simple by treating all the components as if they were equally important to taking the solution market.

Solution Name	Solution ABC	Solution XYZ	Solution 123
Executive Overview*	1	1	1
Customer Presentation*	1	1	1
Datasheets*	1	1	1
Whitepapers	1	0	0
Demos	0	0	1
Sales Tips	1	0	0
Customer References*	1	1	1
Competitive Analysis*	1	0	1
Target Customer List/Profile	1	1	0
Partner Profiles*	1	0	0
Resource Profiles*	1	1	1
Engagement Framework*	1	1	1
Engagement Activity Forms*	1	0	0
Software source code (as req'd)	1	0	0
SOW*	1	1	0
Proposal*	1	1	0
Project Plan*	1	1	0
Sample Architecture*	1	1	0
Sales Training Materials*	1	0	0
Delivery Resource Training Materials*	1	0	0
Sample Customer Support Agreement*	1	0	0
Support Staff Training*	0	0	0
Total %	91%	50%	36%
*—Required Component			

Figure E–1 Solution Maturity Table.

Solution Margin

What is the profit margin on each target solution? This is important if you want to delineate the cash cows from the falling stars.

Putting all three variables together, you can flow the information into a table for ease of comparison (see Table E-2).

Table E–2   Solution Evaluation Data.

Variable	Variable Description	Solution ABC	Solution XYZ	Solution 123
X	Maturity	91%	50%	36%
Y	FY Revenues	$33,000,000	$51,00,000	$18,400,888
Size	Margin	45	30	25

Figure E-2 is a derivative of the information from Table E-2. We refer to the graph in Figure E-2 as a solution map or an S-map.

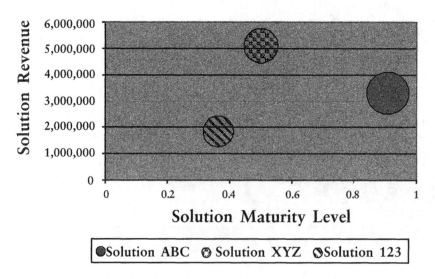

Figure E–2   S-map.

This graph communicates several key points in one crisp picture. First, it demonstrates your highest revenue-generating solution (i.e., the solution that is highest on the graph, in this case Solution XYZ). It also illustrates which solution is most mature (i.e., the solution that is farthest to the right, in this case solution ABC). And, the size of the bubble helps you zero in on the solution that is most profitable for your company (in this case solution ABC). This graph also provides a roadmap of where you want to go, that is, by clearly illustrating the maturity, revenue, and margin for specific projects, it allows you to project where your efforts might improve each variable.

If you were reviewing solution efforts, you would view the following four distinct quadrants as shown in Figure E-3:

> **Continue** (top-right quadrant): Solutions that land here are very mature solutions with high revenues. They should maintain high margins as well.
>
> **Improve or Remove** (lower-left quadrant): Solutions that land here are currently not in good health. They suffer from low revenues and low maturity. Most likely they have low margins as well. Solutions here should face one of two fates: Either they improve their performance or they are removed from the portfolio and the company stops throwing good money after bad.
>
> **Maturity Review** (top-left quadrant): Solutions in this quadrant have high company revenues. However, typically there is very little intellectual property documentation regarding this solution. This makes consistent delivery an issue. Low maturity also jeopardizes any ability to defend the solution and derive the highest possible margins from it. Solutions here should be analyzed to determine what efforts would be required to improve the maturity rating.
>
> **Revenue Review** (lower-right quadrant): And finally, the falling stars. Solutions landing here typically represent past cash cows that are now facing declining revenue streams. Hopefully, margins are still high. When margins begin to decline below acceptable levels, these solutions should be discontinued.

By taking this specific snapshot of your solution portfolio on a periodic basis (e.g., quarterly is ideal), you can assess the health and growth in your target solutions. The clear objective is to move solutions up and to the right as quickly as possible. If solutions are not migrating in a

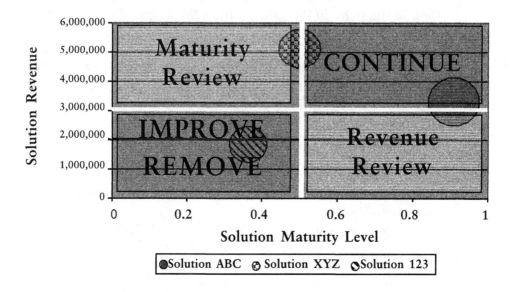

Figure E–3   Solution quadrants.

positive direction, they are clearly suspect. The sooner continuously poor-performing solutions are removed, the healthier your business will remain.

▶ Portfolio Ownership

So, who owns this information and makes sure the portfolio improves quarter to quarter? If we look back to the functional structure we presented in Chapter 4, there are two groups that need to be intimately involved in and responsible for managing the solution portfolio.

Services Marketing

Services Marketing has primary ownership of portfolio revenues. In other words, Services Marketing must be responsible for driving target

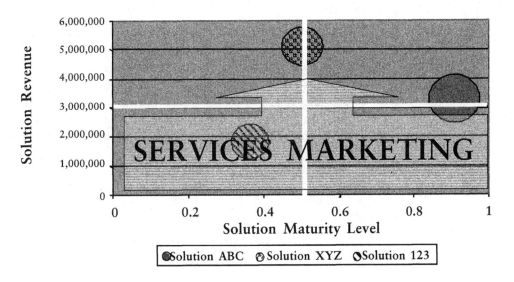

PS Solution Portfolio

(chart axes) Solution Revenue (y-axis: 0, 1,000,000, 2,000,000, 3,000,000, 4,000,000, 5,000,000, 6,000,000) vs Solution Maturity Level (x-axis: 0, 0.2, 0.4, 0.6, 0.8, 1)

SERVICES MARKETING

● Solution ABC ⊘ Solution XYZ ◑ Solution 123

Figure E–4 Services Marketing and the S-map.

solutions into the customer base and acquiring as much revenue as possible. Referring back to Figure E-2, Services Marketing should be looked upon to drive solutions from the bottom to the top as shown in Figure E-4.

If solutions are not seeing momentum in the market place, Services Marketing must be held responsible. This group and the local delivery teams that bid the deals hold joint responsibility for solution margins. Solution margins have a price component and a cost component. Possessing differentiated solutions that command top dollar is the responsibility of Services Marketing. The marketing team and the local delivery team own the price component of margin.

Services Engineering

Services Engineering has primary responsibility for portfolio maturity. Compiling solution IP is the primary charter of this group. Making sure each of the 23 solution components are captured and available is why Services Engineering exists in the first place. Even for the sales-oriented solution components, such as datasheets, Services Engineering should be the taskmaster that owns the successful accumulation of this valuable information.

Services Engineering and Services Marketing have joint responsibility for solution margins. Services Engineering owns the price component of solution margins. Assuring field-delivery organizations are adequately trained and equipped to successfully deliver solutions is within the charter of Services Engineering. By meeting this responsibility, Services Engineering can help keep implementation costs and risks to a minimum, thus improving solution margins. In summary, Services Engineering is responsible for moving solutions from left to right on the solution portfolio graph as shown in Figure E-5.

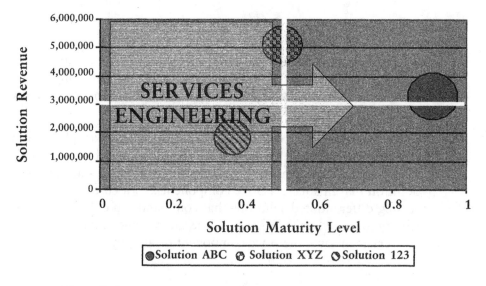

Figure E–5 Services Engineering and the S-map.

Customer Request and Qualification Form

As described in Chapter 5: Selling, a key responsibility of the Services Sales function is to effectively qualify opportunities it has located. This appendix contains a sample form that can be used by Services Sales reps and delivery staff to qualify a customer request.

▶ Request and Qualification Form

Table F–1 Customer Contact Information.

Customer Name	Phone Number
Company Name	Fax Number
Street Address	Email
City	
State	
Zip	
Product Sales Rep	Services Sales Rep
Date Request Submitted	Date Submitter Contacted

Table F–2   Customer Request Information.

Services Being Requested	Implementation Service 123
	Integration Service 456
	General Consulting Services
	Solution ABC
	Solution XYZ
Skills Being Requested	Project Manager
	Technical Skill ABC
	Technical Skill XYZ
	Solution Skill ABC

▶ Customer Qualification Information

For each criterion, place a check mark in the one of the three boxes that best defines the situation. Transfer the rating for that criterion into the rating column. Total the rating column; the higher the total, the more qualified the customer.

Table F–3   Customer Qualification Information.

Criterion	Description			Rating
	GREEN Rating: 3	**YELLOW** Rating: 2	**RED** Rating: 1	
Budget	Customer has proved they have funding for services.	Customer is currently actively seeking funding for services.	Customer has not initiated the funding process.	
Response-Time Requirement	Deadlines for presentations, estimates, and proposals permit standard process to be followed (> 3 weeks).	Deadlines are less than 3 weeks but more than 1 week.	Customer is looking for qualified responses within the next 2 business days.	

Table F–3 Customer Qualification Information. (cont.'d)

Criterion	Description			Rating
	GREEN Rating: 3	**YELLOW** Rating: 2	**RED** Rating: 1	
Project Start Requirement	Start date is open and negotiable.	Start date has been set but can be accommodated.	Current proposed start date couldn't be accommodated.	
Decision Process	Decision-making process being followed by the customer is well understood, documented, and unbiased.	Decision-making process is not clearly understood or is potentially biased.	The decision-making process is biased against our service offerings.	
Decision Maker	Final decision maker is identified. Account team is in contact with this person.	Decision maker identified but no direct contact.	Decision maker not even identified.	
Solution Fit	Customer request closely fits a current solution offering.	Customer request loosely fits a current solution offering.	Customer request does not match any existing solution offerings.	
Skills Fit	Customer request requires skills currently on staff and available.	Customer request requires skills in development or scheduled to be available.	Customer request does not fit current or future capabilities.	
Partner Fit	Have identified all required partners to fulfill customer request. Have partnership agreements in place.	Have identified required partners but do not have agreements in place.	Partners required but it is unclear which ones will be used.	
TOTALS				

Glossary of Terms

Term	Definition	Measurement
Account Expansion	The ability of a vendor to expand its account penetration and its volume of business within existing accounts.	
Advertising Costs	The amount of dollars spent on advertising campaigns including print, radio, TV, and other mediums.	Advertising costs divided by Total service revenue
Alliances/Partnering Costs	The amount of dollars spent on alliance and partner programs.	Alliance and partnering costs divided by Total service revenue
Backlog	The total value of contract commitments yet to be executed.	Total backlog = Previous fiscal year's commitments + Latest fiscal year's sales − Latest fiscal year's revenue
Bid and Proposal Cost	Total dollars spent on submitting a bid, including dollars spent on bid qualification, financial analysis, alliance and partner selection, feasibility analysis, proposal development, proposal submittal, and best and final offer (BAFO).	Total cost for submitting bids divided by Total contract value of bids submitted

continued

343

Term	Definition	Measurement
Cash Flow	The amount of cash generated (or absorbed, if negative) by the organization.	Cash flow from operations divided by Total service revenue
Consultant and Media Relations Costs	The amount spent on external outreach to the press, market research firms, the investment community, consultants, and other market influences.	Consultant and media relations costs divided by Total service revenue
Cost of Services Delivered	The fully loaded direct and indirect costs of billable services. Includes the expenses of any managers that are more than 50% billable (Costs of services delivered = Delivery labor costs + Delivery overhead costs).	Cost of services delivered divided by Total service revenue
Delivery Labor Costs	The direct costs of billable services. Includes the labor costs of any managers that are more than 50% billable.	Delivery labor costs divided by Total service revenue
Delivery Overhead Costs	The fully loaded indirect costs of billable services. Includes the related expenses of any managers that are more than 50% billable (Delivery overhead costs = Fringe benefits + Travel + Delivery-unit management costs + All other related costs with full-time consultants, hourly employees, or independents).	Delivery overhead costs divided by Total services revenue
Delivery Tools	The amount of R&D investment in delivery tools (Delivery tools = Automated methodology tools + Project management + Online skills inventory/resource + Time scheduler + Automated labor voucher + Real-time conferencing + Workgroup sharing + Knowledge database + Library of standard customer forms and deliverables).	Delivery tools divided by Total service revenue
General and Administrative Expenses (G&A)	The general expenses not captured in COS, sales, marketing, or R&D (G&A expenses = Total training costs + Management costs + Other administrative costs).	G&A expenses divided by Total service revenue

Term	Definition	Measurement
Gross Margin (%)	The gross profit generated per dollar of service delivered (Gross margin = Total service revenue – Cost of services delivered)	Gross margin dollars divided by Total service revenue
Hit Ratio	The competitive success rate of the company in the markets it chooses to compete.	Revenue from proposals won divided by Possible revenue from proposals submitted
Infrastructure	The amount of investment in the infrastructure for R&D (Infrastructure costs = Dollars spent for demos and research centers + Dollars spent for internal training centers + Dollars spent for information administrative systems investment and expert centers).	Infrastructure costs divided by Total service revenue
Interest Expense	The difference between operating profit and net income before tax	Interest expense divided by Total service revenue
IT Costs	The total costs for information technology [IT costs = Hardware equipment + Software expenses + Internal service (i.e., MIS personnel) + External services (i.e., costs of third-party service providers)].	IT costs divided by Total service revenue
Labor Multiplier	The average factor by which billable personnel can be charged over and above their fully loaded costs (Fully loaded costs = Direct salary + Direct fringe benefits + Overhead + G&A + Margin). A labor multiplier of 1.0 indicates a breakeven point.	Total dollar amount of personnel hours billed divided by Fully loaded labor cost
Management Costs	Total costs for full-time executive, middle, branch, and technical management personnel that are billable for less than 50% of their time. Does not include marketing management, sales management, or R&D management. Management costs = Management salaries + Management benefits + Management expenses .	Management costs divided by Total service revenue

continued

Term	Definition	Measurement
Market Research Costs	The investment made by the company in market research.	Market research costs divided by Total service revenue
Marketing Costs	The investment made by the company in marketing (Marketing costs = Advertising costs + Seminars and collateral material + Consultant and media relations + Alliance and partnering costs + Market research).	Marketing costs divided by Total service revenue
Net Income Before Tax (NIBT)	The net income generated before tax (NIBT= Operating profit – Interest expense).	Net income before tax divided by Total service revenue
New Client Ratio	Measures a vendor's ability to win new accounts and develop new business (New client ratio = New clients divided by Total clients).	Total dollar value of new client accounts divided by Total dollar value of all client accounts
Operating Profit	The profit generated by operations, also known as operating margin (Operating profit = Total service revenue – COS – Total operating expenses).	Operating profit divided by Total service revenue
Other Administrative Costs	General overhead expenses not captured in management costs or training costs, including expenses relating to overhead, corporate allocations or tariffs, facilities, human resources, accounting/finance, recruiting, training, clerical, administrative, support utilities, etc. (Other administrative costs = Total expenses – COS – Management costs – Training costs – Sales costs – Marketing costs – R&D costs).	Other administrative costs divided by Total service revenue
Project Completion Ratio	Measure the degree of completion against project milestones.	Number of milestones accomplished on schedule divided by Total milestones targeted

Term	Definition	Measurement
Project Overruns	The accuracy with which project costs are forecasted.	Total project costs incurred divided by Total estimated project costs
Rate Realization	The amount of revenue actually earned as a percentage of potential revenue represented by list prices.	Earned revenue (or dollars achieved for billable professionals) divided by Revenue at list (or undiscounted list price divided by fees of work effort from earned revenue)
Research and Development Costs	Degree of investment made to enhance the firm's tools, products, and methodologies (Total R&D costs = Infrastructure + Sales tools + Delivery tools).	R&D costs divided by Total service revenue
Return on Assets	Measures the productivity of assets.	Operating income divided by Average investment in assets
Revenue Growth	Measures total service revenue growth from one year to the next.	Most recent fiscal year end revenue earning divided by Previous FYE's earning
Revenue per Head	The average revenue generated per full-time employee. If subcontractors or third parties are counted in revenue, then include their expense.	Total service revenue divided by Total full-time employees
Sales Costs	The total costs for the selling efforts of each line of business. Total sales costs include salaries, expense accounts, and commissions for sales management, sales people, and sales support.	Total sales costs divided by Total service revenue
Sales Personnel Categories	Categorizes the different types of full-time sales personnel into three broad labor classifications.	Total sales employees = Number of sales people + Number of sales management + Number of sales support

continued

Term	Definition	Measurement
Sales Tools	The amount of R&D investment in sales tools (Sales tools = Product and service information retrieval + Proposal systems + Sales and funnel tracking + Online success stories).	Sales tools divided by Total service revenue
Sales Yield	The sales productivity of the company. (Target values or sales quota versus actuals are encouraged.)	Sales dollar value divided by Number of direct or full-time equivalent sales people
Seminars and Collateral Material Costs	The amount of dollars spent on prospect and/or client seminars and marketing collateral (e.g., brochures).	Seminars and collateral costs divided by Total service revenue
Total Full-Time Employees	The labor classification of full-time personnel. Subcontractors should be included in full-time equivalent (FTE) calculations if they are included in revenue calculations.	Total full-time equivalents = Principals, partners, practice leaders + Professionals + Administrative and clerical
Total Operating Expenses	The sum of all nondelivery operating expenses (Total operating expenses = G&A costs + Sales costs + Marketing costs + R&D costs).	Total operating expenses divided by Total service revenue
Total Services Revenue	Measurement of the different types of revenue; should be listed separately by consulting, solutions, and third-party pass-through.	Consulting: engagement-driven, paper deliverables; Solutions: project driven, solution deliverables; third-party pass-through: Product and service provided by outside vendor
Training Costs	The total cost of training. Training expenses include curriculum design and development, instruction costs, and facilities costs.	Training expenses divided by Total service revenue
Training Days	Average number of working days spent in training.	Number of employee working days spent training divided by Total number of employee working days

Term	Definition	Measurement
Turnover Rate	A measure of attrition. An example of a former employee is a person who was on the personnel roster at the start of the previous fiscal year and was no longer on the personnel roster at the start of the current year.	Number of former employees (annualized) divided by Total number of employees (annualized)
Utilization Rate	Measures the organization's ability to maximize its billable resources.	Total number of hours billed divided by Number of working hours in a year (varies by geography) × Number of billable employees
Walk Ratio	Measures the effectiveness of the bid qualification process.	Number of qualified opportunities that are not bid divided by Number of qualified opportunities examined

Selected Bibliography

"Between the Lines," Macuser, July 1997. The cache version can be viewed at *www.macuser.com/online/casanova.html.*

Davis, Kevin, *Getting into Your Customer's Head,* New York: Random House, 1996.

Homer, *The Odyssey, Translated by W. H. D. Rouse,* New York: New American Library, 1937.

Kaplan, Robert S., and Norton, David P., *The Balanced Scorecard,* Cambridge, MA: Harvard Business School Press, 1996.

Labovitz, George, and Rosansky, Victor, *The Power of Alignment,* New York: John Wiley & Sons, 1997.

Lissack, Michael, and Roos, Johan, *The Next Common Sense,* London: Nicholas Brealey Publishing, 1999.

Maister, David H., *Managing the Professional Service Firm,* New York: Simon and Schuster, 1993.

Moore, Geoffrey, *Inside the Tornado,* New York: HarperBusiness, 1995.

——*Living on the Fault Line,* New York: HarperBusiness, 2000.

Radtke, Janel, "Strategic Communications for Nonprofit Organizations: Seven Steps to Creating a Successful Plan," *The Grantsmanship Center Magazine,* Fall 1998.

Stewart, Thomas, *Intellectual Capital,* New York: Doubleday, 1997.

Index

Services Delivery execution and, 97
sign-off step, 227–228
solution development, 224–226
solution implementation, 226–227
customer presentation, Services Marketing campaign
overview, 151
customer references, Services Marketing campaign
overview, 152
customer request and qualification form, 341–343
customer satisfaction, metrics (reports), 177
Customer Service, O-Map, 55

D

databases, knowledge management, 182
delivery. *See* Services Delivery
professional services functional map, 52
support, Services Engineering, 131
delivery IP, capturing, 122
delivery labor costs, 346
delivery overhead costs, 346
delivery tools, 346
demos, solution review (Services
Marketing), 153–154
design issues
engagement framework documents, 126
infrastructure, 169–171
Services Delivery execution, 95
differentiating characteristics, 22
PS, 22
Services Marketing, 148–150
direct revenue, 40–41
director of business development responsibilities,
75–76
discipline, Services Delivery and, 91
documents
backlog reports, 173
billings reports, 173
bookings reports, 173
engagement activity forms, 127–128
engagement framework, 125–128
financial reports, 175
funnel reports, 172–173
internal distribution lists, 174
partner profiles, 128–129
resource profiles, 128

E

education, 3
characteristics, 5
internal, management responsibilities, 284–285
Services Delivery, 98
electronic newsletters, 174
EMC Global Services
financial performance, 263
service strategies, 261–264
employee compensation. *See* compensation

employee satisfaction metrics (reports), 177
engagement activity forms, 127–128
engagement framework documents, 125–128
engagement life cycle, 53–54
customer workflow
overview, 216–218
request step, 218–219
Services Delivery and, 89
Services Sales, 65–66, 205
negotiation, 72
opportunities, identifying, 67–69
opportunities, qualifying, 69–71
proposals, 71
estimates, Services Delivery, 92–93
evangelizing, Services Marketing, 154–155
execution, Services Delivery, 93
design and development, 95
follow-on, 97
implementation, 95–96
project plan, 94
requirements, 93–94
review, 96–97
sign-off, 96
executive dashboards, 175
executive overview, Services Marketing campaign
overview, 151
expertise, qualifying sales opportunities, 70
external interfaces, 196–197
external mission statements, 25

F

fee-based expertise as core competency, 22
field staff, corporate staff interface,
197–199
financial models, 307
management consulting firm,
308–309
product company, 307
PSO within a product company,
307–308
system integration firm, 309
financial objectives, 29
financial performance
during building phases, 251
summary, 293–294
product technology companies, 263
financial reports, 175
focus, building phases and, 233
consulting services, 241–242
implementation services, 235
integration services, 238–239
productized services, 244–245
follow-on, Services Delivery execution, 97
forecasting demand, Services Sales, 72–74
four qualifying questions summary, 289
funding, qualifying sales opportunities, 70
funnel reports, 74, 172–173

lighthouse accounts, Services Marketing, 156–157
Lissack, Michael, guiding principles and, 30–31

M

Maister, David, mission statements, 24
managed services, 3
    characteristics, 5
management
    costs, 347
    internal education responsibilities, 284–285
    positioning, 264–265
    professional services startup issues, 15
management consulting firms, financial model, 308–309
Managing the Professional Services Firm mission statements, 24
market analysis
    billable rate and, 107
    marketplace landscape, 256–264
market for services, 22
market research costs, 348
marketing. *See also* Services Marketing
    costs, 348
maturity time line, building PS phases, 248–251
    summary, 292–294
metrics
    employee compensation, 78–79
    project metrics, consistent use, 91
    reports
        customer satisfaction, 177
        employee satisfaction, 177
        financial, 176
        operational, 176
        overview, 175–176
    sales, 81
    Services Delivery key metrics, 103, 105–106, 205
    Services Engineering, 138–140
    Services Engineering key metrics, 205
    Services Marketing key metrics, 161, 163, 205
    success factor, 148
    Services Sales key metrics, 205
    solutions assurance review, 180
Microsoft Consulting Services, 2
mission, professional services and, 15
mission statement, 23–24
    audience, 25
    Business Computing Solutions, 23–24
    characteristics of, 25
    external, 25
    format, 24–25
    internal, 25
    Maister, David, 24
    Moore, Geoffrey, 26
    overarching objective, 25–27
    primary objective, 26
    Radtke, Janel, 24–25
    SAR factor, 27–28
Moore, Geoffrey, 9
    mission statement objective, 26

N

negotiation
    customer engagement workflow, 223–224
    Services Sales, 72
new business, Services Delivery and, 89
new client ratio, 348
newsletters, electronic, 174
NIBT (Net Income Before Tax), 348

O

objectives
    business objectives, summary, 292
    financial, 29
    mission statement, 25–27
    parameter setting and, 29–30
    professional services and, 15
O-Map, 54
    Customer Service, 55
    interfaces, 56–59
    Product Engineering, 55
    Product Marketing, 55
    Product Sales, 55
    PS functions, 56
operating profit, 348
operational infrastructure, building phases and, 233
    consulting services, 242
    implementation services, 235
    integration services, 239
operational processes
    implementation services, 235
    integration services, 239
    productized services, 245
operational reporting
    implementation services, 235
    integration services, 239
    productized services, 245
operations, professional services
    functional map, 53–54
organizational charts. *See also* O-Map
    Services Delivery, 108–109
    Services Sales sample, 83–85
organizational interfaces
    external interfaces, 196–197
    field staff/corporate staff, 197–199
    by function, 197
    with larger company, 195–196
    within PS, 194–195
    technical staff and sales/marketing staff, 197
organizational overlap, 279–281
organizational overview, 51–59
organizational structure
    focus, 83
    head count, 199–201
    overview, 81–82
    representative quotas, 82–83
    Services Engineering, 140–142
    Services Marketing, 163–165
    Services Operations, 191–192
    summary, 290, 292
    target revenue, 82
other administrative costs, 348

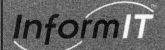